ONCE YOU'RE LUCKY, TWICE YOU'RE GOOD

GEOFFREY ELLIS

Sarah Lacy is a reporter for *BusinessWeek*, where she has worked since 2004. She has reported on startups and venture capital in Silicon Valley since 1999. She lives in San Francisco.

ONCE YOU'RE LUCKY, TWICE YOU'RE GOOD

THE REBIRTH OF SILICON VALLEY AND THE RISE OF WEB 2.0

SARAH LACY

GOTHAM BOOKS

GOTHAM BOOKS
Published by Penguin Group (USA) Inc.
375 Hudson Street, New York, New York 10014, U.S.A.

Penguin Group (Canada), 90 Eglinton Avenue East, Suite 700, Toronto, Ontario M4P 2Y3, Canada (a division of Pearson Penguin Canada Inc.); Penguin Books Ltd, 80 Strand, London WC2R 0RL, England; Penguin Ireland, 25 St Stephen's Green, Dublin 2, Ireland (a division of Penguin Books Ltd); Penguin Group (Australia), 250 Camberwell Road, Camberwell, Victoria 3124, Australia (a division of Pearson Australia Group Pty Ltd); Penguin Books India Pvt Ltd, 11 Community Centre, Panchsheel Park, New Delhi–110 017, India; Penguin Group (NZ), 67 Apollo Drive, Rosedale, North Shore 0632, New Zealand (a division of Pearson New Zealand Ltd); Penguin Books (South Africa) (Pty) Ltd, 24 Sturdee Avenue, Rosebank, Johannesburg 2196, South Africa

Penguin Books Ltd, Registered Offices: 80 Strand, London WC2R 0RL, England

Published by Gotham Books, a member of Penguin Group (USA) Inc.

Previously published as a Gotham Books hardcover edition.

First trade paperback printing, June 2009

10 9 8 7 6 5 4 3 2

Gotham Books and the skyscraper logo are trademarks of Penguin Group (USA) Inc.

Chart on page 16 by Geoffrey Ellis
Illustration on page 164 courtesy of Facebook

The Library of Congress has cataloged the hardcover edition of this book as follows:
Lacy, Sarah, 1975–
Once you're lucky, twice you're good: the rebirth of Silicon Valley and the rise of Web 2.0 / Sarah Lacy.
p. cm.
ISBN 978-1-592-40382-0 (hbk.) ISBN 978-1-592-40427-8 (pbk.)
1. Web site development industry—California. 2. Internet industry—California.
3. Web 2.0. I. Title.
HD9696.83.U63C353 2008
338.4'700670979473—dc22 2007046204

Printed in the United States of America
Set in Scala Designed by Elke Sigal

For Geoff, who knew I'd do this before I did
and always believed in me

CONTENTS

PROLOGUE

It's October 10, 2006, a sunny, if blustery, Northern California day. Chad Hurley and Steve Chen are outside the Google headquarters giggling in front of a video camera. They're clearly unscripted.

"The two kings have gotten together," Chad ad-libs awkwardly before Steve starts laughing at him, backing away from the camera and doubling over in the parking lot. Two kings? Where did that come from?

Chad hams it up more, channeling the current Burger King marketing slogan with mock seriousness: "The two kings have gotten together, the king of search and the king of video. We're going to have it our way."

More giggles all around. And then cut.

You'd be giddy too. Google had just bought Chad and Steve's eleven-month-old video-sharing company YouTube for $1.65 billion. It meant they were now worth an additional $300 million each. And they were no longer on their own, trying to solve those pesky issues like copyright infringement and how to make money.

They had the mighty $195 billion Google juggernaut behind them. But Chad and Steve weren't the only ones reeling from the news. As the two shot the video to be posted on—what else?—YouTube, shock waves were spreading through the fifty-mile stretch known as Silicon Valley.

Just a few miles north of Chad and Steve's exuberant video shoot, Mark Zuckerberg, the twenty-three-year-old founder of social networking site Facebook, was relieved. Suddenly the $1 billion Yahoo! had offered his company a month or so earlier didn't seem so crazy. Better yet, Zuck didn't seem so crazy to turn it down, despite the objections of some of his investors and a good number of employees with stock options.

Some 350 miles south in Los Angeles, Tom Anderson, Chris DeWolfe, and their investors were likely feeling anything but relief. The YouTube deal was an unwelcome confirmation: At $580 million, they'd definitely sold MySpace on the cheap a year earlier. MySpace was now one of the biggest sites on the Web. How big? Some 60 percent of YouTube's streaming videos were being watched from people's MySpace pages. Chad and Steve's business had been built on top of MySpace's success and sold for nearly three times as much. That had to hurt.

Others, toiling away in nondescript offices up and down Highways 101 and 280, groaned, "Here we go again." Thirteen years ago Netscape—an eighteen-month-old company with no profits or business model to speak of—had debuted on the NASDAQ Stock Exchange and got the biggest first-day pop in stock price ever. It was the opening of the floodgates: In the next five years more than a thousand high-tech start-ups would go public, raising $66 billion—a phenomenon that could end only in a fierce crash.

The fear was palpable: Was YouTube the new Netscape? Concern had already been building in certain corners of Silicon Valley and pockets of the business world at large, growing with every report mentioning "eyeballs"—an industry term for the raw number of people who look at a Web site—and the reappearance of young, jeans-wearing idealists aiming to upend industries with the Web. They'd lived through the bursting of the first Web bubble, some just barely, and no one wanted to go through it again.

And the impact on the other Chads and Steves out there? Those other young guys (and perhaps a woman or two) in jeans and Pumas who had quietly spent the last few years of their lives building what they believed would be the next big Web thing? They too felt a mix of emotions on October 10, 2006, swinging between hope and fear, giddiness and wariness. Believing in the Web's innate ability to transform any industry it touched versus hedging and cashing out early while they could. Making sure they didn't look like fools—again. All at once, these twenty- and thirtysomethings feared that YouTube was and wasn't the next Netscape.

Still, even with all the fear and doubt taken into account, YouTube's payday couldn't help but make these would-be Web moguls feel vindicated. Even if the same destiny didn't await them, it was a sign that they'd been right to believe the Net wasn't dead back in 2002, 2003, and 2004 when they started experimenting, at a time when no one was building cool new Web sites. Maybe fundamental changes like proven Internet business models, dramatically lower costs of doing business, and the now billion-person-strong Web audience could make things truly different this time. Maybe they hadn't been so crazy after all.

Now that YouTube was part of Google, the opportunistic among these entrepreneurs saw an opening: Who would be the next "it" start-up? The default answer seemed to be Facebook—particularly once word leaked of Yahoo!'s rejected $1 billion entreaty. But entrepreneurs are optimists by definition, and others weren't ready to cede the title of YouTube of 2007 to Zuckerberg.

Reid Hoffman's site LinkedIn was hitting critical mass after a four-year slog of trying to build a MySpace for businesspeople. What's more, it was one of the few sites that actually charged people to use it. Thanks to revenues from premium services like job listings, LinkedIn was the lone profitable social networking venture out there. By the fall of 2006, its investors were already valuing it at over $250 million.

Another contender was Six Apart, founded in 2002 by then twenty-four-year-olds Ben and Mena Trott in 2003. It was one of the very few companies to find a business model in blogging. By 2006, more than 50 percent of people online were reading blogs—self-published online diaries and newsletters—and they'd proven a disruptive force in politics and business. Six Apart pioneered slick, easy-to-use blogging software; by 2006 nearly any company using blogs for in-house communications bought its software from Six Apart, as did nearly every professional blogger or old-school media outlet looking to get in on the trend. Pundits were starting to describe them as an initial public offering (IPO) candidate in 2007—maybe the first of the Web 2.0 wave. But an acquisition was starting to look just as likely, as it became more and more apparent that blogging was a big part of journalism's future and that Six Apart more than anyone owned and defined professional blogging.

Smaller, but with rabid followings, were Digg and Yelp. Digg, founded by bubble veteran Jay Adelson and Valley party boy Kevin Rose, was a very different kind of news site. The idea behind it was that hundreds of thousands of everyday folks would scour the Web for the best stories and submit them to Digg.com. Think of it as citizen journalism for lazy people who didn't want to write their own blogs, just find stories and mark them as good. Digg's reach and revenues were far smaller than LinkedIn or Six Apart, but on just a couple of million in venture capital it had emerged as a force big media couldn't ignore. Getting a story on Digg's front page would bring a torrent of traffic—and highly desirable young traffic at that. A few years earlier, tech news site CNET balked at adding "Digg

This" buttons to the end of their stories. "We don't do things like that," they condescendingly told Kevin. By 2006, they were begging for buttons—along with *The New York Times, The Washington Post,* and others.

Similarly, Yelp had become a force among the young and hip in San Francisco. Founded by Jeremy Stoppelman and Russel Simmons, friends of Chad Hurley and Steve Chen from the days when all four worked at PayPal, the site was part Yellow Pages, part MySpace, and part Citysearch. Positive or negative buzz on Yelp was soon affecting local businesses so much that they were hungry to advertise on the site and make their own pitch to the influential hipsters with disposable cash. By late 2006, Yelp was in a handful of cities and people were slapping bright red "People on Yelp Love Us" stickers on their storefront windows.

There were also two dark horses in the running to be the next hot Web property: Ning and Slide. Ning is a site where people can build their own mini-MySpaces, tied around some common interest or connection, as, for example, a far-flung group who went to high school together or people who live in New York and love knitting. By the time YouTube was bought, Ning had been building its software for two years and had yet to show the public much in the way of progress. But it had star power: Marc Andreessen was the cofounder and chief technology officer, the very guy who cowrote the first modern Web browser, which later became Netscape. As rumors of the YouTube sale circulated, Marc stole moments from his busy schedule to instant message friends in the know. "Is it true?" he'd ask, almost always followed by a little smiley face emoticon. Just months before, as the media elite met at the epic dealmaking Allen & Company Sun Valley Conference, the whispered purchase price of YouTube was $500 million. For that to triple so quickly, something big was happening to the Web again; he knew it.

Then there was Slide's founder, Max Levchin. Back in 1999, he was the one who lured Chad and Steve to Silicon Valley, hiring them as early employees at PayPal, an online payment company he and Peter Thiel founded in 1998. Max was proud and happy for his friends. But when he heard YouTube's $1.65 billion news, like the others, he was a little jealous. Slide, his online photo-sharing venture, was starting to take off, and like YouTube, it had found its greatest audience on the MySpace pages of millions of people—not just teens but the likes of Justin Timberlake and Hugh Hefner as well.

But building Slide had been a slog—nothing like YouTube's eleven-month runaway success. Upon hearing of Google's acquisition, Max vowed that Slide would be the YouTube of 2007. In November he raised a hefty $20 million in a round of venture capital funding from some of Silicon Valley's most elite investors. Around New Year's, he tried to take a rare weekend off, traveling with his girlfriend to a remote spot in Northern California. He'd reflect, gear up for the big year ahead, and maybe, just maybe, sleep more than an hour or two a night. Only the spot was too remote: no cell phone or email access. They came back two days early. Max simply couldn't start 2007 so far from Slide. This was going to be his year.

By the time YouTube got its payout, Web fever had already been bubbling back up in the Valley. The sites mentioned above and others like them had slowly but surely begun to emerge from Silicon Valley's primordial soup and were catching the attention of investors, advertisers, and investment bankers. They were doing something far different from the first wave of Internet companies. It wasn't about e-commerce or taking prepackaged content from the offline world and throwing it onto a site. This new crop of companies was all about the young geek-turned-hipster techies who were creating them. They were mostly social networking sites built for them and their friends that happened to become companies. There was no inventory. No huge staffs of content creators. No expensive business development guys running around in crisp blue shirts brokering deals with old media powerhouses. No armies of coders whizzing around the office on Razor scooters. In fact, few even had offices.

Forget shopping online. The most important thing to emerge from the Web to date has been email. More than twice as many people use email as shop online. Clearly, connection was the Web's killer application, plain and simple. This was the generation that emailed, texted, instant messaged—frequently all at once. And these sites made those connections easier, more interesting, or more fun. Blogging. Sharing videos. Sharing news clips. Sharing restaurant reviews. Sharing photos. Sharing friends. Every single one of these sites is about meeting people, staying in touch, or witnessing people's own personal quirky forms of self-expression.

These are not Web companies that old media or venture capitalists would ever have concocted or predicted. But by 2006, the wave was here, it was big, and everyone wanted a piece of it. Nearly a quarter of people's time spent online was on these so-called social media sites, yet they were getting only about 6 percent of the online advertising dollars. To old media and the first wave of Web companies, this was a $40 billion opportunity someone was going to get. It was the biggest single untapped area for growth in their industry.

By 2006, this wave had been christened Web 2.0. The term was coined by Tim O'Reilly of O'Reilly Media, the techy book publishing and conference empire, and immediately adopted by analysts, venture capitalists, and the press. A Web 2.0 conference started up in 2005, and by 2006 you couldn't get in unless you were somebody. Before long the term was everywhere. There were thousands of press mentions of the phrase in 2006 alone. Even staid companies like IBM were using it in their press releases. But few people actually at the helm of Web 2.0 sites wanted to claim it—except of course in an ironic, self-mocking way. At a summer party at Jeremy Stoppelman's loft, entrepreneurs gathering for photos quipped, "Say, 'Web two-point-ohhhhh.'" And the closest anyone makes to a serious reference is still accompanied by air quotes and a roll of the eyes. The cool kids call it "Web Twenty."

Part of this is fatigue with everything 2.0 in tech land. But the resistance to being part of the new Web movement—or worse, the new Web bubble—also comes from deep wounds inflicted in the first Internet bubble and its aftermath. Back in the 1990s everyone embraced the moniker *dotcom*. It meant you were cool, with it, you got it. You were part of the new economy that operated by different rules and threatened everyone else. But years later, dotcoms would be pariahs. Dotcoms weren't the sole cause of the great economic expansion of the late 1990s, but they were the most visible and the easiest to blame when it all came crashing down in 2000 and 2001.

The last thing these guys wanted was to build themselves back up again. The jokes and quips all betray a heartfelt fear of anything like hyping yourself or repeating the past. A fear of admitting that you believe in it all again. Or that you are trying to do anything as ambitious as changing the world or starting a "new" economy. These guys were mostly playing it cool. And if they started to take themselves or their companies too seriously, a multitude of bloggers, naysayers, and cynics would remind them of the bust.

Strange as it may be for something so seminal, people frequently remember what actually happened incorrectly. By 2006 it was controversial to suggest we *weren't* in another Web bubble. But consider the facts: At the bubble's peak in 1999 and 2000, venture capitalists were pumping nearly $30 billion into new ventures per quarter. In 2006, it was more like $5 billion. A record 270 venture-capital-backed companies went public in 1999, for a combined $21 billion. In 2006, just 57 venture-capital-backed companies went public, raising $5.1 billion. On average, a company going public in 2006 was more than eight years old. In 1999, it was just four years old.

While it's true that 2006 was a good year for acquisitions, with 336 companies getting bought versus 318 in 2000, that's largely because going public wasn't much of an option. And while those 318 companies raked in more than $68 billion in 2000, in 2006, a larger number of deals netted only $16 billion. And that 2006 number was skewed upward by the blockbuster Google-YouTube deal.

For what was thought of as a bubble, hardly anyone was making or spending much money. Some people argue it is a matter of time until we hit the 2000 levels again, maintaining that we're in the midst of a bubble, only in the stage equivalent to 1994 or thereabouts, so the numbers don't yet back up all the hand-wringing. But there's little proof that there's anything going on other than Silicon Valley business as usual. From a behavioral standpoint, there was nothing inherently unique about how venture capitalists responded to a big new innovation like the Internet. As long as Silicon Valley has been around, bubbles have existed. A new technology emerges—chips, computers, video games, business software—that suddenly creates market opportunity. Entrepreneurs come up with ideas, venture capitalists fund them, and they compete to be the one standing at the end of the game. Remember computer makers like Commodore and Wang? Not so different from all those dotcoms that failed where Amazon or Yahoo! succeeded. Indeed, this cycle is not unique to Silicon Valley. From 1896 to 1930 there were more than 1,800 American car makers. Three survived. Cycles like these are simply how the Valley operates. That's why they call it "risk capital."

Also some big legitimate companies came out of the Internet

wave, like eBay, Amazon, and Yahoo!. And a bit later, Google. Together they add up to more than $300 billion in market capitalization, more than $25 billion in annual revenues, and close to a hundred thousand jobs. And that's just four of the surviving companies. There's a purely economic argument to be made that it was all worth it.

So what made the Internet bubble of the late 1990s so special? The scale of it. Laws changed in the 1970s to permit big institutions like Harvard's endowment or the California Public Retirement System to invest in so-called alternative assets, which includes venture capital. The returns were always higher than those you could get from the stock market. But in the mid to late 1990s, the returns became stratospheric. Suddenly everyone wanted to invest in venture capital funds; the money available ballooned from $12 billion in 1996 to $106 billion in 2000. Single venture capital firms were raising $1 billion at a time—more than double the average amount of just a few years earlier. That meant there was sufficient cash to invest in any promising idea—and in a lot of not-so-promising ones. And companies were raising far more than they needed and throwing it around San Francisco and the Valley just as fast. Six-figure salaries and stock options for everyone! Weekly parties with free drinks! T-shirts, T-shirts, T-shirts!

But more than the money was unprecedented. Just as sweeping was the cultural and widespread economic scale of this bubble. Excitement about the Internet permeated the U.S. economy, captivating the imagination and greed of nearly every American in a way that no other business wave has before or since. While dot-coms were the most visible, it wasn't just silly online catalog businesses that were rolling in the dough and drinking the Kool-Aid. The older tech companies also got involved too. Hewlett-Packard, Intel, Oracle—they all needed a new Internet strategy. Soon non-Valley companies like Wal-Mart were desperate for one. Even cotton brokers in Memphis, Tennessee, started hatching ideas for online cotton-trading co-ops. And this says nothing of all of the networking and telecommunications companies that were starting to provide the necessary plumbing for all that online traffic. This movement was so huge that it affected nearly every company in the United States, new and old economies alike.

And thanks to the great stock market democratization of the time, everyday people could do more than just read about all this excitement—they could buy as much of it as they wanted. The markets used to be the playgrounds of only the very rich, but by the 1990s, companies were ditching their defined-benefit pension programs and instituting defined-contribution plans instead. Through these 401(k) plans, anyone could invest retirement dollars in mutual funds, which in turn invested in stocks and bonds. Folks got quarterly statements showing just how fast those dollars were growing. It seemed so easy. Everyday investors started to get greedy. Millions started playing the markets, investing cash in individual companies. A whole industry sprung up or expanded to support this: Charles Schwab, E*TRADE, AMERITRADE, Scottrade, CNBC. Large financial companies such as Fidelity and Janus started offering mutual funds that were limited to hot Internet or telecom companies.

The quote that summed it all up was issued by one of the most famous Valley venture capitalists, L. John Doerr of Kleiner Perkins Caufield & Byers: "The Internet is the largest legal creation of wealth in history." It was cited ad nauseam as evidence of the Internet's promise and then, after 2000, as evidence of its folly.

The fact that every company and practically every person was caught up into the newest tech craze would make the crash far more disastrous than anything Silicon Valley had seen before. And it wasn't just the jobs or money lost, which were staggering in and of themselves, but the psychological impact as well. On the way up, the Internet was the first invention on the scale of the television or the car that people had seen in a long time—maybe ever, depending on their age. It was a new way to communicate, find out information, be entertained, and buy things all rolled into one. It was mind-blowing. So mind-blowing that you could see it revolutionizing nearly any industry.

And the businesses being built were relatively easy to understand because they were primarily just digital forms of things we already knew, such as a newspapers or catalogs or banks. We were all seeing the world change before our eyes seemingly faster than it ever had before. When the NASDAQ peaked at 5132.52 midday on March 10, 2000, and started its slow, painful descent to less than 1200 two years later, it took with it the promise of lucrative IPOs and acquisitions for half-baked ideas and business plans. It also took a chunk of people's savings and many young people's careers. But worse, it took all that hope and optimism too.

The optimism was so powerful that it wasn't immediately clear that it was all over. People—especially those in Silicon Valley—took a long time to realize just how bad it would get. The new economy had seemed so real that it took months—years—for all that optimism to be beaten out of the Valley. Week after week in 2001, industry magazines such as *The Red Herring* and *The Industry Standard* would feature experts explaining why a tech resurrection was just a quarter or two away. They would tout new sectors as the ones to pick up where the Internet had fallen off. Biotech, nanotech, and wireless each had a turn as the supposed new thing.

As people watched friends and loved ones lose jobs and favorite companies go under, they all wanted to believe these next waves could really turn things around. But nothing had the same mojo as the great information superhighway. In mid-2001 a *Red Herring* headline seemed to say it all, "How Much %^#@! Longer?" By 2002, both the *Red Herring* and *The Industry Standard* would be out of business, laying off hundreds and adding to the carnage in San Francisco and Silicon Valley. According to the economic group the Bay Area Council, the Bay Area lost 450,000 jobs, the equivalent of the entire working population of San Francisco today. In one day during the summer of 2001, JDS Uniphase and Hewlett-Packard laid off a combined 13,000 people.

The devastation involved everyone. Dotcoms, yes, but also the older tech companies who'd staffed up to catch the Internet wave. There were the networking companies like Cisco Systems and Nortel Networks. There were the phalanxes of journalists, investment bankers, lawyers, and accountants brought in to service all this activity. Most of them lost their jobs; many moved away.

This human toll and the pall that hung in the air for years is what people in San Francisco remember most. It made the bust intensely personal. In most circles, for every millionaire you knew, you knew dozens of people out of work, emotionally crushed and scarred. For a time, many people couldn't even get a job waiting tables. If you weren't laid off yourself, you watched it happen. You sat there on a tense Friday afternoon, watching your boss call your friends and coworkers into his or her office one by one. Sometimes they would leave mad, sometimes defiant, sometimes in tears. They would all be escorted out by security. The lucky ones would get a check. A generation of people who just months before had believed they could change the world now knew the hard truth that no one is indispensable in corporate America. And it just didn't seem to end.

The dotcoms became easy targets. They were silly, greedy, wasteful, irreverent. All those $2 million Super Bowl ads weren't funny anymore—they seemed grotesque. No one wanted to admit they too had gone to the weekly *Industry Standard* rooftop parties or bragged about making more money than their parents. In the aftermath of the bust, communters on Highway 101 could see straight through the cavernous Excite@Home campus, with its fluorescent lights still blazing, but nothing inside. It got hate mail for wasting energy. Someone torched the Forbes billboard that proclaimed: PROLIFERATE CAPITALISM.

Venture capitalists were easy targets too. As the financiers for all this, shouldn't they have known better? There was a sense that they had just played a sophisticated game of hot potato with the American stockholder, pushing companies onto us that they knew were worthless and profiting before it all collapsed. In the wake of such anger (and perhaps their own embarrassment for maybe believing a bit too much in the hype), many venture capitalists decided not to talk to the press. Others would begin meetings with "We never really got the whole dotcom thing..." The names of Internet companies they funded were scrubbed from their Web sites, along with some of the partners who funded them. All the people who believed the hardest in the bubble were the ones who piled on the most derision.

Worse than the lost money and the lost jobs was the fact that they had believed. They had all gotten duped. It was a scam and they bought it. There *was* no new economy and all those naysayers they had thumbed their noses at now seemed to be right. The whole experience would have been a hell of a lot easier to swallow and recover from if so many people hadn't believed. Next time, they told themselves, next time they'd be wary. Is it any wonder then that Silicon Valley journalists, analysts, lawyers, and even some venture capitalists start to have palpitations any time a Web company gets some hype? No one was in the mood to believe again, even six years later.

In some ways, that's what changed the most in Silicon Valley in the years after the bust. A few crucial ingredients have kept the Valley at the center of tech innovation for forty years. One is more venture capital than anywhere else. The second is a critical mass of smart people, thanks to the area's preponderance of large high-tech companies and universities. A third is an infrastructure of attorneys, accountants, and publicists skilled at the guerrilla tactics necessary for starting something from scratch. The fourth and most impossible to replicate elsewhere is the culture of risk-taking. That's the only one of the four that really went away after 2000. The Valley was still awash in cash and smart people. Everyone was just scared to use them.

Or almost everyone. This is the story of the guys who weren't.

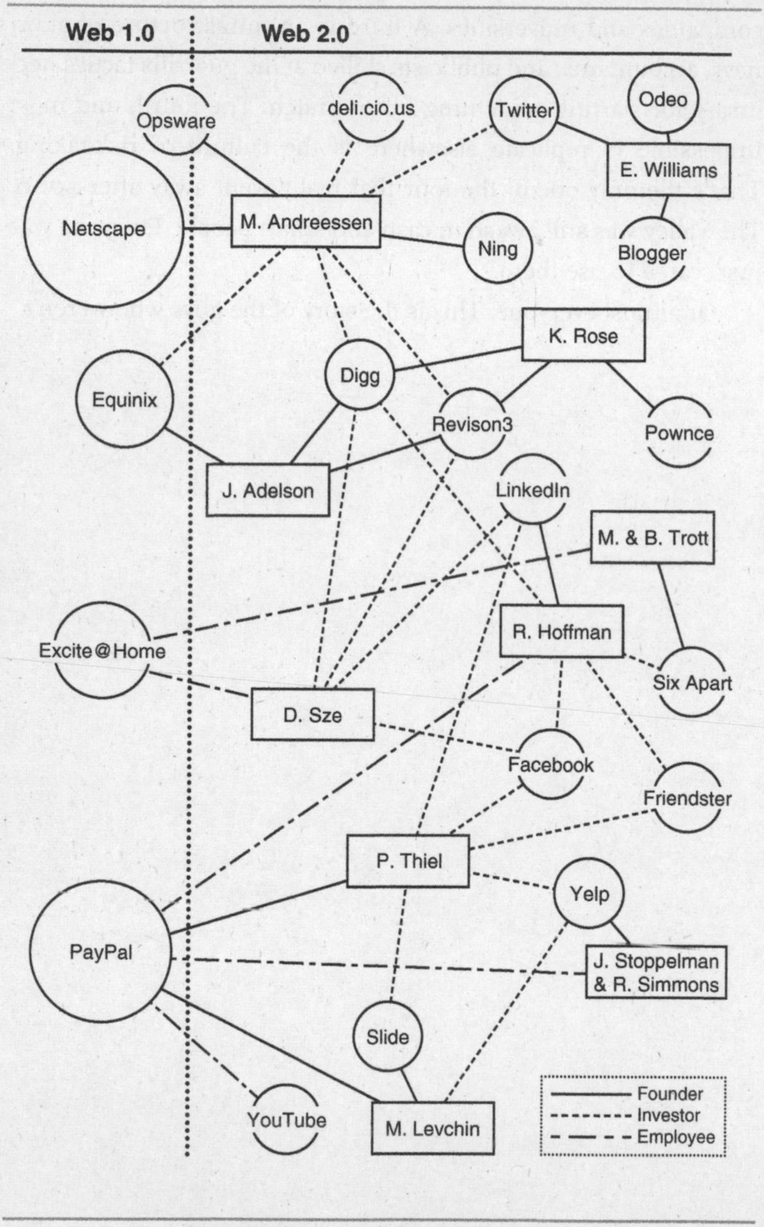

Web 1.0

Web 2.0

Opsware
deli.cio.us
Twitter
Odeo
E. Williams
Netscape
M. Andreessen
Ning
Blogger
K. Rose
Digg
Equinix
Revison3
Pownce
J. Adelson
LinkedIn
M. & B. Trott
Excite@Home
R. Hoffman
Six Apart
D. Sze
Facebook
Friendster
P. Thiel
Yelp
PayPal
J. Stoppelman & R. Simmons
Slide
YouTube
M. Levchin

Founder
Investor
Employee

1

WINNING IS EVERYTHING

Max Levchin is afraid of the water.

He hates this about himself. It's a sign of weakness, and for a guy who prides himself on an ability to work for days without sleeping, nothing is worse than being weak. He can't even admit it without backtracking immediately: "I'm not really scared. I mean, I'm rational enough not to be scared of anything. I just get uncomfortable."

Say he was thrown into the deep end of a pool. Logically, he knows he would be okay. He bikes fifty miles on any given weekend. He runs ten miles a day. "I could probably run a marathon tomorrow," he says matter-of-factly. Swimming a few yards to safety? Yeah, he could physically handle it. Obviously.

But mentally it's another story. As much as Max wishes—even sometimes pretends—it's not true, the simple act of putting his face underwater takes all the courage of facing a firing line. Since age nine, when his mother saved him from drowning in the Black Sea, he has tried not to think about it, let alone talk about it.

That all ends today. It's November 5, 2006, and Max is standing on the edge of the San Francisco Bay in a wet suit, waiting for the bang of the starter's pistol. Some people might conquer a fear of swimming by getting in a pool. Maybe going to the beach. Max is doing a triathlon. When his girlfriend Nellie did one a few months earlier, her goal was to come in at under 130 minutes. Max's goal is not to die.

He's not merely uncomfortable. He's fucking *scared*.

He stretches, psyching himself up. Anything not to dwell on that visceral memory when his snorkel filled with water and he ripped off his mask, only to look up and see he was ten feet below the water's surface and falling fast. Watching the shimmering disk of sun getting dimmer and dimmer. By the time his mother grabbed him, he was half-conscious, loopy enough she looked like a guy with a mustache.

Nope, not thinking about it. "I can do this," he tells himself. His jaw is locked. His intense, unflinching gaze is staring down his enemy.

The starter's pistol fires. Max springs into action. This is the moment he becomes one step closer to invincible. He starts swimming, only to be seized immediately by panic.

"Why am I doing this? I don't have to prove anything to anyone. I have a really good excuse!"

He puts it out of his head and keeps swimming. If he can resist the urge to turn around and head for shore, he'll conquer this fear. He'll take control. He knows it. Max passes the first buoy on the course and his limbs start feeling heavy. It occurs to him how easy it would be to just relax. Slip down into the water. Fall asleep. He looks at the rest of the course and isn't sure how he can make it.

He panics again.

This time it shows. A lifeguard in a kayak glides up to him, watching him closely. Max gets pissed. "I don't need your help!" he says to himself and continues plowing through the water, stroke after stroke after stroke. The next ten minutes are pure macho athletic force of will. If trying to conquer childhood trauma is too overwhelming, he'll just focus on proving this asshole wrong.

As Max rounds the last buoy, he suddenly realizes he's going to make it. He's swimming! His intensity turns giddy. He starts laughing maniacally. He's laughing so hard he's inhaling water, then painfully coughing it back up, but he can't stop. The lifeguard is still paddling alongside, only now eyeing Max like he's nuts.

Max climbs out of the bay, grinning. Just before he jumps on his custom-made titanium bicycle, he takes a moment. He feels something he doesn't feel often: satisfaction. "I survived. Good job, Max!"

He knows his mom will call in a couple of hours. She'd been dead-set against all this. They'd fought during his weeks of training in a lap pool at the gym—each day marked by that terrifying moment of shoving his head underwater. They'd even stopped talking about it for the weeks leading up to the race. He smiles, thinking about it now.

As Max turns back to gloat on his accomplishment, suddenly everything changes. He sees only about a dozen people left in the water out of the hundred or so that started the race. "Fuck," he thinks, "I should have tried so much harder." He's so distracted by the idea that he bikes the next few minutes with his gloves still in his mouth.

He bikes hard. He runs hard. He finishes the race at 126 minutes—a respectable time. He beat Nellie at least. But he knows it's not great.

His mom calls almost immediately afterward.

"Are you okay?"

"Yep."

"Did you swim?"

"Yep."

"All the way?"

"Yep."

A pause.

Then "Did you catch a cold?"

Max takes a few days off and starts training for the more rigorous Escape from Alcatraz Triathlon in April. "The first time was all about survival," he says. "Now I want to win."

Long before Max Levchin was an Internet millionaire standing on the shores of the bay in a wet suit, he was a skinny Ukrainian immigrant with a self-described jewfro rummaging through the Dumpsters of Chicago. He had collected quite a haul over the summer of 1991: a mattress, a broken black-and-white television set, free weights that had seen better days, and some long sharp knives he presented proudly to his mother. Horrified, she shrieked the knives were unsafe, since so many "crazy Americans had AIDS." Back into the Dumpster they went. But the other treasures remained, and during that summer at least, the most important was the TV.

Today Max couldn't care less about the medium—he doesn't even own a television. But back in the summer of 1991, he was just weeks away from his first day of American high school. And he was determined to start it without any vestige of a Russian accent. His family had had only $700 when they climbed onto the jet, leaving everything they knew behind, so English lessons or anything like that was out of the question. But as soon as he saw the TV Max realized he'd found the perfect free tutor. After all, those crazy, possibly-AIDS-infected Americans love their TV, right? Surely it held the keys to all the idioms and slang that his English teachers in Russia would not have known. Once he could pry into the television with some makeshift tools and get it working, that is.

Every night, in the cramped, drafty apartment his family was sharing with a distant relative, Max would watch the only channel he could get, face pressed up to the screen, mouth hanging slightly open, his eyes locked on sitcom characters' lips. He made notes of what they said, the way they said it, the way their mouths moved, practicing every night in the mirror before he went to sleep.

Finally school came. He mostly kept to himself, as usual. But by band class, Max was feeling confident. He'd mastered American English, and as a longtime clarinet player, he was entering his domain. When his teacher Mr. Harris called on him to introduce himself, Max stood and gave his name and a few other Max Levchin facts. Midway through his terse report, he noticed a strange look cross Mr. Harris's face.

"Max, can you come see me a second?" he said as class was ending. Max panicked. He'd worked so hard to be perfect—what could he possibly have done wrong? It wasn't a feeling he was used to.

"Where did you learn English?" the teacher asked.

Max responded: "Whatchu talkin' 'bout, Mr. Harris?"

Mr. Harris kindly suggested he switch from *Diff'rent Strokes* reruns to the nightly news. Embarrassed but undeterred, Max did, and his near-flawless English steadily improved. His journey into the heart of modern American capitalism, however, wouldn't begin until years later. Like his early Dumpster diving days, the journey was hardly a glamorous one. But, as with everything Max does, it would be marked with the same steely-eyed determination.

He may not have known what to call it, but by college he wasn't just a hard-core geek, he was a hard-core Silicon Valley entrepreneur. He'd been coding since his preteens in the Soviet Union, starting on a rudimentary programmable calculator. By high school his extracurricular coding even prompted a call from the Feds. Good thing his parents spoke limited English. Max was let off with a warning. His parents were always nagging him to do more around the house, instead of sitting there all day and night tapping out cryptic words on a screen.

His interest grew more intense the older he got. By the time Max entered college at the University of Illinois, everything that had ever fascinated him—music, literature, girls, friends, martial arts, the clarinet—paled in comparison with writing code and finding ways to turn that into cash. One of his first attempts was a company called SponsorNet that he started with two other University of Illinois math geeks, Luke Nosek and Scott Banister. This was back in the days before Netscape, when the only people online were government workers and academics. Luke, Scott, and Max were aiming to match up dorky college students with advertisers hungry to reach them, like the ill-fated malt liquor beverage Zima. The conduit was an early version of the Internet banner ad. Unfortunately Max, Luke, and Scott knew nothing about the ad business. Worse: an early competitor did. It would eventually become the multibillion-dollar Internet ad network, DoubleClick.

SponsorNet ultimately failed. Still, it was a gutsy effort. These were the days before Internet start-ups. The three financed the company with credit cards and had to move into actual office space because there was no other way to get a high-speed Internet connection. The only way to get a server was mail-ordering it from Palo Alto. Max would stay up all night coding, with Scott parked over his shoulder advising him on how the technology should look and feel.

When SponsorNet failed, Luke and Scott didn't stick around Urbana-Champaign. By now it was the mid-1990s and Netscape had happened. The browser itself was important, but far more transformative was the new idea of the Internet start-up. Marc Andreessen—a University of Illinois student just a few years older than they—had proven a smart kid could pick up and move to Silicon Valley and in short order wind up a millionaire. It wasn't just Luke and Scott. Nearly every smart coder Max knew was dropping out of school and driving west to the land of Hewlett-Packard, Apple Computer, and of course, Netscape.

Max was envious. He was already on his third company, and he was anxious to start his fourth one in the start-up mecca of Palo Alto, California. Where Stanford kids came up with the ideas for companies in their dorm rooms. Where billions of dollars in venture capital were just waiting for good ideas to back. Where ranch-house garages had become historic landmarks for the so-called new economy.

Unfortunately for Max, dropping out of school just wasn't an option. "Your grandmother would die," his mother told him, effectively ending the conversation. Max's mother was one of the few people who could expect total compliance when she issued such an edict. It was his mother, after all, who abetted his early computer addiction by sneaking a clunky IBM minicomputer out of the classified Soviet lab she worked in, wheeling it several blocks to their cramped apartment every weekend so Max could code.

And Max's near drowning wasn't the only time his mother had saved his life. She also whisked Max and his brother, Serge, out of Kiev just before the cloud of radiation over Chernobyl spread. She was working as a research assistant for the Soviet government and overheard about the leak well before it was publicly announced. "I have to get my kids out of here," she thought immediately. Only problem: Max was in the hospital. His dad went to get him, but it was midnight and the orderlies wouldn't discharge him. They told his dad to come back in the morning. He muttered the Russian equivalent of "Yeah, whatever," slung Max over his shoulder, and left. Eleven-year-old Max and his brother were on their way to live with their grandmother in Crimea for a year and a half. As the four Levchins trudged toward the train station that night, a strange warm rain started to drizzle down, acid rain. "This is very bad" was all the parents muttered as they hurried the boys along.

By the time their train arrived in Crimea, news of the meltdown had gotten out and Soviet guards blocked their path. "You've been contaminated," they said, telling them they had to go back home. After much back-and-forth the guards measured the Levchins with a Geiger counter. They were clean, save Max's right foot. They turned down the sensitivity on the counter—it still went crazy. They turned it down again. "Wooo! Wooo! Wooo!" Some part of Max was definitely radioactive.

"Right leg bone marrow contamination," the guard said. "Maybe we have to amputate."

"What?" a terrified Max yelped.

His mother interceded. "Why don't you try again?" she said and instructed Max to take off his shoes.

Sure enough, it was all coming from the shoe: specifically a rose thorn he had stepped on back in Kiev that was still lodged in the sole. He never saw that shoe again.

Max is far too macho to call himself a mama's boy. But given all this history, when his mother put her foot down, he respected her place. And she was not budging on this. Higher education wasn't just college in the Levchin family. It was already bad enough that the grandson of renowned Soviet scientists wouldn't get a doctorate. Silicon Valley would just have to wait. Max considered hunkering down, overloading on classes, and just pushing through college as fast as possible. As it was, he wasn't sleeping nights. But his entrepreneurial ambitions couldn't be put on hold for even a few years. With a cadre of computer scientist cronies he kept starting companies. Like SponsorNet, most were spectacular failures, but no sooner would he close the doors than he'd turn to a friend and say, "So what are we doing next?"

By 1998, Max, his college girlfriend Carol, and one of his coding protégés Eric Huss had graduated. No more excuses. It was time for Max to move to a place where everyone was just as smart, driven, and hungry as he was, and to prove he could make it there. Actually, Max really wanted to prove he was smarter, more driven, and hungrier than anyone else. But to start, he would settle for just fitting in.

He called Scott and told him that in a matter of days he would be arriving to crash on the floor of Scott's Palo Alto apartment. Scott was elated. "I thought we'd never get him out here," he says. Max convinced his mother after promising to buy a cell phone he could ill afford. He rented a yellow Ryder truck that was just smaller than a big rig. It was hardly to carry his personal belongings scavenged from the trash. Instead, the truck held every piece of office equipment cobbled together from his various ventures: servers, computers, desks, chairs. In hindsight he admits it was silly. He would probably have done better to sell it all and start new in the Valley, but at the time he just wanted to hit the ground running the second he arrived. He'd tell people, "I'm leaving to go start a company in Palo Alto." What exactly that company would do was secondary for now.

Day after day, Max pushed his friends across Highway 70, through Illinois, Kansas, Utah, Nevada, moving closer and closer to California. It was a ramshackle caravan. Eric's Toyota Tercel was attached by a single joint to the back of the truck, making it impossible to do anything in reverse. Following that was Carol's Toyota Camry. They couldn't go fast enough for Max, who drove the truck the entire time, while Eric and Carol took shifts driving the Camry. Bathroom breaks were allowed only when they stopped to refuel. Food was only what could be purchased in gas station marts. They did stop to sleep—an indulgence, says Max—but not until they'd driven until one or two A.M. Seven hours later, they were back on the road.

This relentless pace was taking its toll on his relationships. Calls from his worried mother were driving up a $200 cell phone bill—a big chunk of the meager $1,000 he had saved up for his California future. And Max and Carol couldn't stop bickering, leaving him to wonder how he could wriggle out of their plan to get an apartment together in Palo Alto. Indeed, the relationship didn't last. But more to the point, it was taking a toll on the truck. Just outside Elko, Nevada, it died, and as Max, Eric, and Carol pulled over, they saw a sign bolted onto a post: LOCK YOUR DOORS. DO NOT GET OUT OF THE CAR. MAXIMUM SECURITY PRISON AREA.

They hunkered down, called AAA, and waited. The truck was so big that it required a special flatbed tow truck. AAA only had a few of them, so it would take several hours. Ignoring his friends, Max hunched down in the cab of the truck amid the pile of beef jerky and empty water bottles and played chess on his Palm Pilot until the battery died. Then he just stared, angry there was nothing he could do to speed things up. They ended up getting towed thirty miles to Elko.

Now when he tells this story, Max notes that this city happens to be the brothel capital of the world, raising his eyebrows and making a comical, leering sort of expression. He has a habit of saying anything creepy or nefarious in a Boris-and-Natasha-style Russian accent. It was the type of fact he might have learned during one of his all-night binges of reading Wikipedia. But that trivia held little fascination for him at the time, as he lost another twenty-four hours waiting to get the truck fixed. He just wanted to get back on the road.

Two days and several dozen bags of beef jerky later, he was finally close. Davis, California, just a few hours from Banister's Palo Alto pad. It was four A.M., but he was determined not to stop until he got there. He wasn't even tired; he was exhilarated. He was learning all the ways truckers communicate, flashing lights to tell someone to pass you and the like. The closer he got, the giddier he became. If he'd had one of those trucker horns, he probably would have been pulling it right about now.

But Eric and Carol were beat. They pleaded with him to stop. Eric had long since given up reaching Max on the crappy Radio Shack walkie-talkies they'd bought in Kansas City. And they were both too cheap to make a cell phone call. So he pulled next to him on the highway, rolled down the window, and screamed, "Dude, it's four A.M.!"

This was pretty extreme for the incredibly shy Eric. So, begrudgingly Max listened and pulled over. That night, they ate at a restaurant Max would soon regard as the finest restaurant he'd ever experienced. He got an egg-white omelet. An egg-white omelet! Just try ordering that in the Midwest. Here, nobody even blinked at the request. They checked into their hotel, and once again, it was the nicest one he'd ever stayed in. So plush. So well kept! He'd balked when he saw the room rate, but now that he was here cozied up in the nice, clean bed, it seemed well worth it. (As it turned out, this grand splurge was a diner called Lyon's and a Hampton Inn. Even after he became a millionaire, Max would regularly eat egg-white omelets at Lyon's in Palo Alto, just to remember that night.)

All this was only the beginning. It was happening. Later that day he'd be in Palo Alto—the land of Internet start-ups. A piece of Max couldn't help feeling as if he'd already made it. Each company he'd started had come closer to making something real, and there was no doubt in his mind that trend would continue. No doubt. His last company had sold for $100,000. At twenty-one he was already a success! Granted, that cash was still locked up while the transaction closed, which was just as well because it was more money than Max could fathom what to do with. Truth be told, a sum like that terrified him. It was important only for keeping score.

As it turned out, he would never touch that money. It's only when he recounts this story in 2006 that it dawns on him the money is still somewhere in a bank in Illinois, likely earning quite a pile of interest. In just four years, $100,000 would go from being unfathomable riches to pocket change.

Thousands of wide-eyed geeks made similar pilgrimages to Silicon Valley in the late 1990s, but few had success on par with Max. The company he'd start that summer, along with a Stanford graduate named Peter Thiel, was PayPal, the multibillion dollar online payments company. Nothing about PayPal was easy. For starters, there were all the normal dotcom start-up rigors. Things like building a working product at warp speed to preserve that so-called first mover advantage, building a mass consumer brand overnight, and continually having to raise money to make that possible. But making matters worse, in 2000, PayPal had legitimate reasons to fear for its survival. Its biggest customer base was some 13 million eBay users who'd seized on PayPal as the easiest way to pay for the $5 billion in goods they were buying and selling over the auction site every year. Finally eBay woke up and bought a rival payment system called Billpoint. Visa—also unhappy with PayPal's success—quickly partnered with Billpoint to bolster it and hurt "the Pal," as Max called it.

Max's personal albatross was fraud. A gang of Russian mobsters took to using PayPal to steal credit card numbers and launder money. By mid 2000, he and another engineer were working day in, day out to stay one step ahead of the thugs in an hour-by-hour cyber arms race that threatened to erode all the customer confidence PayPal had worked so hard to build. Such fraud had already taken out competitors like Bank One's eMoney Mail, PayMe, and PayPlace. But Max and a team of seventy-five engineers were fighting back hard. "We would either defeat fraud or fraud would defeat us," he told *Newsweek* as he watched money launderers take out his competitors.

Max would go days without sleeping and sometimes without showering. When the smell got bad enough, he'd grab a shower at the PayPal offices, then throw on the same pair of jeans and a new PayPal T-shirt from a trove in the back of the office and get back to coding. At any given time, Max's workload could be measured by the growing pile of these used shirts at his almost-unlived-in Palo Alto apartment. Among the results? The Gausebeck-Levchin test. Next time you go to a Web site to purchase something, check out the box with crisscrossed lines and crazy letters and numbers. You know, the one you have to look at and copy the text into another box to prove you're a real person? Max was the first to use that.

But it was all worth it. Max and Peter's monetary success was assured when PayPal ranked among the very few tech companies to go public after the stock market collapse of 2000 and the terrorist attacks of September 11, 2001. A year later, eBay would offer it $1.5 billion, once it was clear Billpoint was going nowhere.

Unlike most of the fluffy dotcoms of the late 1990s that were little more than overhyped catalog businesses, PayPal was doing something hard and real. It enabled the world of e-commerce to grow and thrive by building a way for people to easily wire money around the Internet, no credit cards required. In fact, the original mission was even broader: a new payment system with none of the normal borders of the physical world. It'd be independent of space and time constraints—in contrast to, say, mailing a check—and free of government and national borders. PayPal was so important to this new economy that it would continue to grow even after eBay bought it—ringing up $38 billion in online payments and bringing in revenues of $1.4 billion for eBay's 2006 fiscal year, a growth of 37 percent over 2005. Analyst Scott Devitt gushed to BusinessWeek.com in January 2007, "It is one of the best acquisitions of the Internet." Like FedEx, Xerox, or Google, PayPal is a verb, exhibiting an impact and a staying power few wide-eyed geeks ever get to experience.

Of course, the money is nice too. Few people know exactly what Max and Peter netted off the sale. It has been pegged at $35 million for Max and $60 million for Peter. Part of it depends on when they sold their eBay stock, which nearly doubled in the year after the deal was done and has mostly risen since. It's safe to say it was below $100 million, although it's also safe to say the two have made a good deal more money since, at least on paper.

Just imagine it's 2002 and you are Max. You are twenty-seven. The last four years of your life have been a complete blur. You find yourself left standing in a Valley that's cratering into a recession so deep it wouldn't really rebound until 2007. But now—just ten years after your family immigrated to the United States and shopped in Dumpsters—you find yourself with more money than you know what to do with. You never have to work again. Your loved ones never have to work again. Better than that, you have a legacy. You made a difference. You made a meaningful contribution to the Internet, the most important new medium to emerge since television.

Max was miserable.

It's hard to feel sorry for him. But for Max, success on this scale was almost worse than failure. He could hardly turn to a friend and ask "So what are we doing next?" the way he used to when his ventures tanked in the University of Illinois days. PayPal had been *it*, the big score. He had won. And it was over. Despite every reason to be happy, he was sinking into a post-PayPal depression that nothing seemed to fix. Not money. Not travel. Not the new puppy, his current girlfriend, Nellie, gave him. Not even free time to spend with all his friends and family he had neglected over the past five years.

Not even what others might regard as a dream job helped. Max was an entrepreneur in residence at Silicon Valley's top venture capital firm, Sequoia Capital—one of the handful of firms to make a bundle off PayPal, not to mention Yahoo!, Apple, Cisco Systems, Oracle, and soon Google. It's about as cushy a job as you can get in Silicon Valley, where working evenings and weekends are de rigueur and no one seems to log just forty hours a week. Basically, Max got a paycheck, an assistant, and an office at Sequoia's plush Menlo Park offices. His job was to sit around and think brilliant thoughts about what company he would start next and about other companies the firm was considering investing in. It was low pressure, high glam. The Silicon Valley equivalent of being put out to stud.

But it just wasn't Max. Most articles chronicling this point in his life simply describe it as a period of boredom. That's true, but that was only part of it. He was locked in an identity crisis, a very peculiar Silicon Valley breed of midlife crisis. For entrepreneurs like Max who came of age in the throes of the dotcom bubble and bust, it was like twenty years of work experience had been compressed into four or five. He was twenty-seven years old, single, childless, and still checking out girls and test-driving fast cars. But in terms of career experience he was a grizzled vet.

He couldn't figure out who this new Max was, and unfortunately he had far too long to dwell on it. Everything he'd ever defined himself by had changed. He was wealthy. He had free time. He could sleep all he wanted. He could even take up a playboy's hobby like film producing, wine tasting, or weekend zero-gravity flights. The kid who grew up in communism was now catapulted into a quintessential American success story in one of America's most capitalist spots. It was exhausting, thinking about it all the time—*agonizing* about it all the time. Ironically, this year after he sold PayPal—when he wasn't working—is the only time in his life he ever felt burned out.

And there were few people Max could discuss his feelings with. His parents had no concept of his net worth and were clearly uncomfortable with it. His core group of friends had shrunk down to just a few—the inevitable result of hiring all your friends, then having to be a demanding boss. Even if he had trusted more people, Max could hardly go around a Valley in which one out of every three people were out of work and complain about all his good fortune.

You have to understand: For all that drives Max Levchin, at his core it's all about competition. It's the basis for most of his close friendships. When he and Peter hang out, they race to see who can solve a math equation the fastest, or literally race on the streets and hills of San Francisco. On the eve of San Francisco's annual Bay to Breakers footrace in 2006, Max was in North Beach until the wee hours of the morning sipping subpar Chianti and talking about classical music. Fighting off a cold, he really didn't want to wake up a few hours later to run the width of the city. It all depended on whether Peter was going to do it. Sick or not, Max can't resist an opportunity to beat Peter. But if Peter bails? Big deal. He'll bag it. There's really no point in going. (Peter did bail; Max gratefully slept in.)

So it's fitting that he usually refers to PayPal as "the Pal," because it has become just like any other friend Max lives with and constantly strives to outdo. To cede that his greatest success was behind him at the ripe old age of twenty-seven would leave him no reason to wake up in the morning. What? Just be the PayPal guy for the rest of his life? Worse, that sole big hit was a product of the Internet gold rush, when total idiots managed to make a fortune. No matter how many people stroked Max's ego or how many things he could buy, he couldn't shake the fear that maybe, despite all the hard work and sleepless nights, he was nothing more than a fluke. A product of the times. Or worst of all, a one-hit wonder, just plain lucky. It soon became clear that there was only one way out of his funk: He had to start another company. And it had to be bigger and better than PayPal in every way.

Just thinking about it, Max would get the familiar rush of that overeager twenty-two-year-old who arrived in Silicon Valley with a Ryder truck full of office equipment in 1998. It didn't matter what happened, he was going to start another company. He picked up the phone. This time he wasn't calling his mother. He called Russel Simmons. Russ—no relation to the hip-hop impresario with the same name—had known Max since their University of Illinois days. He was the first engineer hired at PayPal and the only one to report directly to Max throughout the company's history. He's also one of the few people that Max describes as smarter than him. Russ had taken his PayPal millions and was living in Hawaii. Early in 2004, Russ would get a call from Max, who said, "I'm starting something new. You have to come to Palo Alto immediately."

2

BUBBLING BACK UP

"Dude, move back to Palo Alto and we'll start it."

"No, start it first, then I'll move back."

"No, move back first and then we'll start it."

This was the ongoing conversation between Russ and Max over the first few months of 2004. Russ was still in Hawaii and wasn't coming back unless this next big thing was real. Russ never really knew with Max. Back when he moved out to Palo Alto to be the first engineer of PayPal, he wasn't exactly sure either. Russ was several years younger than Max, but had already finished college and was in the middle of grad school. Moving meant dropping out early. Other University of Illinois kids would look at him and say things like "Really? You're following Max Levchin? Is that guy for real?" Max was known for confidently talking a good game, but no one was quite sure if the uber-intense Ukrainian who never slept really had the goods to build something big, something worth moving across the country for.

Clearly he did. Still, it wasn't enough that Max had proven everyone wrong. Max always took comments like these personally.

Back in 1999, he was trying to recruit a math whiz named Nathan to PayPal. He was an old friend of Russ and Yu Pan, the second engineer Max had lured across the country. Russ, Yu Pan, and Nathan had all gone to Illinois Math and Science Academy and the University of Illinois. Max didn't know Nathan well, but he knew Nathan was intense and brilliant, and there's little Max prizes more.

Max was hanging out at Russ and Yu Pan's Palo Alto apartment one night. It was one of those typical geek pads, complete with a whiteboard in the living room. Yu Pan and Nathan were drunk "like you wouldn't believe," Max remembers. "They are brilliant and barely standing with immense amounts of vodka everywhere." (Max himself never gets drunk. He claims to have three kidneys, so his blood filters faster. Russ loves to call bullshit on this. His point was bolstered years later when Max went to the emergency room for a dizzy spell and an X-ray seemed to show two kidneys, albeit one of them being very large. Max counters that two of them had partially fused, but really he still has the filtering power of three.)

Presumably, Nathan had only two kidneys because he was drunkenly trying to prove some mathematical something on the whiteboard, but he was slurring so badly Max could barely follow. Still, Max is pretty convinced Nathan discovered something that night that would only be published for the first time a few years later. That's how smart Nathan was. Unfortunately for Max, Nathan's next brilliant proof was why Russ and Yu Pan would never make any real money from PayPal. It was an oddly skeptical argument at a time when most of the Valley was in love with stock options.

"How much of the company does Yu Pan have?" Nathan slurred.

"That's private," said Max. Yu Pan drunkenly blurted out his number of shares.

"There's no chance he'll ever make any money. No one will except the founders," Nathan insisted, scribbling away on the whiteboard, showing how much ownership would get diluted per round of funding, what the company might be worth by the time it went public or got bought, and so forth.

Max couldn't take any more of it. He blurted out, "Yu Pan will make a million dollars. I guarantee it."

Nathan quickly worked up what PayPal would have to end up being worth to make that possible.

"Well, that's what we'll have to get to," Max said, deadpan.

Even a guy with three kidneys could have dismissed this later as the booze talking. But to Max, this was a serious pledge. Suddenly his bar for PayPal's success changed from "make more than my last venture" to "Yu Pan must make $1 million." When the company went public, it was the first thing Max checked. Yu Pan made well over a million. So did Russ. Even Nathan, who joined the company much later, neared a $1 million windfall. Max estimates that PayPal created between fifty and a hundred millionaires, depending on when people sold their shares. And those are real millionaires, the kind with money in the bank. Not the paper kind who lost their shirts in the bust. People actually named their kids after Max.

Hell, even the owners of Max's favorite sushi joint made money. He went to eat at Naomi Sushi in Menlo Park on the day of the IPO and they wrote PayPal's ticker symbol, PYPL, on his check and smiled. They spoke only broken English, but apparently were fluent in the ways of Silicon Valley. They figured, Max assumes, these PayPal guys came in a lot and ordered plenty of sushi. They all seemed happy. And in the chaos of 2001 that seemed as good a stock tip as any. Every time Max and his friends went in, the owners would write PYPL and that day's closing price on his check. And smile.

In 2004, Max had no idea what this new post-PayPal thing would be. His plan was to set up an incubator—Valley speak for an office where engineers and businesspeople gather to pool their resources while they come up with the next big thing. If anything was more universally ill advised than starting a new dotcom as the

Valley was just getting its strength back, it was starting an incubator. Incubators had been big in the bubble, because back then, anything online had a fair chance at getting bought or going public. The most ignominious of all the incubators was Idealab! (Yes, in 1999 style the exclamation point was actually part of its name.) Idealab!'s hubris was so great during the bubble that it even started planning its own IPO, never mind it had no actual revenues to speak of unless you counted shares in overhyped companies like Pets.com, Boo.com, and eToys.com. Idealab! managed to shoehorn a small bit of money into PayPal, but it's a fact mostly whitewashed from the corporate history. That's how tainted Idealab! and other incubators were.

Max hardly cared. He knew he was smart, he thought Russ was even smarter, and he had money. They'd sit around churning out brilliant ideas until something stuck. Max would take one for himself and fund the others. He knew one other fact about it before they started: The company that emerged would be even bigger and better than PayPal. Max was going to do everything in his power to make sure. Russ knew this. He also knew that at twenty-five he was hardly ready to retire. And to be honest, he hadn't made quite *that* much money from PayPal. So by March, Russ capitulated and came back to San Francisco, and the incubator was born. Initially they wanted to call it Midtown Doornail, an anagram for World Domination, which was a popular phrase in the PayPal days. But after some concern about how that would go over on international employees' work visas, it was scrapped for the more conservative MRL Ventures, Max's initials. But soon everyone just started calling it the Maxcubator. Yu Pan joined the Maxcubator, but left when Chad and Steve coaxed him into being one of the first hires at YouTube. Jeremy Stoppelman signed up too. Jeremy was yet another PayPal alum who'd tried out Harvard Business School after the eBay sale, but quickly missed the Valley's excitement and moved back.

Russ, Max, and Jeremy had all undergone quite a transformation from the late 1990s, when the geeky programmers first arrived in the Valley. Of the three, Jeremy was probably the most with it. His hard-core geek days ended in his freshman year of college when some girls came by and asked if he wanted to go out. Without thinking, he told them he'd rather stay in and play video games. They left, and he suddenly realized he'd turned down girls for a computer. D'oh.

Russ and Max were still pretty nerdy in the late 1990s. "Mega geeky," as Max would say. Russ still gets visibly excited when he talks about math, and in the early PayPal days he looked the part, with a long dark stringy ponytail. Max was still rocking his 'fro and had large glasses. Add to that the toll of many late nights spent coding and no showers. Not exactly babe magnets. Each has photos of the others from those days on their hard drives. "Mutually assured destruction," they call it.

But by the time they started the incubator, all three had gotten hipster makeovers. Jeremy had close-cropped dark, wavy hair. Max's hair was shorn down to a respectable quarter inch or so. And Russ finally lost the ponytail, trading up to a shaggy haircut that always seemed to result in strands falling in and around his blue eyes, rock star style. Add designer jeans, Pumas, and a supply of tight-fitting T-shirts with witty sayings, and the geeks were now practically ladies' men. Add the bank accounts, and they definitely were.

And don't forget the ultimate Web 2.0 accessory: puppies. Darwin (Jeremy's vizsla) and Uma (Max's wheaten terrier) rounded out the Maxcubator. Darwin fit that old adage of dogs looking like their owners. He was thin, wiry, and tan—just like Jeremy. Russ loved to joke that Uma was the furthest thing from Max, though: fluffy, girlie, and kind of dumb. Indeed, while Max might greet you with a grim expression and a solemn nod of the head, Uma will run across the room, tail wagging and tongue flapping, to express how happy she is to see you.

Together, they all filled up a well-worn San Francisco office. You had to take a scary ramshackle elevator to get to the incubator's second-floor offices. Over time they developed a bit for new visitors. Russ would lean against the wall with all the controls on it. And just when the elevator lurched, making a harsh metal-on-metal screech, Russ would casually flip the light switch behind his back. It was a test of someone's guts. If the person screamed—good luck getting hired at one of their companies. At the very least, you got a slug in the shoulder. You needed a strong stomach to start an Internet company in 2004.

They spent their days eating classic start-up fare (read: coffee, Red Bull, hummus, Easy Mac, and beef jerky), brainstorming about the Internet, and trying to find their way to something new. Finally two solid ideas emerged. One would become Russ and Jeremy's new company, Yelp, and one would become Max's new company, Slide. (Snappy one-word company names are big with this set too.) Max invested his own money in both sites and still retains the largest ownership stakes.

Yelp is like a Web 2.0 take on CitySearch, which was itself a Web 1.0 take on the Yellow Pages. Yelp is more useful than either of the others. In the Yellow Pages, companies pay for placement. You have no idea about a business's quality. And on Citysearch, unnamed freelancers write up reviews. Nearly everything seems to get four stars. Yelp applies the wisdom of crowds to the problem. Mobs of everyday people write reviews of anything: a bar, a club, their doctor. The reviews are frequently funny, detailed, and engaging. You can look up a given bar and see the whole community's warring views on whether it's great or it sucks. The ins and outs of what people loved or hated about it, often down to the minutest detail. Presumably a mass of people will come up with the right review. But just in case, you can go to someone's profile and check out his or her other reviews to see if you can trust his or her judgment. If you find someone you really resonate with, you can befriend that person and follow his or her—usually her—specific reviews more closely. Yelp was one of the few sites that has a disproportionate number of women hanging out on it. Attractive, hip women at that.

Slide is harder to grasp. The basic technology is about grabbing images from all over the Web and delivering them to your computer on a smooth-gliding, stock-ticker-like slide show. By far the biggest use of Slide in its earliest days was for tricking out millions of people's MySpace pages. The main reason MySpace beat Friendster and went on to become one of the largest sites on the Web was the endless possibilities for self-expression on your page. You could add music, videos, even write HTML code to make sure your page looked like no other. Early on, MySpace limited the number of photos you could post, but you could pop in a Slide slide show and endless shots of you mugging with your friends would crawl across your profile page. At any given time a million MySpace pages are running Slide slide shows. You could also add these slide shows to your blog or even an Evite invitation to a party. Strategy-wise, it was exactly what YouTube had done so well, though photos weren't quite as exciting as video, so it didn't catch on quite as fast.

The Yelp guys are pretty nonchalant about how their company came about. At lunch one day, they were brainstorming about a site where you could ask your friends for, say, their favorite date restaurant. Yelp was eventually born. But Slide partakes in the proud—if little known—Silicon Valley tradition of the great founding myth. The iconic slice-of-life story behind nearly every start-up. For example, the one about Pierre Omidyar starting eBay so his wife could swap PEZ dispensers. In reality, most of them are only partially true, including the eBay example.

In Slide's case, the story for reporters goes like this: Max was restless after selling PayPal and was anxious for his girlfriend Nellie to pay more attention to him instead of shopping online. So he built a clever piece of software that would go scour the Web for the latest women's shoes and bring them back to her computer scrawling across the screen in a slick slide show. She could cuddle with Max, for instance, and just glance over to see the latest finds.

But according to Russ, long before it was called Slide, it was called the babe ticker. Confronted with Russ's version of events, Max gets an embarrassed grin and quickly backpedals, saying in a way both stories are true. He did build the tool for Nellie, but she was unimpressed. He didn't care much about looking at women's shoes either. So one night at dinner he and his best friend, James Hong, were brainstorming about what else he could do with it.

"What would you like to look at?" James asked.

"What do you *think*?" Max said. By this he means "hot girls." And he was talking to the right guy. James is the cofounder of HotorNot.com, a site where you can post pictures of yourself and people can rate you on a scale of one to ten. (James is a 9.3, but he admits it's probably skewed up because he owns the site.) It morphed into a dating site just as the last bubble was crashing, and although low profile, it is extremely profitable, to the tune of several million dollars a year. "What if I could get you a feed of women ranked nine or above from HotorNot?" James asked. Max liked this idea a lot. The babe ticker was born. It still runs on several engineers' screens at the Slide offices. Probably a good thing few women work there.

In Valley circles, much has been made of the PayPal mafia's quick and early success. By 2006, Yelp and Slide were doing well, but other ventures run by PayPal alums were doing even better. Reid Hoffman, a former PayPal exec, had been building LinkedIn for four years. LinkedIn is like a MySpace or Facebook for the business world. As with those sites, you have a profile that tells people facts about yourself. And as with those sites, you invite people you know to join your network.

But there are restrictions. You have to have someone's email address to ask him or her to be your friend. And unlike MySpace, where you can cruise around, chatting up anyone you want, on LinkedIn you ask your network to introduce you to someone you don't know. Another crucial difference: Until very recently, there were no photos. Instead of listing your favorite bands or movies, the profiles contain your jobs and people who "recommend" you. LinkedIn's founders wanted to make sure it stayed about careers and work life, not dating. That emphasis meant LinkedIn grew more slowly, but it has also made it one of the few social media sites that's designed for adults and never feels like a meat market. It has also resisted being a fad. That means it's less hot than MySpace or Facebook, but may have more staying power.

Reid was one of the first people to get social networking back in 2002, when a handful of companies were started including Friendster, LinkedIn, Tribe, and a few others. LinkedIn managed to outlast all of them. It has 9 million users and in addition to advertising revenues offers so-called premium services, unlike most of its peers. For a fee, LinkedIn will deliver a message to people you don't know but would like to. You can also post a job opening and scour your extended network for viable candidates. It's only the beginning of hundreds of applications Reid wants to roll out on LinkedIn. As of late 2006, this early foray into fee-generating services had already gotten the company to profitability and a valuation of $250 million. A company that wanted to buy LinkedIn would have to spend a good deal more than that. Industry insiders were already talking about the possibility of a late 2008 IPO. LinkedIn could become one of the first stand-alone $1 billion plus companies to come out of Web 2.0.

And then there was YouTube. It was the most culturally transformative of the bunch, getting regular mentions on late-night talk shows and joining with CNN to host the 2008 Democratic presidential debate. And it was the first Web 2.0 site to make more than $1 billion for its investors, netting PayPal alums Chad Hurley and Steve Chen a tidy $300 million each. Keith Rabois, an early LinkedIn employee and PayPal alum, invested in YouTube and suggested Roelof Botha, PayPal's former chief financial officer, take a look at it as well. Roelof had joined the elite venture capital firm Sequoia Capital as its newest partner after PayPal sold, and YouTube was one of his first deals. Not bad for a rookie.

Meanwhile, Max's cofounder, Peter Thiel, had emerged as an even bigger force in the financial side of the tech world. Peter met Max back in 1998 at a Hobee's off the Stanford campus. Hobee's is like a Denny's with a Northern California makeover—that is to say, they serve avocado slices on a huge pile of scrambled eggs. It's a family-owned local chain and they dot all the geeky corners of the fifty-mile stretch between San Francisco and San Jose. If you are an engineer and you live in the area, you've been to Hobee's. If you are Marc Andreessen, you go through stretches where you eat two meals there a day.

Peter was a thirty-one-year-old Stanford graduate who logged a few years in a prestigious New York law firm before becoming bored. He'd fled back to the West Coast to invest a small fund of money. The freshly arrived Max cornered him one day on Stanford's campus after a speech, wanting to pitch Peter on a business idea about how to wire money between Palm Pilots. Hence the date at Hobee's.

Max was late to breakfast, as usual. When he did show up, he wowed Peter. Peter not only invested but became the company's CEO. Peter dazzled Max as well, and only impressed him more the more time he spent with him. One night when PayPal was still mostly just an idea, Peter and Max were at dinner with some potential investors. Someone at the table was bragging about his chess prowess. Very calmly Peter, a U.S. chess master, challenged him to a game, right then and there. It was a mental match across the dinner table. The board was in their heads. Peter won, and Max was in awe. Max loved to be blown away by someone's brilliance, and Peter loved to amaze people with his. It was an ideal match.

But when they sold PayPal in 2002, their paths diverged. Unlike Max, who vowed to build an Internet business bigger and better than PayPal, Peter was done with start-up life once they sold, at least for a while. Instead, he started a hedge fund called Clarium Capital and within a few years grew it into one of the largest and most prestigious on the West Coast. He would more than triple investors' money in the first few years. He also started a venture fund on the side, called The Founders Fund. Its ethos grew out of his experience with venture capitalists and was rooted in giving founders better terms and getting out of their way.

The PayPal mafia even had Hollywood success. Jeff Skoll was one of the first eBay executives who became friends with the PayPal crew when eBay bought the company in 2002. He started up Participant Productions on a lark, and it has been one of the most profitable production companies in Hollywood. Among its first four films were *Syriana, Good Night, and Good Luck, North Country,* and *An Inconvenient Truth.* Skoll's success convinced Max and Peter to start dabbling in Hollywood, bankrolling the 2006 indie flick *Thank You for Smoking,* along with David Sacks, PayPal's former chief operating officer.

While Sacks continued to play the Hollywood game, he also launched a new social networking site for families, called Geni.com. It allows people to fill out their family trees and link them to the family trees of spouses and in-laws. Anyone on the tree can add to the tree, the idea being that over time you discover people you're related to that you didn't know. It's a bold idea, one of the first Web 2.0 start-ups aimed squarely at families. Peter Thiel, naturally, backed it early on. And in Geni's first venture capital round with

Charles River Ventures, it got a nosebleed $100 million valuation. The CRV partner who wrote the check was George Zachary, Skoll's early partner in Participant Productions and a friend of Max and Peter's. By 2006, the PayPal mafia was an incestuous world where, for now, everyone seemed to be making lots of money.

Was there something in the water at PayPal? Its alums seemed to have the Midas touch. On one hand, this much success couldn't be just luck. But it couldn't all be talent either. The odds that in 1999—the most competitive market for engineers and Web guys ever—Max and Peter just happened to recruit all of the smartest, most talented people were pretty low.

Much of the PayPal mafia's post-Pal success is cultural. It goes back to the whole notion of believing in the Net. The PayPal crew—along with those on the Google campus and in a few other pockets of the Valley—simply had an experience of the bust different from that of everyone else. They lived through it, and it wasn't easy. They watched restaurants around them go under and friends lose jobs and leave town. But the bulk of their world was PayPal, and PayPal was still growing as the rest of the Valley was crashing. Even the post-9/11 economic slide couldn't take down PayPal, as it became one of the few tech start-ups to have a successful IPO in the fall of 2001. Their bankers and lawyers were simply amazed. About the time the rest of Silicon Valley was finally realizing just how bad this downturn would be, the PayPal guys were at their IPO party, whacking away at a dollar-sign piñata and competing to see who could do the longest keg stand. It was surreal, downright anachronistic.

Peter remembers an off-site meeting the company had in April 2001, as the company was prepping to go public. PayPal wasn't wildly profitable. They weren't profitable at all, in fact. They had large companies trying to drive them out of business. And they'd burned through a pile of cash. But their business was still growing even amid the onset of dotcom nuclear winter. And—knock wood—that seemed to be enough even as companies were closing their doors all around them. No one was sure this IPO would take. PayPal and a few others with the guts to try would be like canaries in a coal mine. Employees were happier than most of their peers, but confused and nervous still.

Always the economic philosopher, Peter addressed them, seeking to make sense of it all. He articulated what he called the liberal view: that the Internet age had been a tremendous period of personal growth and learning; people were pushed and stretched and could now take all that back into the so-called old economy. In other words, the bubble was good. He articulated the Darwinist view: All of these companies were stupid and deserved to die. As with a forest during fire season, the dead brush was going to be cleared out. In other words, the carnage was good. Then there was the nihilistic point of view: There was no sense to be made out of any of it. Just be glad you were spared.

Peter rejected them all. Instead, he gave his view: "You can never lose sight of the fact that every death is an absolute tragedy. Every company failure is an absolute tragedy. We have to do whatever we can to make sure this one succeeds."

Keeping their jobs was good. Getting to cash in their stock options was great. But the real gift from the PayPal IPO was this crew got to keep their optimism. They had been sobered enough to realize they had to work hard to build a Web business and there were no guarantees. But they watched PayPal beat the odds at the worst possible moment. At the bleakest possible time, it sold for $1.5 billion.

On a human level, it meant they all stayed friends. The friction that inevitably results from the arduous task of building a company and then steering it through turmoil was reduced to mere water under the bridge. They had the luxury of remembering the good times. Each of them got to live the moment of the IPO party at a time almost no one else did. They got to watch PYPL crawl across the NASDAQ ticker for the first time and gleefully calculate their net worth. Max would call it the happiest day of his life; he still has a picture of him and Peter, with paper crowns on, beaming. So happy, Nellie would re-create the IPO party in PayPal's garage for his thirtieth birthday. This time he was sure to do a keg stand—he had been too overwhelmed the first time. "I think that in most failed start-ups, people don't remember any of the good times. But that also goes in reverse," Peter says, looking back. In other words, the PayPal guys could hardly remember the bad times.

A few years after the IPO party, Peter was raising money for his hedge fund Clarium Capital. He had plenty to tell potential investors about the market and his strategy, but one question stumped him. "Do you consider yourself a lucky person?" one investor asked him. It's a trick question, Peter thought. If he said yes, that sounds superstitious. What's next? Astrology and tarot cards? On the other hand, if he said no, that seems sort of strangely un-self-aware. Like PayPal's success was all Peter and Max and no other outside forces.

He thought for a moment, ever the chess master considering his next move.

"I consider myself to be very fortunate," he answered. It accounted for the serendipity of his being in Silicon Valley in the mid-1990s, but still acknowledged it wasn't just that.

Luck is a big question in the Valley. It might be the only place on earth where just creating a single $1 billion company wasn't enough. An entrepreneur had to do it twice to know he was actually good. And three? Well, that was Jim Clark, the brash entrepreneur who started Silicon Graphics, Netscape, and Healtheon. He was the only person to start three billion-dollar-plus companies and is a legend in the Valley for that reason. And even Clark needed the bull market of the late 1990s to get market caps that high. You could count on two hands the guys who'd done it twice. On the other hand, failing several times didn't necessarily mean you were bad. It was agonizingly hard to quantify. Most everyone knew luck played some sort of role, but where exactly did it end and your skill begin?

Perhaps Max and Peter were fortunate, but almost everyone who went to work for them was lucky. There were thousands of Silicon Valley companies they could have joined and all seemed to have promise. In fact, PayPal was one of the least sexy. Had they joined any other place, and they might have been too burned to try again. Jeremy Stoppelman saw that firsthand when he left the Valley to go to Harvard Business School, just after PayPal was bought. All around him were people who'd picked up and moved to the Valley in search of quick riches and not fared quite as well. They were now training for careers in more traditional corporate America. No more dumb risk taking. Meanwhile, all Jeremy wanted to do was get back to Silicon Valley. He couldn't believe the cultural chasm between people who'd been in pretty much the same place at the same time. It's a big reason he dropped out, moved back, and joined the Maxcubator.

It's not that the PayPal crew had the lock on new Web businesses from 2002 to 2004, when consumer Web businesses started to bubble back up. It's just that they were some of the only people consciously setting out to build new businesses. The rest of what would become the Web 2.0 crew were merely experimenting with fun projects. People like Mark Zuckerberg of Facebook, Joshua Schachter of del.icio.us, Kevin Rose of Digg, Brad Fitzpatrick of LiveJournal, and Ben and Mena Trott of Six Apart were either in college, in jobs they hated, or laid off. They wanted to do something cool, because few new cool Web sites were being built by anyone else. The Googles and News Corps of the world weren't buying hot new Web properties when they started playing around. There was no Web 2.0 wave. The term didn't even exist yet. Most of them hoped to make enough money off ads or user donations to pay for the costs of running the sites or maybe, *maybe* pay their rent.

Take Ben and Mena Trott, possibly the only people who might build a billion-dollar company off the industry-changing blogging trend. It started largely as a labor of love, literally. Ben and Mena started dating when they were seventeen. They went to Santa Clara University together and in 1999 graduated, got married, and found themselves smack in the middle of a world of wide-open opportunities. It's hard to imagine a more opportune time or place to start a career—for a while. Ben, a programmer, went to work at Excite@Home. It had 2,500 employees and was worth billions. By the time he left, about a year later, it had 1,000 employees and was on the road to bankruptcy. Mena joined a start-up hoping to build an educational portal that would allow parents to keep up with what their kids were doing at school. The company's investors tried to turn it into a far more mundane online-tutoring company and it soon went under. Burned by the new economy, they both joined a small design firm. But when the firm's biggest customer slashed its budget by 80 percent, it too closed its doors.

So in 2001—just two years after they graduated with a world of six-figure salaries in front of them—the Trotts were out of work. They moved into a two-bedroom apartment on San Francisco's foggy Clement Street. At that time *blogging* was hardly a household term, but Mena was getting very into it. As a designer who "just likes things to be pretty," she wanted better software, so Ben, an engineer, built it. Mena collaborated, coming up with the designs. They called it Movable Type and posted it for free online; the early blogging movement grabbed onto it. By May 2004, thousands of people were using Movable Type. Ben and Mena made the hard decision to start charging for their blogging software and needed to form a company around it. They settled on the name Six Apart, because Ben and Mena were born in the same year, just six days apart. Going corporate was a risky move, particularly because the people they might alienate had forms for complaints: the very blogs that Movable Type enabled. Mena wrote a post explaining that the users had grown into the thousands and they couldn't possibly support the software on donations anymore. "Looks like I'll be dumping Movable Type soon," snarked one commenter. Other comments and posts were far worse.

Backlash aside, the move paid off. Six Apart powers 20 million bloggers, with some 100 million combined readers. Nearly any company that has an internal blog uses Six Apart's software. Any newspaper or magazine trying to get with the times uses it too. Everyday people who had quit their jobs to try to make a living blogging also use it. Together, Mena and Ben crafted the way the blog looked and felt. When they bought college blogging community LiveJournal in 2005, nearly 50 percent of people visiting the Internet were reading blogs and Six Apart had a place as perhaps the only hot company in one of the hottest new Internet pastimes. By 2006 Six Apart was valued at hundreds of millions of dollars.

But back in 2002, when all this was just getting started, building a billion-dollar company was the last thing on their minds. The only venture capitalist who seemed to care about blogging or Six Apart was Andrew Anker from August Capital. Andrew was not your typical venture capitalist. He had been the firm's dotcom guy—specifically interested in content companies, not e-tailers. Even after 2000, he still was. He refused to be one of these VCs who erased the record and started scrambling to make investments in a more sober part of the tech economy, like enterprise software. Andrew still wanted to fund Internet companies, frustrating as it was just waiting for them to come back. He got fascinated with blogging and used Ben and Mena's software. He called them and asked if they were interested in meeting. They weren't. In fact, they wanted nothing to do with the traditional Silicon Valley set. They didn't understand how venture capitalists work ("Do you have to pay them back?"). And they had lived in the Bay Area through the bust. "We associated a lot of what really went wrong with venture capitalists," Ben says.

Instead, Six Apart sought out a Japanese company to fund them. And Andrew? He decided if he couldn't bring Six Apart to August, he'd just go to them. In 2002, he quit the firm and joined Six Apart as one of its first non-Trott employees. Clearly the world had changed, and if he was interested in the next wave of innovation online, the place to be wasn't at a VC firm. (August would invest in Six Apart later—at a healthy $100 million plus valuation.)

Ben and Mena were typical of the newest group of Web entrepreneurs, which was just starting to emerge as Andrew was begging the Trotts for a meeting. Web entrepreneurs break down into generations. There are no hard-and-fast demarcations, but if you step back, you can see distinctions between the groups. The first generation were people like Marc Andreessen, who started Netscape before there was such a thing as an Internet start-up. This generation drew on a kinship with the young software and computer nerds from the '80s like Bill Gates of Microsoft, Steve Jobs of Apple, and Larry Ellison of Oracle—largely dropouts and misfits. Then there were the first real Internet guys: Jerry Yang and David Filo of Yahoo!, Steve Case of AOL, Jeff Bezos of Amazon, and Pierre Omidyar of eBay. They were mostly Ivy League–educated geeks who loved algorithms and sticking a finger in the eye of staid old-economy companies, even as they employed scores of business development execs to court these companies into partnerships. They generally played by modern Silicon Valley rules, raising hundreds of millions and enjoying celebrated public market success. People from companies such as Google and PayPal are sort of the sandwich generation, a small group. They started their businesses at the peak of the bubble, amid all the enthusiasm in the world, but unlike so many others had real enough businesses to survive the crash and still come out on top. They valued good engineering first and foremost, not sales, business development, or the lure of IPOs.

Then, starting in about 2002, came the Web 2.0 crowd. Most of them finished college, although there were a few dropouts as in any Silicon Valley wave. They were a bit too young to be the founders in the Web 1.0 wave, but were old enough to have been dotcom rank-and-file employees and shareholders. They graduated into the world of the late 1990s, in which they could make more money at their first job than their parents. But they were also the most likely to get laid off. They like computers, but are of the generation when liking computers started to become okay, socially acceptable even. (Kevin Rose's favorite T-shirt: "Stop laughing, computers are cool now.") So while they may be late bloomers, they weren't the pocket-protector-wearing nerds such as Bill Gates or even Max Levchin. This generation consisted of people like Mena and Ben. Kevin Rose. Mark Zuckerberg and Brad Fitzpatrick. Hip, irreverent kids, yes. But savvy, cautious ones too.

But the earlier generations would play a huge role in their Internet lives, ensuring that this wave of companies would go about their business in a manner totally different from those of a few years earlier. For every youngun with a cool new project, there was a guardian angel of sorts from previous start-up cycles, making sure he or she didn't get screwed. These guardian angels would frequently find their young charges.

A perfect example is Josh Schachter and del.icio.us, a tagging site. Tagging is simply when someone likes a site and marks or tags it. By collecting and organizing all those tags, del.icio.us created a different kind of search engine, one that showed what people were into. Josh was working on Wall Street at the time, about as far as you can get from Silicon Valley, culturally speaking. Still, he was a techy. He built del.icio.us in his spare time and flew to an annual geekfest/summer camp called Foo Camp to somewhat sheepishly present it in 2003. Marc Andreessen was there. He was impressed. A few weeks later, he cold-called Josh. (Not too different from the cold call Andreessen got in 1994 from Jim Clark that led to Netscape.)

"This is Marc Andreessen. What's your address? I want to send you something."

Josh assumed it was a prank, but gave him his address anyway. Even if it were the real Marc Andreessen—you know, the god of the modern Internet browser?—he expected maybe a T-shirt. Marc sent him servers. Later on when Josh agonized over whether to sell to Yahoo!, Marc urged him not to. "You should never sell as long as you are still growing," he told him. But that was 2005. Entrepreneurs like Josh believed in the Net enough to start companies, but not enough to turn down $30 million or so.

Andreessen would similarly reach out to other smart start-ups, always staying out of the Silicon Valley limelight. He backed Digg and some of the so-called open source software companies, who were making the cheap software essential to powering this new generation of Internet companies.

Other behind-the-scenes godfathers of Web 2.0 were emerging as well. Two of the biggest were—no surprise—from PayPal: Reid Hoffman and Peter Thiel. Between them they backed Friendster, Facebook, Digg, Six Apart, and, of course, Yelp, Slide, and LinkedIn. (Amazingly, the one company both would miss was YouTube; their friend Roelof snapped that one up while they were busy investing in other companies.)

So-called angel investors, wealthy individuals who invest the first hundred thousand in innovative ideas, aren't new in Silicon Valley. But these guys were different. They were more than angel investors. They were more than just advisers, mentors, godfathers. This younger generation respected them because they'd been there not twenty years before, but just six years before. And they were friends of the younger group. They were trustworthy. They weren't just sources of cash and experience. They were "friend-tors."

These friend-tors told them things they'd learned the hard way that this younger generation needed to know. These friend-tors explained the importance of control, emphasizing that venture capitalists aren't friends. The evils of giving up too much equity too soon. The dangers of filling their board with big industry names who were likely to be more loyal to investors than creators. Why the younger generation shouldn't raise as much money as possible, because with every dollar they take they lose more control of the company. Why bringing in the "adult" CEO may not be the answer, even if he does have more experience.

A common element of crime dramas is the giant bulletin board that shows the structure and interconnections of a criminal syndicate, with photos and names pinned up showing the complex hierarchy of soldiers, bosses, and known associates. In the early '00s, you could construct the same thing in Silicon Valley, as entrepreneurs quietly started to build new sites and their wealthy friends—not venture capitalists—began cutting them checks for a few hundred thousand dollars here and there to keep the experiments going. The idea was that they would all retain control. If they had to give up equity to someone, it'd be someone who understood things, who'd been there.

But these entrepreneurs who had arisen from the dotcom rubble turned to wealthy friend-tors not just because they were like-minded. These were often the only people to turn to. In 2002 and 2003 most venture capitalists simply weren't interested in funding the next crop of consumer Internet companies. After all, Kleiner Perkins had taken a chance on Friendster and gotten burned. Those investors who came back to the table wanted a piece of more mature dotcoms, companies such as dating site eHarmony or online restaurant reservation portal OpenTable.com. Started just before the bubble burst, these companies had raised enough cash to hunker down and survive and had now built solid businesses. That's incredibly different than betting on a new unproven company that could at best promise you lots of eyeballs. It was all the venture set was ready for.

So before companies like Digg, Six Apart, Yelp, Slide, YouTube, and Facebook would become the Web darlings of 2006, they were just low-key clusters of ideas and projects between friends. It was an incestuous little group, and a microcosm for how Silicon Valley works at its best, that *je ne sais quoi* that no other region can replicate. If it had been up to venture capitalists or the politicians to jump-start the next wave of Internet companies in the Valley, we'd still be waiting.

And the reticence cost them dearly. One by one the new Web godfathers would get the most lucrative stakes in the hottest Web companies. Sure, venture capitalists eventually invested in a company like Facebook. But they invested late. That meant Mark Zuckerberg was able to hang on to a whopping 30 percent ownership of the company. Had he taken Yahoo!'s $1 billion purchase offer, he would have netted some $300 million overnight. Compare that to Peter and Max. They'd had to give up so much to investors that when PayPal sold for $1.5 billion, their net was more like $60 million and $35 million, respectively. This time the entrepreneurs would be the ones to make the big bucks.

But after the bust, venture capitalists hardly cared that the hottest deals were being stolen right out from under their noses. They were still burned. New ideas were not welcome unless there was a clear path to revenues and profits. But that's not how the consumer Internet works. Consider Google: No one had a clue how they'd make money and the founders didn't particularly care. They invested all their efforts into making searching better. Today Google makes more than $10 billion a year in revenues and more than half of that is profit.

Eyeballs, then cash. It was the last myth of the dotcom era, and these rebel entrepreneurs and their backers were secretly clinging to it. And by 2006 it was starting to look like a good bet.

3

FUCK THE SWEATER-VESTS

As the nascent Web 2.0 movement was taking off, it wasn't that easy for everyone to believe again. For every optimistic Peter Thiel or Marc Andreessen trying to convince a Web 2.0 protégé not to sell, there were far more Jay Adelsons. Back in 1998, Jay was just like Max, a wide-eyed Silicon Valley entrepreneur starting a new company and hoping to change the world. But by 2001, their paths had diverged tremendously. While Max was whacking a dollar-sign piñata at the PayPal IPO party, Jay was growing more bitter, jaded, and angry every day as he watched his multimillion-dollar net worth and rosy dreams of making the world a better place evaporate. People like Jay could relate to Web 2.0 desire to take the money and run. Because they wish they had. To understand why someone like Max was so unique, you have to understand the far more common bubble-and-bust story of someone like Jay, someone so battered that believing again was nearly impossible.

The company Jay started in 1998 was Equinix, one of several networking companies hoping to make money off the growing Internet traffic by providing the essential computing power, pipes, connections, routers, and switches that made the Internet work. For a time, Equinix seemed to have everything going for it. Staggering profit forecasts? Check. Outfits like Forrester Research were saying Equinix would be in the middle of a $14 billion market by 2003. Funding from a top venture firm? Check: Benchmark Capital. Benchmark partner Andy Rachleff was the local god of networking. Andreessen, who had already made a pile of Netscape dough, also threw in some cash. A killer Rolodex? Check. Equinix would eventually count the who's who of hot dotcoms and major telecom firms as clients, not to mention investments from old technology powerhouses Microsoft, Cisco, and WorldCom. High-minded rhetoric? Check. In 1999, Jay told the press, "Our business is absolutely essential for the Internet to grow at this pace."

If you've never heard of Equinix, you're not alone. It was hardly a sexy dotcom. Those didn't make sense to Jay. Not that the Internet was boring—it was the coolest thing Jay had ever seen. But in 1999, the Web was just an online catalog, or worse, a badly designed online catalog. Rooftop parties and nights swilling champagne at the Bubble Lounge were hardly his style. Jay is what they call the ops guy, someone who oversees all the nitty-gritty techy details of running a new economy company. It's a hallowed but ultrageeky position in the Valley, integral to making sure all those sites getting the big headlines actually worked. You had to have serious chops to do it right, but most ops guys are sort of self-taught. Jay himself majored in film and broadcasting, not engineering or computer science. So like most ops guys, he had a bit of chip on his shoulder.

Not that the glitz wasn't a little seductive. Jay watched as dotcoms bubbled up and minted cubicles of insta-millionaires. Early on, Equinix was next door to Google and Jay remembers pressing his face against the glass, watching Googlites tie-dye shirts at a lawn party, thinking, "I wish we could have a little of the dotcom fun." But it just wasn't Jay. He considered himself a conservative businessman, and the dotcom rage was anything but conservative. His wife, Brenda, had just given birth to their first child, and he wasn't about to do anything reckless.

Only in the bubble could Equinix have seemed like a safe bet. Dotcom parties, swag, and TV commercials may have had a steep price tag, but building out the backbone to run the Web was stratospheric. Trillions of dollars kind of stratospheric. Consider this: Pets.com was one of the biggest and most notorious cash junkies, burning through $25 million for its 2000 Super Bowl spot alone. But in the end Pets.com spent "only" about $100 million. Equinix chewed through nearly $700 million. While Equinix is one of the few of these companies still in business today, and is currently worth about $2 billion, most of its life has been a struggle for survival.

Equinix's 2000 S1, a form filed with the SEC in order to sell shares to the public, is like a trip down bubble memory lane. In just two years in business, the company had already raised nearly $500 million—and still needed more cash fast. What did it have to show for all of that? About $170,000 in revenues and three so-called Internet Business Exchange centers, where all this Internet hosting and connecting would take place. That was a far cry from the thirty such locations the initial press reports had promised. Nothing about Equinix's supposedly more sane business model was proven. It was all a gamble that projections about the need for an enlarged Internet backbone were accurate, and that given enough funding, Equinix would be the company to profit from it.

Equinix was smack in the middle of the Valley's "No, it's not really a crash" delusion. Like others, it continued to raise more money, some $400 million between junk bonds and its fall 2000 IPO. Although Equinix was one of the first telecom and networking start-ups to tap the junk bond markets, it wasn't alone. In fact, these deals were not remarkable enough at the time to warrant much press.

That kind of cash and wishful thinking was enough to put off Jay's own personal corner of the bust for about a year, but not indefinitely. Like so many first-time entrepreneurs in the bubble, Jay made the mistake of losing control. By 2000, he was still one of the largest stockholders in Equinix, but he had given up his board seat to make room for the company's new "grown-up" chief executive, Peter Van Camp, formerly of UUNET, the Internet services division of WorldCom. Although Jay retained his titles of cofounder and chief technology officer, his influence had waned considerably—he didn't even report directly to Van Camp. Still, when the company went public in August of 2000 at about $12 per share, Jay watched his net worth rise to $55 million, and it all seemed worth it. At the time he thought he'd eluded the fierce reckoning that had hammered so many other less conservative businessmen.

Turns out, the reckoning was just delayed a few months. By the end of the year, all of those Internet companies—Equinix's potential customers—were going out of business in droves and taking all those rosy market predictions with them. Equinix had invested near $700 million building out expensive hosting and connection centers with guaranteed seventy-two-hour power generators, bulletproof glass, and biometric hand readers, just in time for Internet growth to slow and all of technology to sink into an economic slump. Prices plummeted, competitors went under, and a business model that had always existed largely in theory became even shakier. Jay had ideas for how to adjust to the new times, but had little influence on Van Camp, who was more executive than technologist.

The way Van Camp saw it, Equinix was fighting for its life. This job that had seemed a fun opportunity when he took it was all of a sudden a test of will and survival. "Phase one of the company was dead," Van Camp says. "As we evolved out of that, it evolved away from Jay. The benefit of leading a company through a time like that is the choices are very clear to you. If something has intangible value, it doesn't get supported." To Van Camp, Jay and his R&D department had intangible value. "Jay is a great spokesman, but he doesn't grasp the day-to-day. He doesn't dive deep into what it takes to really build a company," he says.

Jay watched idly from his Equinix corner office as the stock slid to $.30 and the company did a reverse 30-to-1 stock split just to make sure they wouldn't be delisted from the NASDAQ. Frequently, a C-level executive would get a sizable new grant of shares as part of his compensation, but Jay didn't. By January of 2003, his $55 million paper fortune was gone.

Even worse, he'd unintentionally inflicted the same pain on his loved ones. When it came to Silicon Valley IPOs, the rage was the so-called friends-and-family stock that large shareholders could dole out at their own discretion. Everyone wanted it, and in 2000, Jay figured there was no better gift to give someone he loved. He warned them to do it at their own risk. "I can't guarantee you'll make money, but look at what happened in past IPOs," he told them. They all lost their shirts. "Basically I hurt every friend and family member I had," he says.

Years later he's still finding out the extent of the carnage. He recently learned that his stepbrother's biological father invested half a million in Equinix, figuring the fact that he knew Jay, knew how hard he worked, made it as close as he could get to a sure thing. "It's very brutal," Jay says. "It's like, wow, on the one hand they had such confidence in me. But on the other hand, look at all these lives I hurt just by introducing them to this." (Although Equinix's stock has since rebounded, the massive 30-to-1 reverse stock split still rendered these early shares worthless.)

The indignities didn't stop there. As the tech economy worsened, there was a new blow every day. Van Camp internally started referring to Equinix as just two years old, dating its birth back to when he joined. And he banned an annual founders' day party, celebrating instead the day the company went public. "To most people, there were these two weird founders, Al and Jay, who weren't in control of anything," Jay says.

At one company meeting, Van Camp mentioned Equinix's being "two years old," and one of Jay's most loyal employees, Jeff Rizzo, stood up and confronted him.

"I keep hearing about how we're doing great things for a company that's only two years old," Rizzo said. "Those of us who've been here since 1998 are a little distressed to hear that the company didn't exist then."

"I was referring to when we first started recognizing revenue," Van Camp stammered.

"Our first paying customer was Blue Mountain Arts, and we got a check from them in mid-1999," Rizzo said. In his mind, he could still see the big novelty check executives waved around to mark the occasion. Rizzo sat down and a hushed "Ooooooooooh" fell over the crowd. It was a rare moment Jay actually smiled in Van Camp's presence.

The lowest point for Jay came in the fall of 2001. Equinix's revenues were growing, but its losses were growing faster. Van Camp had decided to lay off half of the company's staff, including every last one of Jay's direct reports. Jay insists they were targeted first. The supposed technology company was essentially cutting its entire research and development staff. These were heavy hitters in the geeky networking world; people who had made their names writing the protocols behind HTML and domain-naming functions before coming to Equinix. People Jay had personally worked hard to recruit, and who gave Equinix street cred in the techy world. "It was such an anti-tech leadership I foolishly brought to the company," Jay says, practically spitting the words. The hardest part was that he had no one to blame but himself. He knew he didn't have the experience to be a CEO of a multibillion-dollar public company, so he hired someone he believed did. Interview a random cross section of idealistic twentysomething founders from the bubble and it's a regret you hear over and over again: mistakenly placing one's trust in a corporate CEO who never really got the Web.

Jay asked about Nicole Williams, his assistant who had made his life livable in these miserable days. Van Camp said she was spared, and it helped. At least Jay would have one ally in the company. With a heavy heart he enlisted her to help with the gut-wrenching day of having to lay off his friends. The only layoff meetings Van Camp sat in on were Jay's. Jay scowled. Van Camp wouldn't even let him have that private moment. Says Van Camp, "There's a lot of scrutiny around doing layoffs properly, and I sensed many of these people were as much Jay's friends as they were his employees."

In meeting after meeting, it was all Jay could do to keep it together, not break down crying, storm out, or throw a punch at Van Camp. All of his hard work, vision, and innovation was coming down to this. It was bad enough that he had lost his fortune; now he was losing his dignity. By the end of the day he was a sobbing mess. "These aren't just my friends, but these are superstars of the Internet!" he was thinking. Two had even come to the United States on visas to work at Equinix, and now they would have to be deported along with their families.

Nicole came up to him, teary-eyed herself. He hugged her, trying to retain some semblance of the together boss. "Nicole, it's going to be okay," he said soothingly. "We're going to get through this and hire them all back."

"Well, you will," she replied.

"What do you mean?" he asked.

"I'm gone too," she said, still stunned.

While Jay had been in his day of meetings, another executive had decided to cut Nicole too, without even letting him know. He was left completely alone. It was when he was in this stunned state that someone from HR approached him and said, "So we think you might want to consider taking a package," Corporate America speak for: It'd look bad for us if we fired you, so what will it take to buy you off?

Jay had to think about it. He was miserable, and the days just got worse and worse. As he commuted home, all he could think was "I should have left before all of this happened." No one would have blamed him. Hell, his friend and angel investor Marc Andreessen had told him to sell some of his shares long ago, when they had value. To this day his wife brings this up, saying, "You had one of the smartest men in the world telling you to sell and you didn't." Even as it was falling apart, Jay just believed in his company too much.

But it wasn't his company anymore. The world and Equinix had just changed. He was only thirty and had plenty of time to start over. He could do something totally different, even move back East and open a coffee shop. The stress and work of Equinix had crippled him more than metaphorically; it had given him a painful form of early-onset arthritis. He had to take medication daily that so weakened his immune system he would catch any cold making the rounds. By the time Jay got home to discuss it with Brenda, a fighting spirit arose from nowhere. It said loud and clear: "Fuck you, assholes. I am not leaving my baby. This was mine. I'm taking it back and I'm going to make things happen my way."

But he never did take it back. Jay, Brenda, and his kids soon left San Francisco to move back to New York, where her family was from. He still worked at Equinix, or more appropriately took a paycheck from them, frequently making public appearances instead of Van Camp. But it was just too hard to be where all the carnage had happened. He sums up the feelings of so many people who lived in San Francisco during these times when he says, "The boom went by in a split second, but the bust took forever to get through." He sold his dream house in Noe Valley—making more from that than he did his four years at Equinix. He had once loved everything about his life in San Francisco. Now, he vowed he'd never return.

And until about 2005, that was where Jay's Internet story ended.

It's August 2006, just five years after the peak of his Equinix misery. Jay has had a bit of a San Francisco hipster makeover. He's wearing an untucked black-and-gray-striped shirt, jeans, and Pumas; his hair is rumpled. The shaggy beard and braided leather belt he sported when he started Equinix are long gone. And he's beaming. He's in the wings of a stage at a club in San Francisco; the club is packed with thousands of entrepreneurs, bloggers, media, and even "fanboys," all waiting to hang on his every word. He's savoring the moment.

He climbs onstage, welcomes everyone, and formally inaugurates his new company Revision3, to much cheering. Forget short ten-minute Internet programming or user-generated content, Revision3 is aiming to be a full-time video Internet network with long-form original programming, like an online ABC, NBC, or CBS. And Jay intends to be a new kind of Internet media mogul. Unlike video sharing sites like YouTube, these aren't repackaged clips. It's original programming, the kind you couldn't find on TV. It's aimed at smaller slices of the general public who don't get anything out of distilled, homogenized programming like *King of Queens* or the many, many iterations of *Law & Order* and *CSI*.

Revision3 shows are edgy: The characters swear and they talk about things that only a few hundred thousand people might care about. But it's serving neglected audiences that advertisers increasingly want to reach, such as young, college-educated males making $75,000 plus a year. The vision is nothing short of the long tail of television, analogous to satellite radio, only free.

Although Jay is just now hosting a big party and talking about it, Revision3 has been around for a few years. Not only that, Jay is also chief executive of Digg.com, a growing force in the online news world. Jay introduces his "stars" to the crowd—the biggest of which is undoubtedly Kevin Rose, the cofounder with him of Digg. Revision3 produces Kevin's weekly video podcast, *Diggnation,* that has hundreds of thousands of rabidly loyal viewers. Kevin climbs onto the stage, his hair disheveled even more than usual and his black tie all askew. He high-fives Jay, and the crowd goes nuts. They are at this moment the kings of geek chic.

It's a big night for Jay. He's almost in giddy disbelief. After everything that happened, here he is at the helm of the next wave of Web companies—this time even sexy companies! He is at his own open-bar dotcom party! (Well, open bar for an hour. It's not actually 1999 and it's still Jay.)

As the evening winds down, he's leaning against the bar, talking to Bram Cohen. Bram is hardly your Harvard MBA entrepreneur either. He has a mild version of Asperger's syndrome and is usually clad in some sort of video game T-shirt, keeping to himself. But tonight he's excited. He is the brainiac who created a program called BitTorrent, which revolutionized how to send large files over the Web by taking tiny pieces of them from lots of sources, sending them through cyberspace in these manageable chunks, then putting them back together when they get to their final destination. Although it's best known as a tool for stealing movies and software, it's also the kind of breakthrough that's making video distribution like Revision3 possible. BitTorrent too is now being turned into an online media company.

"If you told me a few years ago I'd be CEO of two Internet companies, both growing and making money, I'd never believe it," Jay confides in him, beaming. "I mean, what are the odds?"

"Tell me about it," says Bram. "Can you believe *I* run a company?"

Jay is still living in New York, commuting once a month to run Digg and Revision3, and Brenda has flown in as a surprise to share this moment with him. It's almost surreal for both of them. It's no doubt also a bit surreal for Jeff Rizzo and Nicole Williams. The ally who stood up for his boss at Equinix is now chief technical officer at Revision3, and Nicole is now Jay's right-hand person at Digg. In 2005 he begged her to move back to California from Washington, D.C., to take the job. "Whatever you need," he said of the salary and benefits. She agreed.

Of course, one euphoric evening hardly washes away the past. A big reason the two companies are doing so well is that Jay has done every conceivable thing in his power differently this time. He thinks about Equinix daily. He doesn't look back and laugh at the experience either. When he talks about it he still gets angry, hurt, and sometimes emotional. One day in January 2007, we were having brunch at San Francisco crepe joint Ti Couz. The night before, Jay stayed out late partying with Revision3 folks and dancing with Jessica Corbin and the crew of Fempire, an all-girl Internet channel he wants to bring to Revision3—a company that could use a good dose of estrogen.

He's sporting a Digg hoodie and a hangover (typically Kevin's department). Jay hasn't been at Ti Couz since the days when he lived in San Francisco and he's grinning when his food comes, pausing before answering a question with "I can't tell you how happy I am about this crepe!" But when Equinix comes up, his demeanor transforms completely. "Believe me, I thought I was done with it," he says of being an entrepreneur, emphasizing each word heavily. "The only way I would ever [start another company] was if every single one of these potential issues—political, financial, control issues—everything was managed and I could guarantee—*guarantee*—this would not happen again."

Another big reason is Kevin Rose.

Jay and Kevin met back in 2002. Kevin, a bushy-haired, easily excitable twenty-four-year-old, was hosting the most popular show on the geek basic cable network TechTV. He decided to pay a visit to the very place where the world's biggest Internet networks converge: an Equinix Internet Business Exchange center. Jay was his on-air tour guide. Oddly enough, even as he was being marginalized inside the company, he was still the Equinix spokesman. Not betraying the pain he must have been feeling, he grins and does his corporate PR shtick, showing Kevin around the state-of-the-art facility, which Kevin gushingly calls "one of the coolest places I've ever seen."

For people who know Kevin and Jay, watching that clip is like watching one of those flashbacks they do on sitcoms or movies that show the moment when central characters met. (Think Joey and Chandler, Jerry and Kramer, Obi-Wan and Anakin.) They quickly developed a mutual man-crush on each other. Kevin, a frustrated journalist, was always jealous interviewing people who were actually *doing* something. Here Jay had built this thing that helped run the Internet. "That's some cool stuff," he says on the clip. And Kevin? Well, Kevin was young and effortlessly endearing. He had no training, was horrible at reading a teleprompter, but on camera he just worked. Jay had been a communications and broadcasting major in college and saw in Kevin the guy he'd wanted to be. It's clear in the clip that he's entertained by him and also a bit jealous.

Back then, on national television, they were eerily polite to each other. Today they can't be in front of any audience without throwing each other under the bus. And the bigger the audience, the better. Jay almost always plays the wiser older brother whose job is to keep this emerging Web 2.0 rock star in his place, while Kevin rolls his eyes and plays the "you so don't get it, Dad" hipster. Take the time when one of Digg's investors, David Sze, called Kevin the "dreamiest guy in the Web 2.0 scene." Kevin acts like he's embarrassed, but clearly loves the attention. Jay responds from New York via a conference phone, calling Kevin out as a metrosexual.

"You're the one who spends *hours* on your hair," says Kevin.

Jay fires back with a new target: how embarrassing it is that Kevin still "sags his pants"—that is to say, wears them lower than his boxers. "Kevin," he says, his voice dripping with condescension, "You're twenty-nine now, time to stop."

"Hey! At least I wear boxers," Kevin retorts. "Briefs," he mouths, pointing at the phone. It goes on for a while.

A few weeks after this bit, at Digg's version 3 launch party, a very nervous Kevin had just finished a demo for the Web 2.0 elite in Anu, a crowded Web hangout. Jay sneaks back onstage and projects an embarrassing picture of Kevin in far geekier days on the massive demo screen. Kevin gasps and almost breaks something getting back to the laptop to shut it down. Jay howls with laughter.

The actual day version 3 launched, Jay was in particularly high spirits. By late afternoon, the only noise at Digg headquarters is coming from Jay's desk. Dressed in his usual button-down shirt with a geometric design, jeans, and Pumas, the long, lean New Yorker is sitting on his sparse desk with his feet in his chair—legs bouncing up and down on the seat. He still has all the excitement of a kid on Christmas morning, long after his staff has crashed from exhaustion and the waning effects of caffeine. "Look at my eyes!" he shrieks, opening them wide to prove how bloodshot they are. "I can't sit! I'll fall asleep!"

Eventually Kevin wanders over, groggy and bundled up in a copper-colored puffy jacket with a light brown Puma cap yanked down over his eyes. He collapses in a chair. He was sleeping under his desk and still has some sort of imprint on his face to prove it.

"I only got three hours of sleep," he moans dramatically.

Jay lets him soak up sympathy for about five seconds, then says, "Kevin, tell everyone why you only got three hours of sleep." No, Kevin wasn't putting finishing touches on the site before the big day; he blushes and 'fesses up that he was out with "a lady friend" until two A.M. Jay mocks him, sure, but he also shoots Kevin a look of sheer fanboy envy.

Every time you see Jay with Kevin or with anything related to Digg or Revision3, he is clearly having more fun than he has ever had before. But a big reason he's so at ease is his confidence that neither Digg nor Revision3 will be another Equinix. He has adopted a new motto since he was a young, idealistic twentysomething: "Fuck the sweater-vests." Sweater-vests are venture capitalists, corporate America gatekeepers, investment bankers—not necessarily all of them, but the majority. Like the ones who screwed him over in the Equinix days. "They always wear sweater-vests when they golf and stuff, in their clubs I can't get into," he says with disdain.

Sweater-vesty is an oft-used adjective in Jay's world, and it's always accompanied by a grimace. He's making a bumper sticker for his car. On it is an argyle sweater-vest in a circle with a line across it and the legend: FUCK THE SWEATER-VESTS. From the time he told Kevin what to do with his first investor check, Jay views protecting Kevin from the sweater-vests as his God-given mission in life.

Digg started as one of the dozens of ideas Kevin would have for a new Web business on any given day back in 2004. He was living in Los Angeles, still doing the gig on TechTV, now called G4. It was horribly depressing. The network had been bought by Comcast, gutted, and retooled. Kevin was one of the "lucky" ones left, but didn't feel like it. Every night he'd go home to the Santa Monica apartment he shared with four other people and explore around online. He was a tech news and gossip junkie and was always frustrated by the jewels that mainstream editors and Web sites missed. That's when the idea occurred to him: an army of Kevin Roses could do such a better job.

Kevin had stayed in touch with Jay over the years. One night at Blowfish Sushi in San Francisco Kevin was going on and on about the idea—a site where people could dig up the best stories and vote on them. If they sucked, people could bury them. He was riffing on about all the possible features. Typically when this happened, Jay would just listen, thinking to himself, "He should really have someone follow him around and take notes." But this time the idea was too good—Jay took out a notepad himself and started scribbling.

Or that's Jay's version. Like squabbling brothers, they have slightly different versions of the early Digg days. (Indeed, the two have different versions of nearly every story they tell.) The way Jay tells it, he had to stay on Kevin to get him to follow through on Digg. The newly born Revision3 would pay Kevin a salary so he could finally quit G4 and focus on Digg, filming techy shows for Rev3 here and there.

The way Kevin tells it, he needed advice and a salary but not so much prodding. He says if Jay remembers correctly, he was far too into Revision3 to care much about Digg back then. Kevin, on the other hand, was Digg-obsessed. He couldn't stop thinking about it. It was even causing problems with his long-term girlfriend, Sarah Lane—a sassy blonde also of TechTV. For the underground geek audience, late-bloomer Kevin and Sarah were like Brad and Angelina. On one episode, they did a segment showing all the digital cameras they were going to demo on their upcoming romantic vacation to Ireland. "Way to go, Kevin!" fanboys would text in chat rooms.

Sarah wanted the two of them to move forward, buy a house. She gasped one night at dinner when Kevin told her how much of his savings he had spent on Digg and that he was considering quitting his cushy job. He reluctantly chose to pursue Digg over Sarah, hurt that she didn't believe in him more, and it led to their breakup. It's something Kevin hasn't quite gotten over, although it hasn't stopped him from being the resident Brad Pitt of the geek world. (One Sarah Lane successor? Busty brunette Lala from the popular video podcast *Tiki Bar TV*. After much podcast-to-podcast flirting, she was soon seen with him at a Revision3 party, clad in a red tube top, giggling on his arm and doing shots with him most of the night.)

But regardless of where the push came from, Kevin clearly did all the heavy lifting in the beginning. He quit his job and withdrew most of his savings to get Digg up and running. A thousand bucks went to a coder named Owen Byrne, who actually built it. Server space, rented online, was going to run him $99 a month. The domain name set him back the most: $1,200. Ouch.

The site launched on December 5, 2004, and Kevin lived it for months: constantly making sure people weren't stuffing the Digg ballot box, so to speak, with fake votes to get their story higher. Harder still was simply keeping it up and running as traffic soared. In February 2005, when Paris Hilton's Sidekick got hacked, the story was voted to Digg's front page, and that link was the first one to come up when anyone Googled "Paris Hilton Sidekick." The deluge of traffic overwhelmed Digg's servers and crashed the site for days. And in a few months, a listing on Digg's front page would bring such a flood of traffic it itself could crash blogs and other news sites. Soon enough it would become one of the biggest referral sites to major national news sites. *The New York Times,* CNET, and others would add "Digg This" buttons at the bottom of stories, hoping to lure some of that sweet traffic.

But so far this was all just momentum and promise. Building a business is something else entirely. By the fall of 2004, Digg needed an official CEO and Kevin would consider no one but Jay. He trusted him more than anyone else. After all, Jay had believed in his idea from the beginning. Even Owen, his freelance coder, insisted on being paid in cash, not stock. Kevin knew Jay got Digg and he knew he needed him—battle scars and all. Already Jay had set Kevin up with the most in-the-know angel investors in the Valley, including Reid Hoffman and Marc Andreesen. Both had happily invested, and a few hundred thousand had kept Digg flush and growing without the need to give up much independence. Without Jay, Kevin probably would already have sold Digg for a couple of million or lost control of it altogether. Kevin formally asked Jay. Jay asked Brenda. Kevin even asked Brenda. But in the end everyone knew this was just a formality.

"Come on, dude, you know you're going to do it," Kevin told him.

He was right, of course, but for Jay to quit his Equinix job (finally) and become Digg's official CEO, he would need a salary. He was now the father of three. That, plus a surge of traffic that was greedily eating up servers, pushed Digg to finally—finally—visit the land of the sweater-vests. It was music to the ears of Sand Hill Road. By mid-2005, the Web 2.0 craze was beginning, and Jay had been fielding cold calls from investors for some time. He decided to wait until August, the time when the bulk of venture capitalists jump into their Gulfstream jets and take the month off. "The lazy ones," as Jay says with disdain.

As much as he hates their kind, Jay relished the two-week period he made Kevin wake up early, don a nice shirt, and drive up and down Sand Hill Road pitching Digg to hungry investors. This time he held all the cards and he knew their game. They visited some twenty firms and experienced an all-too-common occurrence for the returning Net entrepreneur: VCs didn't get what they were doing, but were dying to give them money anyway. Some even told them, "This is a market we have to get in and we have to get in now." Jay described it as a palpable aura of desperation. He was offended at the idea of Kevin's baby just being someone's ticket into a market. One firm was flummoxed enough to ask an executive from the now out-of-vogue Friendster to come in, evaluate Digg, and explain it to them. Others asked how Digg planned to convert its site into something that could be the next Yahoo! or AOL. "They are still back in the 1998 belief system that it's all about portals," Jay said afterward, laughing. The two would leave meetings stunned.

Then they hit Greylock Partners. Located in an obscure San Mateo office park, several miles north of the Sand Hill strip, Greylock is a venerable East Coast firm that has had some solid Valley hits, but nary a big dotcom win among them. David Sze was working to change that. He had heard about Digg and was curious to meet the guys behind it. Jay and Kevin sauntered in wearing almost head-to-toe hipster black.

"Who are these guys?" Sze thought to himself, amused. They had a bit of the too-cool-for-school aura to them. (Indeed, Jay has been known to wear sunglasses indoors from time to time.) Sze was different than most of the venture capitalists they'd been pitching, and not just because he was dressed more like the UPS delivery guy than the typical blue-shirt-and-khakis VC. For one thing, he had actually worked at a dotcom. Sze was one of the first employees of Excite@Home, the granddaddy of all bubble flameouts. He had lived through all the mistakes and giddiness firsthand. He got Jay's trauma and he could relate.

But he also thought about investing differently. The Digg boys wanted to raise only $2 million, a paltry sum to a venture capital firm sitting on billions in assets. Each partner had to personally deploy $10 million or so a year, ideally on one or two deals. A deal for $2 million was hardly worth their time. But Jay had seen the evils of too much money at Equinix. When start-ups have it, they spend it. He didn't want to see Digg get corrupted that way. Shockingly, David agreed. He couldn't even really explain why. He shrugged, saying he just believed in the guys and the company and knew it was the right thing for them. He had confidence that if the company worked out, the reward would be worth his time. That was enough.

Another condition: The Digg boys wanted to focus on building a cool product people loved and not start worrying about revenues yet. They would outsource some ad sales to pay the bills, but that was it. "No problem," said David. He asked Jay about how he saw the potential exit—Valley speak for how investors will make back their money, typically through an acquisition or IPO. That was a tough one for Jay. He had hated being part of a public company and blamed it for most of what had ruined Equinix. He did not want that to happen to Digg. Nor was he anxious to sell out to a company that wouldn't get it. He had this fantasy that Digg would stay pure and cool forever. "There is no need for another corporate bureaucratic sweater-vesty piece-of-shit formerly cool company. Not this one. The days of those are over."

So he answered David honestly. "I can't operate with that in mind. I think there will be an exit one day and you will get your money and you will be very happy, but I want to keep the goal of democratizing the media for now." He added to himself, "This time, if the right offer comes along after what happened last time, they can kiss my ass. I don't care; I'm taking the money. My family comes first." An outsider might argue Kevin and Jay had the swagger, the parties, and the attitude of a classic dotcom, but they harbored none of those late 1990s delusions that they were invincible.

Within a few days Digg was $2 million richer, and amazingly, Kevin retained a whopping 39 percent of the company. David was the only other person to join the board, leaving Kevin and Jay as a two-to-one voting majority for any big company-changing decisions. As he signed the terms of the deal, Jay smiled and breathed a sigh of relief. If Digg was a hit, he knew his protégé wouldn't endure the same fate he had.

4

LEMMINGS AT THE GATE

Jay Adelson may be the only one yelling, "Fuck the sweater-vests!" but he's not alone in the sentiment. Most of the haters are far less creative. Calling venture capitalists lemmings all chasing one another blindly off a cliff may be the most overused insult in Silicon Valley history, followed closely by the term *vulture capital.* These phrases encapsulate the distrust a lot of entrepreneurs and start-up onlookers feel toward VCs. It's a combination of hating them and mocking them. There's the fear that VCs viciously use the weaknesses of others to their advantage but at the same time are bumblers who have merely won some kind of cosmic lottery where they get to make millions a year doing very little but following one another's lead.

But how deserved is the rap? That's hard to answer. Venture capital is one of the last vestiges of California's Wild West. A partner in a venture firm decides to invest in a company on the basis of a lot of information—for example, detailed financials and extensive customer interviews—or on as little information as a breezy PowerPoint between friends. It's not a loan, so the money is never repaid per se. Rather, the venture investor swaps stock and usually a board seat for the cash. They make their money by selling those shares when that start-up sells to a publicly traded company or goes public itself; then they pass the returns to their investors, typically large pension funds and institutional investors. (They keep a good deal for themselves too.) Since they are basically betting on an idea or a best-case scenario, a few million can buy a huge percentage of a young company. Most of their bets will be worthless. But one jackpot can return the entire investment on a several hundred million dollar fund—and then some.

Even within finance, most industries consolidate as they grow. The bigger companies buy up smaller ones in order to get more market share faster than opening new locations, hiring a new sales force, or building new products. But amassing pure market share doesn't matter so much in the venture capital business. It's more about getting in those one or two deals that'll become the big home runs, and that's best done with a small cadre of in-the-know partners. So as the overall amount of venture capital grows, the industry doesn't consolidate, it just gets bigger and more fragmented. Where there used to be about three hundred firms several years ago, there are thousands today. And there's a huge discrepancy when it comes to returns. The top 10 percent of venture capital firms make nearly 90 percent of the money. That means there are a lot of posers, or in the language of disgruntled Valley folks, lemmings.

Venture capital is also intensely private, unorganized, and at the most elite levels, very clubby. Since it's all private money—in other words, not traded on an open stock exchange like the NASDAQ—it's mostly outside the purview of the Securities and Exchange Commission. There are few rules. Deals and terms are based less on the company itself and more on who holds the most power at that given point in the economic cycle: the venture guys or the entrepreneurs. This balance of power continually swings back and forth over the very slow life of a given fund, about ten years. When things are going well, entrepreneurs are in the driver's seat. VCs are hungry to get in great deals before they go public or get bought for a load of cash. When times are tough, the purse strings tighten up, and suddenly the entrepreneurs are skulking up and down Sand Hill Road, begging for a meeting.

When the bubble burst, venture capitalists looked around and saw thousands of Web companies that suddenly had no shot at going public or getting acquired. So they had to get a little brutal. Funding was cut off. Companies were shuttered. And deal terms got harsher and harsher. Many venture capitalists just wrote off their losses and started to look for what might be the next big wave. (Biotech? Maybe nanotech?) If these Net companies weren't going to deliver a return, better to shut them down now, write their value down to zero, and build their portfolios back up from there. Companies were sold for pennies on the dollar invested, and the common wisdom was a fund invested in 1999 or 2000 would be lucky merely to make its money back.

That wasn't a good thing for venture capitalists, but venture capital funds are graded on a curve. In other words, their investors wouldn't compare a fund invested in 2000 to a fund invested in 1995; they'd compare it to other funds that started investing in 2000, or so-called vintage 2000 funds. And when the best vintage 2000 funds broke even, that was a pretty low bar. Most of the big Silicon Valley venture firms would be just fine.

What's more, the individual partners would continue to make millions. Venture capital firms get paid in two ways. The most well known is by selling their shares in a company when it goes public or is acquired by another public company. But their investors also pay the firms an annual management fee. It's typically about 2 percent of the total fund they are investing. When funds were under

$100 million, that was just enough to keep the lights on. But in 1999 and 2000, the funds were closer to $1 billion, and those annual management fees were swelling to more like $200 million to split among five or six guys. In 2002, when Andrew Anker was debating about whether or not to leave August Capital and go to Six Apart, he had done hardly any deals and sat on only a few boards. But thanks to those management fees, he was bringing home a cool $3 million a year.

Entrepreneurs didn't have such a safety net. Every time a company goes out to raise another chunk of cash—or a round of venture capital—the terms get renegotiated. After the bust, the few companies that could raise additional cash had to swallow some pretty ugly new terms. Now that few dotcoms had a prayer of going public, the paper value of a company that had been considered worth, say, $300 million would be written down to a fraction of that. Called a cram-down round, it did just that: crammed down any existing stockholders' ownership to practically nothing, while the new investors got the bulk of the ownership in the company. Almost always those previous investors included the founders and all the employees. They'd be dependent on venture capital investors to allocate them more stock if they wanted to have any ownership at all. To be fair, most of the good venture capitalists would allocate some shares—after all, they didn't want to own the *whole* company. Entrepreneurs worked harder with skin in the game.

There were also truly onerous terms, such as liquidation preferences. If an investor has a liquidation preference, it means he gets paid first in the event that a start-up is actually worth something. That's pretty standard. But in the wake of the bubble, a lot of investors were getting greedy and insisting on so-called multiple liquidation preferences. Imagine an entrepreneur took $10 million in funding and worked his tail off to build something; then Yahoo! decided to buy it for $30 million. If his investors had a multiple liquidation preference, they'd be guaranteed to get three or more times their investment before the entrepreneur or his employees saw a dime. Congratulations on tripling our money. Here's nothing for you.

To be fair, venture capitalists are in a business. They are entrusted with money from pension funds or wealthy investors and they have a fiduciary duty to make a big return on it, commensurate with the risk inherent in backing an unknown, unproven company. Any entrepreneur should know that he can't get millions of dollars with no strings attached. With every dollar of venture capital he takes, he is selling his company bit by bit. And the buyers didn't always have the same interests as the entrepreneur.

Taken together, all of this creates an ugly truth of the venture business that was made crystal clear in the years after the 2000 NASDAQ bust: While all or most of a founder's net worth was likely tied up in a start-up, VCs were essentially playing with the house's money. They not only had bets across dozens of companies but were taking home salaries of a couple of million dollars per year *no matter what*. Even if every single company in their portfolio crashed and burned. So it was part of a venture capitalist's job to sit on a board and say, "Nah, let's not sell for $100 million. Let's let it ride," then shut the company down weeks later when the economy tanked. For an entrepreneur, this was frequently emotionally and financially devastating.

Most VCs knew they were making some enemies in the bleak years. They also knew things would come back in favor of entrepreneurs at some point, and such terms would ease. Entrepreneurs would have the power again, sure, but VCs would always have the money, the lifeblood of the high technology start-up game. It was simply how the Valley worked. But venture capitalists made one big miscalculation: They assumed that when dotcoms came back, entrepreneurs would need their money. They didn't.

Not even the most prescient venture capitalists could have predicted how cheap starting a Web business would become in just a few years. Sure, to really build out a big business, an entrepreneur would eventually need venture capital. But he could get pretty far on just a few million, and many could scrape that together from wealthy friends. By the time entrepreneurs really needed VC-level cash, their businesses would be far enough along that they could name the terms.

When Netscape was founded in 1994, entrepreneurs like Marc Andreessen and Jim Clark had to buy pricey Sun servers, Oracle database software, data storage equipment from EMC, Cisco routers, plus very, very expensive bandwidth—the computing power necessary to shove trillions of bits across telecom networks. They also had to hire a lot of expensive programmers to write millions of lines of code. It would take $2 million just to prove it all worked, and another $10 million or so to get the site launched. To make it a real business? Another $30 million, $40 million, easy. Total: at least $42 million.

By 1999 or so, the only thing that had fallen in price was bandwidth, as trillions of dollars were being spent to build out more telecom networks to carry all that fast-growing Internet traffic. Total costs actually went up. An entrepreneur still had to buy all that software and hardware from the tech elite, and probably more of it, given that more people were online. He would also have to add in substantially higher price tags for smart engineers (this was the peak of the salary curve, especially for engineers) and stratospheric rent (in Silicon Valley, at least $80 per square foot). And of course he would need a lot more money for branding and marketing in such a hypercompetitive market. Back then, it took $5 million to prove it would work; another $10 million to $15 million to launch it; and another $30 million to $40 million to build it into a real business. Total: at least $45 million.

Compare that to the origins of Digg, just about four years later. It took Kevin less than $10,000 to prove it would work. He paid $90 per month to a company to host it—cutting out much of the costs of servers and all that pricey software. And building the site? He no longer required an army of highly paid engineers. Just one guy in Canada whom he met online and paid $12 an hour. By the time Digg even set foot on Sand Hill Road, it already had a well-defined product and hundreds of thousands of rabid users. All that on just $500,000.

Mark Zuckerberg is an even more extreme example. He started Facebook in his dorm room. So real estate and employee costs: zero. Sure, there were still costs associated with bandwidth, servers, and keeping the site up and running as new colleges joined and traffic soared. But the costs had come down enough that Zuckerberg could slap a few banner ads on the site and cover those expenses easily. The site was profitable when it raised its first round of investor cash.

Entrepreneurs didn't even have to do anything as formal as ad sales. When Ben and Mena started Six Apart, they funded it all through donations. If people liked their software, they used it and sent the Trotts a check. Ditto for Brad Fitzpatrick, who started LiveJournal in his dorm room at the University of Washington. He wrote LiveJournal as a tool to communicate with his friends: "Keg in my dorm. Come over if you want." As in the case of Facebook, people from other schools started using it as the blogging revolution was taking off. As the surging traffic gobbled up bandwidth and servers, Brad simply posted a note asking for donations. In exchange, he'd send them a T-shirt. He gave his friends "internships" to manage it all. Brad was a millionaire before he graduated.

Another miscalculation venture capitalists made: A lot of entrepreneurs *did* make a good deal of money in the late 1990s. And, as detailed in previous chapters, that created a whole new generation of angel investors. Angel investors with grudges against VCs, at that. When entrepreneurs like Mark Zuckerberg or Kevin Rose needed money, they turned to these friend-tors first, and the costs were so low that the money could last them a good while. In many cases, venture capitalists were totally shut out of those key early stages of a company's formation, the time when they would normally build up the most lucrative ownership stakes. When it came to the Web, they were turning into late-stage investors whether they liked it or not. In a few cases, they were shut out all together. When Marc Andreessen set out to build his third start-up, Ning, he personally invested $9 million of his Netscape and Opsware winnings. He was his own angel investor, and effectively his own venture capitalist as well. In 2007, when Marc and his cofounder Gina Bianchini finally set out to raise outside money, they pitched large investment banks such as Lehman Brothers, skipping over traditional VCs completely.

Similarly, Brad never raised any outside funding for LiveJournal at all. When the company got so big he couldn't handle it with his skeleton staff, he sold it to Six Apart in 2005—notably, another start-up. He could have sold to a much larger Internet company for more. This was right when blogging was hot and few sites had the audience of LiveJournal, especially with its coveted high school and college demographic. But Brad wasn't sure that big companies like Yahoo! really understood LiveJournal. Plus, he still wanted a job and knew he wouldn't exactly fit in with one of the tech old guards. At Six Apart, he was the guy who has a few beers on a Friday afternoon, then races his coworker's Segway around the office. Or fills out joke expense forms for "hookers and blow" just to see if Ben would sign them. (He did, and the whole thing ended up with an angry Mena running through the office waving the form, yelling, *"Beeeeeeen!"*) Sure, you could argue Brad sold too early and that LiveJournal could have been a huge company on its own. But he didn't care. At just twenty-six he had millions in the bank, significant holdings in Six Apart, a big San Francisco house, and little responsibility. And he had never held a single meeting with a VC.

These entrepreneurs simply held all the cards. Those who did take venture capital funding had VCs by the cojones. Exhibit A: Mark Zuckerberg. Even before he arrived in Silicon Valley in 2004, Zuck had met Sean Parker, a twenty-five-year-old grizzled vet who cofounded Napster at just eighteen. He'd just been ousted from his latest startup and gave Zuck, as he was called, a crash course in how venture capital really works. Sean set him up with ex-PayPal CEO Peter Thiel, who was now running a small venture fund for some quick cash, and that was all the money the company ever really *needed.* By the time Facebook raised cash from the traditional venture firm Accel Partners, it was already dominant on about thirty college campuses and the company was profitable. That meant Zuck could command a nosebleed valuation of close to $100 million. The higher the valuation, the less ownership he had to give up. Zuck was able to hang on to more than a third of the company and an unconditional voting majority on the board.

At the time, a lot of onlookers saw the details of the deal as a sign of Accel's desperation to be in a hot Internet company. In hindsight, even if the partners had strolled down Palo Alto's leafy University Avenue in Facebook-blue body paint, it would have been worth it. Facebook's valuation went from a steep $100 million when Accel invested to an even more unimaginable $500 million two years later when David Sze of Greylock got in. Less than a year later, the company turned down a $1 billion acquisition offer from Yahoo! Accel and Greylock weren't looking desperate anymore. They were looking prescient.

By 2006, the same investors who mocked Facebook's valuation years before were starting to do even lamer things that smacked of Web 2.0 desperation. Like hire young associates to go hang out at hip San Francisco bars and strike up conversations with potential entrepreneurs. "It was almost like adverse selection," explains Andrew Anker, the Six Apart exec and former venture capitalist. "If you're really onto something good, why would you give up any of it before you have to?"

It was simply a new world, and in the venture capitalists' haste in 2000 and 2001 to cut their losses, many of them had made a crucial error in thinking. They miscalculated how fast deep pockets could become irrelevant. Without money, what did they have? There's the shopworn shtick on Sand Hill Road that VCs are more than just cash—that they bring valuable contacts in the industry, that they can help entrepreneurs recruit experienced vice presidents to help run their businesses, that they make sage board members. In some cases, it's true. After all, YouTube, a Sequoia company, sold to Google, another Sequoia company. Sequoia made the most money on the deal. Any wonder how those two came together? But for the early days of a Web company, little of that mattered. Far more important was hanging on to control of the board and of as many shares as possible, and the longer the founders could put off raising money, the more likely that was to happen.

But the cost of running a business—even a dramatically lower one—is just one side of the balance sheet. If founders wanted to keep the lemmings at bay for long, they'd need some sort of income too. Since costs were so much lower, they didn't need much. But they did need something. And the easiest way to get it was by slapping ads on their sites. Many of the late 1990s class of Internet companies also sought to build businesses with advertising revenues. But this time around, it was far easier. Part of it was the mere fact that time had passed. By the early 2000s, more than a billion people were spending copious amounts of time online, increasingly with high-speed broadband connections. Even old economy companies who spent the year after the bust gloating over the humbling of the Net soon realized online advertising hadn't been simply a fad. If big consumer brands wanted to reach people—especially young people—they needed to start shifting a sizable chunk of their ad budgets back online.

Meanwhile, in about 2000, Google quietly changed everything by cracking the search advertising code. To be fair, a company named Overture (later bought by Yahoo!) figured it out first, but Google applied the idea to its superior search engine, and perfected it. For a small fee, advertisers could buy search keywords. Say, Amazon wanted to make sure every time someone searched *Harry Potter* they saw an Amazon link. Before paid search ads, they had to hope that Google's search algorithm would rank Amazon higher than competitors. Now they could bid for the words *Harry* and *Potter*. If they paid the most, the Amazon link would show up in a box labeled "Sponsored Link."

It was genius. Google had safeguarded the integrity of its search results by keeping them not for sale, but gave companies a way to buy their way to the top of the list at the same time. And the system of bidding for keywords would ensure that more coveted keywords got a higher price, while less popular ones at least brought in something. And because it was broken up in per-word chunks, paid search ads were a rare advertising market for both big companies with billions to spend and small businesses that couldn't afford more than a hundred dollars or so. Both groups ate it up and a new multibillion-dollar market was born.

Paid search advertising also truly exploited the Web's interactivity for the first time. Advertisers had lost faith in boring banner ads, assuming people just tuned out the top of their Web pages. But search ads could be aimed directly at users looking for a particular thing. People would click on them and be directed to the advertiser's site. Advertisers paid by the click and could track where those clicks went. They could easily see how much their marketing was costing and exactly how much it yielded. And in the early days, paid search ads were cheap enough that marketers could experiment with them without much risk. Today, paid search accounts for more than 40 percent of the online advertising market, and those dollars are still growing along with the overall market.

Clearly, it's the biggest chunk of Google's $10 billion in annual revenues, with less than 5 percent coming from other services like business software. But the search giant had another idea that enabled the Web 2.0 explosion. It was called AdSense. AdSense brought the no-frills, almost insta-revenue of paid search ads to other smaller sites like blogs and fledgling Web businesses. Google would sell text, image, or even video ads for a site. And then thanks to the magic of HTML, the ads would automatically show up on that site. When someone clicked on them, the site—and Google—would make money.

What's more, Google would use its search engine to match appropriate sites with appropriate advertisers. Say Hewlett-Packard wanted to advertise a new printer on blogs that do gadget reviews. Employing its vast network of computers and servers, Google could automatically make that happen. Google would price the ads based on how many people click on them or how many people flock to a given site. And then at the end of the month, Google would send the site a check. For the advertiser, it was like buying keywords, only they were buying key sites. For the Web site, it was a dream come true: revenues without having to lift a finger. To be sure, smaller sites might generate just pennies per ad. But for larger sites with a lot of traffic, Google ads can mean hundreds of thousands of dollars in annual income, even millions. It was the early lifeblood for sites like Digg and YouTube, giving them a stream of income from the beginning.

And as Internet advertising continued to mature, this outsourcing of ad sales was only the beginning. Other firms would soon launch, taking the AdSense idea and tailoring it for specific types of Web sites. Henry Copeland started Blogads in 2002, specifically placing ads for bloggers wanting to quit their day jobs, making millions for popular political blogs like Daily Kos. John Battelle, a former journalist and publisher of the bubble magazine *The Industry Standard*, founded Federated Media in 2005, a more high-end ad shop that bigger blogs such as TechCrunch and sites such as Digg would use to handle their ad sales, typically once they outgrew AdSense.

Then in 2006, Google set a new online advertising precedent again when it struck a unique deal with MySpace, which was quickly emerging as one of the largest sites on the Internet. Google would sell ads on all those millions of MySpace pages, guaranteeing MySpace $900 million over several years and of course taking a cut for its trouble. Desperate not to lose any more of the Internet advertising game to Google, Microsoft countered by striking a similar deal to sell Facebook's banner ads for three years, paying them a guaranteed $300 million. And nearly a year later, Microsoft doubled down on the new Web, striking an ad deal with Digg, in the range of $100 million or so. Suddenly, sites like these weren't just about promise and eyeballs. They had real robust guaranteed revenue streams. Deals like these had been impossible in the first bubble because online advertising was so new. But by 2006, an infrastructure had grown up to support it.

Just as important as the cash, these quick and easy revenue streams enabled a psychological shift in Web thinking. No one *wants* to be advertised to, so on any site there was a natural tension between the so-called user experience and the ads that paid for it. After the crash, venture capitalists started demanding that Web businesses have a business model from day one—the whole "let's build an audience first" experience had proved just too risky. But this focus on revenues made for some pretty lackluster sites littered with flashy pop-up ads, pop-under ads, and annoying ads that would load in between pages.

But the new kind of ads meant that just by setting aside a tiny bit of space on the page entrepreneurs could frequently bring in enough cash to cover their low expenses. If they needed more money, they'd just free up more space or raise their rates as traffic grew. It almost ran on autopilot, freeing them up to once again focus on building a killer product that users would love. Everything they did was all about the user and innovation. Entrepreneurs became rabid about this. As YouTube's popularity grew, advertisers were clamoring to show short thirty-second spots before videos. But Steve Chen refused, arguing that it would turn people off.

It also meant the blue-shirt-wearing MBA types didn't have the same role they did when they first flooded out of Ivy League schools and swarmed San Francisco during the bubble. They were the business development or "biz dev" guys. Their job was to jet around making deals with large old economy companies while the coders stayed back at the office, toiling all night to make sure the sites worked. The biz dev guys were once gods at dotcoms. The Web was so new and there was such an emphasis on amalgamating eyeballs that dotcoms would sign sometimes expensive partnership deals to be the dotcom presence for a bevy of old economy companies. It was the kind of thinking that led to the AOL-Time Warner merger. But because this new wave of Web companies was so focused on user-generated content and building communities of everyday people, they hardly cared what old media or any other stodgy business thought. These new Web businesses were started by coders, and the businesses were focused on product and engineering. "All the CEOs as salesmen failed," says Peter Thiel. "That lesson has been learned."

There's an important caveat in all of this. None of these instant-revenue ad-outsourcing deals solved the problem of figuring out a sustainable high-growth revenue model to support the nosebleed valuations of a hot Internet start-up. It simply put it off.

For MySpace, Facebook, and Digg, outsourced banner ads alone wouldn't do it—even when they were bringing in hundreds of millions. And while Google-style contextual ads worked great on a search engine where people were trying to find something, they weren't nearly as powerful on a site where people just wanted to connect with friends.

If a start-up was going to be Silicon Valley's next Google, it wasn't enough to have the best technology or even the biggest audience. The Web has seen many transformative social and cultural trends that didn't yield big businesses, like Napster and KaZaA. Only slightly better are companies like TiVo, which utterly transformed how people view media, but ultimately haven't been able to capitalize much on that success.

Anyone who lived through the bubble and bust knew that figuring out how to make money couldn't be put off forever. The next breakthrough in Web advertising would still need to be found. And on sites where people just wanted to hang out with their friends, figuring out ways to shove ads in people's faces without alienating them was going to prove a thorny problem.

5

THE MOB GIVETH AND THE MOB TAKETH AWAY

Reid Hoffman of LinkedIn is one of the only people in the scene who actually uses the phrase *Web 2.0* with a straight face, which is a shame because the term is actually very fitting. As the acceleration in Web advertising shows, these new Web companies were both building on the first crop of dotcoms and doing something distinctly different. Reid explains a difference between Webs 1.0 and 2.0 that's more basic than the differences in capitalization or business models. During the Web 1.0 days, the Internet was a new, distinctive thing. Going online was seen as a reclusive, socially detached experience. These were the days when the term *virtual reality* was big. Internet users were stereotyped as pasty-faced geeks terrified to go out in public, typing away in chat rooms and using codelike, inscrutable lingo such as LOL, IMHO, and OMG.

By the time Web 2.0 came around, the Internet was no longer its own distinct land. It was woven into people's everyday lives. This was partially due to advances in networking and computer technology. As high-speed connections, wireless Internet routers, WiFi-enabled laptops, and Web-enabled cell phones became more common, people could be online instantly and anywhere, not just at a desk. It changed how they used the Web. Instead of opening an encyclopedia, you could open up Google. Instead of checking a newspaper for a movie listing, you could just check Yahoo! (much to the chagrin of encyclopedia salesmen and newspaper executives everywhere). And when sites such as MySpace, Facebook, and LiveJournal popped up, they gave people a way to access friends, family, and coworkers online more efficiently too.

A good social networking site makes all the intangible things that go along with being friends—like staying in touch, organizing get-togethers, and swapping photos—more efficient than in the regular, offline world, just as the telephone did for people a hundred years earlier. A great site enables connections that might never have happened in the offline world, but should. Suddenly, socializing online was no longer about hiding from the real world, because the two were becoming indistinguishable. "Think about if you tried to do something like Yelp in 1996," Reid says. "So few people would ever join, and they'd be the kind of people who were 'going' to the Internet." Hardly the urban, affluent, fashion-forward San Franciscans who dominate the site today. As Mark Zuckerberg puts it, Facebook isn't trying to *create* a social graph; it's trying to mirror or depict the social graph that already exists in the real world today.

Of course it's not easy. Technical factors such as innovation, design, and technology get these companies only so far. A great Web 2.0 site needs a mob of people who use it, love it, and live by it—and convince their friends and family to do the same. Mobs will devote more time to a site they love than they will to their jobs. They'll frequently *build* the site for the founders for free, because they get something out of that site that's far greater than money. When done well, social networking, media, and user-generated content sites tap into—and exploit—core human emotions. Blogs and sites such as YouTube, Yelp, Revision3, and Digg are ostensibly about getting the entertainment and news that you want. But it's the stroking of your ego that makes them so powerful. Having thousands of people read your opinion on something or your minute-by-minute life story. Having dozens of people mark your Yelp review as "funny" or "cool." Your video clip becoming a YouTube phenomenon or your Digg submission getting voted front-page-worthy. People you don't even know love you.

But more important than entertainment, self-expression, or ego-boosting is the human need to connect. This is a far more powerful use of the Web than for something like buying a book online. That's why these sites are frequently described as addictive. Machines are used to exploit what makes humans so uniquely human. Only a certain subset of people is addicted to, say, online gambling or online shopping. But everyone is addicted to validation and human connections.

And as Web 2.0 came around, the Internet was also becoming more mainstream. Soon it wasn't just for geeks, as in the Web's early days, or teenagers, as in social networking's early days. One billion and a quarter people were online. In the United States alone, the percentage of people online had grown from 10 percent in 1995 to 70 percent ten years later, nearly half with high-speed connections. Forty-eight million have posted content online—that's more people than watch *American Idol* in a given week.

It's hard to overstate how powerful this mass, two-way nature of social media and social networking is, whether it works to build a site up or tear it down. The Web community is both this generation of Web companies' greatest strength and its greatest challenge. Web 2.0's reliance on all things community may be an even greater contrast with the first wave of Internet companies than the dramatically different economics of Web 1.0 and 2.0.

Sure, the first generation of Web businesses took advantage of a lot of the medium's inherent uniquenesses. E-tailers had the advantage of not having to build out a chain of brick and mortar stores. eBay dealers got the plus of eBay's vast global community of shoppers. Media companies could cut out costs like paper printing and distribution, some 70 percent of a daily newspaper's expenses. And all of these vendors would enjoy the huge reach of the Web. But few sites in the Web's early days were really using all of the Net's potential for interaction. At best, sites like Amazon.com might track what you browsed and purchased to make recommendations for you in the future. Or Yahoo! might remember where you live and automatically bring up local weather and sports scores the next time you logged on. Such behind-the-scenes customizations were considered groundbreaking at the time. But that was nothing compared to having the audience actually creating, fueling, and proselytizing for the site.

This may seem like a curious path for the Web to take, from companies pushing goods, services, or information via the Web to companies building sites that would allow everyone to push them to each other. It was hardly one that seemed obvious or planned, but just as the business models of the first bubble laid the foundation for Web 2.0 economics, so too did a handful of early sites like eBay, Craigslist, KaZaA, and Napster create the first seeds of community online. The two greatest influences were a couple of underground movements called open source software and peer-to-peer file sharing. And ironically, both were mostly born in stodgy old Europe, not in the Valley.

The more important of the two was open source software. Call it a last bastion of romanticism in the maturing, increasingly cutthroat world of the business software. Open source programs are typically written by far-flung coders working all over the globe to solve some problem, frequently for the intellectual challenge of it alone. The best-known example is Linux, an operating system for computers, servers, even mobile phones and calculators. It was created by a Finnish student, Linus Torvalds, in the early 1990s, and while a set group governs the code, hundreds of thousands of engineers have contributed to it over time, many of them from the privacy of their own homes, coding away through the night and rarely ever meeting any of the other Linux builders.

In the past when you bought a piece of software you got only the finished product, such as iTunes or Microsoft Word. You take what they give you. With open source software companies you get that, but also all the underlying code that makes the program work. The idea is that the user can monkey around with the code, fixing any bugs, adding features, tailoring it to meet his needs. And frequently users submit these fixes to the code back to the community for approval, making it better for everyone. There's another big benefit too: Open source software is cheap—sometimes free—because it's written in this highly collective manner. Frequently, people just download it and get to work.

Sounds kinda hippieish, right? Peace, love, and open source? That's a big reason traditional software companies—and by extension, venture capitalists—weren't worried at first. But it has become big business these days. More than a quarter of the business world's servers run Linux. When Mozilla, the nonprofit maker of the open source Web browser Firefox, started in 2002, it had a skeleton crew of full-time coders, an army of volunteers, and a modest goal: take down Microsoft's ubiquitous Internet Explorer. The same Internet Explorer that had run Netscape out of business years earlier, which was appropriate because Firefox was based on the old Netscape code.

The browser was ready to go, but it occurred to one of Mozilla's founders that if a sprawling network of volunteers could write and debug the browser, why couldn't a sprawling network of volunteers market it? Surely there were advertising executives, PR people, and college kids who were just as into this mission and couldn't write code. Why couldn't they be mobilized into a grassroots army to spread Firefox? It worked. Hundreds of thousands of bloggers added "Download Firefox" buttons to their sites, while thousands of others chipped in for a $250,000 two-page ad in *The New York Times*. A group of college students in Oregon made a 220-square-foot crop circle out of the Firefox logo. Even the logo itself was designed by a volunteer. As a result, Firefox grabbed 10 percent of worldwide browser market share in about a year, while a rival browser sponsored by deep-pocketed Apple struggled to get just one percentage point.

Clearly, the Web enabled the rise and proliferation of open source. With high-speed, always-on Internet connections, anyone could be part of the movement, and companies in turn could use those connections to download the fruits of this collective labor. But the rise of open source enabled the rise of Web 2.0 just as much. The most obvious way was drop-dead-cheap software, a must in the early days of the Web's resurgence, when founders were lucky to cobble together a few thousand dollars from friends. Almost all of Web 2.0 uses open source databases, application servers, and coding languages, not to mention cheap, no-frills servers running Linux. It's the biggest single reason costs fell 90 percent in a matter of years.

But inexpensive, flexible software wasn't the only thing Web 2.0 got from the open source movement. In its reliance on a far-flung community of mostly unpaid rabid contributors, it borrowed from the open source movement's very ethos and soul. No other place had mastered and utilized community the way the world of open source software had. It had managed to knock every big software company back on its heels one way or another. It *forced* them to change, mostly for the better. By 2006, Microsoft was frantically working Firefox-like features into its browser, and more beleaguered companies like Novell and Sun Microsystems even started giving away code for free in the hopes of enjoying some of those good community vibes. Both Linux and Mozilla succeeded because they made people feel like they were part of a movement, something bigger than themselves. That is hard to do, but is a far bigger motivator than a paycheck. Now Web 2.0 was hoping to use that same playbook to beat the Yahoo!s, AOLs, News Corps, and Viacoms at their own game.

It's all about the wisdom of crowds in the Web 2.0 and open source worlds. Just as a mass of Kevin Roses can build a better front page to a newspaper, so too can a mass of unnamed coders build better software. It would be almost hypocritical for these grassroots sites to use anything else. Had open source not taken off, Web 2.0 might still have emerged. But it would have taken longer, cost more, and the cautious, tight-fisted hackers who came up with its greatest ideas likely wouldn't have been part of it. It probably would have looked a lot more like Web 1.0. Maybe you could call it Web 1.5.

At the same time open source was taking off in serious geek circles, peer-to-peer networks like Napster, KaZaA, and BitTorrent were using far-flung communities to swap music and movies for free all over the world. Open source was using community to make the Web work; Napster and KaZaA were using it to make the Web *cool.* Although these sites were called havens of piracy, their explosive growth provided one of the earliest examples to everyone—venture capitalists, everyday Web surfers, and big media—of how powerful networks of average everyday folks could reshape whole industries overnight.

You can't talk about peer-to-peer without talking about Niklas Zennström and Janus Friis. This European duo have been at the forefront of every bite the Web has taken out of big traditional industries, and they've always used sprawling networks of everyday folks linked together online to beat large companies at their own game. The first was KaZaA. While Niklas and Janus set out to build something big, it certainly wasn't intended to become a case that would make it all the way to the Supreme Court.

Niklas and Janus met in a very un-Web way, through a newspaper classified ad in Denmark. This is ironic because the Swedish-born Niklas first encountered the Internet way back in 1991 and was an instant believer in its nascent power. He was studying at the University of Michigan in Ann Arbor. When he finished his studies, he returned to Sweden and signed up to work for a start-up hoping to compete with the big local phone company by rolling out fiber-optic cables and Internet service throughout Europe. Once he was finished wiring Sweden, the company moved Niklas to Denmark.

That was 1996 and it was there that he placed an ad in the local newspaper for someone to run the company's local help desk. Janus was just twenty-one and had been working on the competitor's help desk for about a year. He answered the ad, and Niklas hired him, mainly because Janus would know the ins and outs of how the competitor worked. Niklas needed someone who could jump in with little training. But Janus was young and inexperienced. Niklas figured he'd have to be replaced as the company grew.

Instead Janus got promoted. When Niklas left Denmark to continue expanding the Internet access business throughout Europe, Janus soon followed. The two began working closer together and were a bit of an odd couple. Niklas is old-school, with dual degrees in engineering and business. He'd worked in the corporate world for several years, wore suits, and knew how to play the game. Janus not only lacked a college degree, but had dropped out of high school in ninth grade. It bored him. Obviously, Janus was smart. But more important, Janus was completely unrestrained by corporate norms. Every time Niklas told Janus why something couldn't be done; Janus would ask, "Why not?" He was like a little ray of Silicon Valley shining into the gray European business world.

So in 1999, as Internet fever spread to Europe, the two started to wonder why they were working for someone else. They quit their day jobs and started KaZaA. Although a bit late to the dotcom game, KaZaA was very forward-thinking. Most of the Internet world at this time was still obsessed with the idea of portals: Sites such as AOL or Yahoo!, which aggretate a large amount of information—stock quotes, weather, news, links to other sites, and so forth—would put all this media and information on one page that would essentially be your gateway to the Internet. The AOL-Time Warner merger was all about shoving some of the world's greatest content into this portal, as was Disney's 1999 acquisition of Go.com.

Niklas and Janus thought that notion was absurd. Instead, KaZaA would be a platform where anyone could put content online and have distribution of it worldwide. Unlike Napster, the focus wasn't strictly on music. The idea was that millions (today, more than a billion) of people connected online could collectively be a better news and entertainment service than any one company. Clearly there is a European socialist basis to the idea. It obviouly targets the capitalist U.S. media conglomerates. But whatever the source, KaZaA and other peer-to-peer networks like Napster were the first instances of user-generated content on the Web.

Janus and Niklas hoped KaZaA would be big, even socially transformative. But they had no idea they would be pulled into a revolution. More than 300 million people downloaded KaZaA's software and opened up their personal stores of media to strangers everywhere. Unfortunately, big media still had a say in all this, and the Recording Industry Association of America declared war on these so-called peer-to-peer networks. When Napster was shut down, KaZaA only got bigger. And unlike Napster, KaZaA wasn't run on a central server, so shutting it down wasn't as easy. KaZaA won its case in Sweden's Supreme Court, so as long as the company had no business dealings in the United States there was little the RIAA could do to thwart them.

That said, KaZaA wasn't much of a business. From the get-go Niklas and Janus had hoped to sign deals with all the content providers, but clearly this wasn't going to happen. And to stay legally safe, they'd opted not to travel to the United States, making any potential negotiations tougher. So they sold KaZaA rather than keep fighting the battle. Still, the power of peer-to-peer networks had impressed them.

After KaZaA, the two founded Joltid, a company that built peer-to-peer networks for others. Joltid was being run by Niklas in Sweden, a development team in Estonia, and Janus working out of his home in Demark. They were a bare-bones operation, and by far their biggest cost was all those international phone calls. Niklas assumed there had to be a cheaper option. Before KaZaA he'd personally worked on developing something called voice over Internet protocol, or VOIP. The idea was to make phone calls over high-speed Internet networks instead of antiquated copper phone lines. It was something that seemed great in theory, but back in the 1990s no one seemed to be able to make it work. Niklas assumed the problem had been solved by someone, and started trying out different VOIP services on the market, most offered by big telecommunications or Internet companies.

But neither Niklas nor his engineers could get any of them to work. The problems were techy. In short, too many calls would max out a system, but it was too expensive and took too long to build out a network of so-called access points to ease the burden of all that traffic. That's when it hit Niklas and Janus: a peer-to-peer network would instantly and inexpensively solve that problem. They quickly built out a solution and gave it the quirky name Skype.

On Skype, people can make free or very low cost calls in exchange for sharing some of their personal bandwidth to help others make calls. The idea is similar to someone's generating power for his home with solar roof panels and selling what he doesn't need back to the grid. The notion was radical enough that no one would fund it. Niklas tried to raise money for an entire year, mostly in Europe, since he still couldn't travel to the United States without risking KaZaA-related legal woes. He remembers it as a painful experience. Some investors didn't return calls; others ordered him to leave their offices once they heard what he wanted to do. Most telecoms probably weren't too threatened by it either.

They should have been. By August 2003, Niklas sent some text messages to his friends telling them to check out Skype.com. They told their friends. That was the extent of the marketing. Within a month they had 1 million users. Two years later, Skype had grown in value enough for everyone to notice. By 2005, a thriving business flush with all the venture capital investors it could ask for, it was emerging as the VOIP player to beat. By the fall of that year, eBay made Niklas and Janus a $2.6 billion offer they couldn't refuse. Today, Skype has had more than half a billion downloads.*

If peer-to-peer networks could take on something as nonobvious as a telephone company, Niklas and Janus couldn't help but think back to their original vision for KaZaA: upending the world of entertainment. Although their day jobs were still working for Skype, in 2006 the two started Joost, a start-up aiming to merge television and the Internet, tapping the old CEO of Joltid to run it. Unlike KaZaA and even YouTube, they're seeking out content agreements with big media companies first. Now it's such an obvious business they have to jockey for position with Amazon, Google, and a host of other start-ups. But amazingly, Joost is one of the few

*eBay may have overpaid. On October 2007, eBay reassessed the value of its Skype assets—essentially admitting to investors it paid $900 million too much. Niklas stepped down.

using peer-to-peer technology to skirt a lot of the technical problems, just as they did with Skype. It's a highly competitive market, but Janus and Niklas have proven they *get* community. In today's power-to-the-people Web era, that makes them a force that can't be ignored.

The communities that drove open source software and peer-to-peer file sharing may have been socially and economically transformative, but they were hardly mainstream. Despite Mozilla's experiments in marketing Firefox, open source was mostly the province of geeks who could code. And most peer-to-peer networks were still considered shady or unstable. Many people don't want to open up their computer and its contents to the world. Plus, most peer-to-peer networks require a software download, as opposed to working solely over the Web. It was largely the Web 2.0 movement that took the powerful idea of community and made it legal, palatable, and easy for a mass market.

Just as with peer-to-peer networks, user contributions are key. Blogs need everyday folks to write them. Yelp has no content if people don't post reviews. Digg is nothing unless people contribute and vote on stories. MySpace, Facebook, and LinkedIn all need people to post their lives on those millions and millions of profile pages; otherwise who would go to them? Without people's photos, Slide would be one empty slide show. But you can also be a passive user in the Web 2.0 world. You can just use Yelp as a Yellow Pages while others write the reviews. You don't have to spend hours searching the Web for cool stories to be part of the Digg mob, you can just read the site. In the Web 2.0 world, people creating content and consuming content are all part of the community. And in this world, community is all-important. It is the single most powerful positive or destructive force.

There's no playbook for building a great community. It's all about listening to the users and knowing when to give in to them and when to stand firm with your vision. It always involves a great deal of trial and error and bobbing and weaving. But done right, these companies have something valuable that big media giants or the earlier Web wave simply can't replicate. Done wrong, they are toast. And it's not a one-time thing. Good communities take round-the-clock care and feeding.

Consider Yelp. When Russ and Jeremy first started the site, they never thought people would write reviews. They thought people would use the site to ping their friends and ask them to recommend, say, a good dentist. Then perhaps these recommendations would get organized in some big database. Reviews were sort of a subfeature. They also thought men would like the site, so they used colors like blue and gray that would resonate with guys.

But then a funny thing happened: Thousands of women flocked to the site and spent hours writing funny, engaging reviews. Russ, Jeremy, and their largest shareholder, Max, were stunned, but they quickly reacted, redesigning the site so reviews were the focus and changing the color scheme to be more lady-friendly. It paid off. Cute, funny girls in their late twenties and early thirties brought in lots of guys. Especially when Yelp started getting its community together for offline parties at hip clubs around the city, and all those girls showed up.

Had Russ and Jeremy set out to create a site for hip girls, maybe casting it in pink and getting sponsors like Sephora, it probably would have come off as contrived and no one would have joined up. After all, what do these guys know about what girls want? Instead, they followed the crowd and adjusted the site accordingly. They hired hip girls, and you can now buy panties from the site in signature Yelp red or an "I ♥ Yelp" red tank top—certainly never part of the original business plan.

The new Web scene is littered with examples like Yelp that

show how listening to a community and following its lead can make a site more valuable. But there is one big example of a site that didn't do it and failed: Friendster. The site no one in the Web 2.0 scene wants to become. It soared during early days, at one point getting a $300 million purchase offer from Google. But it was ultimately eclipsed by MySpace. The only time a less technically sophisticated company from Los Angeles—*Los Angeles!*—has beat out a Silicon Valley start-up, insiders bitterly recount.

Friendster's founder, Jonathan Abrams, cashed out several million dollars' worth of shares when he raised venture capital money in 2004. The valuation was more than $50 million—far higher than it would be a few years later. In a Wall Street–like culture, Abrams would be considered shrewd, with a classic "buy low, sell before it tanks" mentality. But in Silicon Valley, no one wants to emulate Abrams. Friendster was the first promising dotcom to come out of the rubble of the Internet bust. And it failed. That crushed any budding optimism there was about the consumer Web for a good two years. Even today, comparing a company to Friendster has become shorthand for "calm down, your site is just a fad."

Abrams got a lot of social networking right, with features that dozens of companies have emulated. But then Friendster made two crucial missteps. The biggest was that the site couldn't support the crush of traffic when it took off. It didn't act quickly enough to add more servers and update the site's inner workings, so the Friendster loyal got frustrated and logged off. There too is a lesson about open source software: Friendster used some open source technologies, but wrote it in Sun's power-hungry Java, not the more nimble open source scripting languages.

The other mistake was trying too hard to control everything. Critics of Abrams say he was too rigid in what people could or couldn't do on his site. Friendster saw itself as a dating site. Its early users were people in their twenties, mostly in San Francisco, looking for dates. When younger people started to use it, Abrams squelched it. He got in the habit of killing off profiles if they did not fit his criteria for the site. Social media sites need to have a benevolent dictator whom users will love and rebel against, but mostly love. Friendsters hated Abrams. MySpacers, on the other hand, love Tom. Tom Andersen is the co-founder of MySpace, but he's known simply as Tom or MySpace Tom to anyone who has been to the site. Users may make gentle fun of him, but he's like a friendly mascot for the site. Tom is automatically everyone's first friend on MySpace. You can ditch him if you like, but he *wants* to be your friend.*

An example: A Christian group wanted to make a Friendster profile for Jesus so they could identify other believers as "friends of Jesus." Abrams reportedly killed such profiles, saying only real, living people could sign onto the site. (Despite repeated requests, Abrams has refused to be interviewed about Friendster for this book.) On MySpace, you can start any profile under anyone's name. This can be tricky. At some high schools mischievous students have created dummy profiles for teachers. Think back to all those notes you passed with drawings of a mean teacher, or something you drew on a chalkboard behind the overhead projector screen. Now imagine that all online. Ouch. But if that is what the community wants, that is what they get.

There is a curious dynamic in Web 2.0 land. The more these entrepreneurs built tools and forums for democratizing the Web, the more they create tools that could be used against them. For instance, when Ben and Mena first started to charge for Movable Type, bloggers everywhere trashed them. Without Ben and Mena's software, bloggers wouldn't have had that very public forum. Privately, the two are horrified at a lot of the bad behavior that takes

* Danah Boyd, "Friendster Lost Steam. Is MySpace Just a Fad?" *Apophenia Blog*, 2006.

place on blogs. Nearly everyone on the Six Apart staff has a story of someone with an odd user name who has come after them, guns blazing, without having ever met them. One declared that he had been Ben's nemesis in high school. "I didn't even know I had a nemesis," the ultra-shy Ben says.

"He didn't!" snaps Mena. "He barely talked to anyone!"

A more extreme example of an online mob gone bad was the debacle of the Facebook News Feed in August 2006. The News Feed is one of the most impressive technical feats the company has ever pulled off. It automatically collects every change in your friend universe. Someone you know changes his or her photo. Someone changes his or her marital status. Someone posts a new blog. Someone adds a new friend. You get the idea. You log into Facebook and in front of you is the equivalent to an AP News roster about what's happening in your microcosm of the world. Every single thing.

Zuck was ecstatic about this feature. His dream for Facebook is to help people make sense of what's around them. This was a clean and efficient way to do it, and it was something that MySpace didn't have, for good reason. Such a move was a risk in terms of traffic and ad revenues. By culling information from all the profiles and putting it on one page, Facebook would be cutting down on the number of pages people had to visit and the amount of time they needed to spend on the site—the two most important metrics to show advertisers how popular a site is.

As it turned out, he was taking an even more basic risk: pissing off his users. Within a day of its debut, hundreds of thousands of Facebook users joined online coalitions protesting the News Feed, claiming it invaded their privacy by making their Facebook doings public. The irony is, as each person joined these anti–News Feed groups, the News Feed picked it up, broadcasting it to their friends. So they too joined. The News Feed enabled the rapid growth of the population trying to eliminate it.

Zuck couldn't help being a little happy. For one thing, traffic and page views actually rose substantially amid the chaos. The News Feed was undeniably a powerful and useful tool even for those who hated it. He didn't do away with it, but he and his team coded all night to incorporate more tools to turn it off or control what it contained. Still, the company learned a valuable lesson: Facebook wasn't just *their* company. The Facebook staff has been incredibly open and conversational through blogs and other tools whenever any change has come up since. They don't have a choice.

Then less than a year later, there was Digg's great community revolt, which threatened to push it into a Napster-like legal mess. In May 2007 someone submitted a story to Digg that contained a string of codes that allowed you to hack copyright provisions on an HD-DVD player. The story rapidly rose to the site's front page, getting a record-breaking 15,000 votes, or "diggs." About that time lawyers representing a consortium of DVD and media companies slapped Digg with a cease and desist order. Digg complied and pulled the story, assuming users would rather the site stay in business. After all, freedoms are a tricky thing. Digg already bans stories that link to hate crime or pornographic sites. This story was also promoting illegal behavior.

The community didn't see it that way. They saw it as censorship. Or worse: as bowing down to the man. Kevin had made his reputation among this geek underworld as the techy kid who could show you how to hack stuff. That's what his popular podcast *The Broken* was all about. That's why these geeks idolized him. Even the more conservative Jay had his "Fuck the Sweater-vests!" rallying cry. Now suddenly Digg was squelching such hacks and bowing down to the man? The site gave way to a total free-for-all. Thousands of Diggers started posting random fake stories containing the verboten code, and thousands more promoted them to the front page. By midnight, the front page had been overrun. Digg had a choice: shut down the entire site, pulling every single story and suspending thousands and thousands of its most loyal users' accounts, or capitulate to their will.

Either was dangerous. Ignoring what their most rabid users were saying would be suicide in the social media world. But if they capitulated to the mob, they'd not only open themselves to lawsuits but could set a dangerous precedent. Even a benevolent dictator ultimately has to do what's best for the site, even if his subjects don't like it. As all hell was breaking loose on Digg's front page, the weary crew didn't have long to figure out what exactly that was.

Ultimately Kevin made the call: better to piss off corporate America than Digg's community. He wrote a post saying, "After seeing hundreds of stories and reading thousands of comments, you've made it clear. You'd rather see Digg go down fighting than bow down to a bigger company. We hear you.... If we lose, then what the hell, at least we died trying." Kevin even repeated the taboo string of letters and numbers in the subject line of his post—just to prove he was still the same badass, noncorporate Kevin after all.

It was of course submitted to Digg's front page and received 28,000 diggs—easily an all-time record. The furor mostly died down, but at the price of Digg's potentially being hit by a major lawsuit. It was like nothing seen in Web 2.0 world yet. Most bloggers simply wrote about the news agog. Wrote Om Malik on the popular GigaOM blog, "It's hard for me to form an opinion on this right now, for I am watching this drama unfold in near real time with morbid fascination."

Although Digg hasn't yet been sued, this situation went well beyond "community is king." In this case, community was the despot, and hardly a benevolent one. It served as a warning: All that labor may be free—but that doesn't mean it doesn't come at a cost.

6

THE RETURN OF THE KING

It's November 2006, at the Web 2.0 Conference at the Palace Hotel in San Francisco. Hundreds of people are crammed into the hallways, buzzing, occasionally making what they consider fresh "isn't this just like the bubble?" quips. Thanks to the hefty price tag of attending and the fact that it has been sold out for months, few up-and-coming engineers building brilliant new Web sites are here. Or as Kevin Rose puts it derisively, "No one who's actually doing anything is here."

Kevin does make a cameo appearance, but only because his press people force him. He does a fifteen-minute speaking gig, with his usual two-day patchy beard, ruffled hair, and hipster garb. He gives a mediocre walk-through of some screenshots showing Digg's inner workings and then jumps offstage, out of the hotel, and back to work. Instead of a room full of Kevins, the hallways are filled with a gang of deal makers and elder statesmen who want to see and be seen. Swarming around them are people hoping some of the Web 2.0 chic will rub off on them.

It's not as if the halls were filled with high-tech nobodies. Marc

Benioff, chief executive of salesforce.com, a scrappy company that has sent shock waves through the business software world, was there; as was Jeff Bezos, the Web 1.0 kingpin who built and still runs Amazon.com; and Danny Rimer, the superhot London-based venture capitalist who backed Skype, MySQL, and any other hit to come out of the old world. David Sze, the VC who prefers fleece to sweater-vests and funded Digg, Facebook, LinkedIn, and others, was there too.

And there were the bloggers. John Battelle, former chairman of bubble magazine *The Industry Standard*, is somewhere between businessman, journalist, and Web 2.0 cheerleader. His new company Federated Media sells ads for sites like Digg so the companies don't have to. He's moderating the whole event. In the evenings, he works the room, a bourbon on the rocks in hand.

Nick Denton of Gawker Media is dressed in his characteristic all black and is avoiding the limelight, mostly making snarky comments in the corner. He too has a fake conference ID, borrowed from Zach Nelson, chief executive of the hot business software start-up NetSuite, which is set to go public in 2007. Denton had augmented his gossip empire, which skewers Washington, D.C., New York, and Los Angeles, with a new site to mock Silicon Valley, called Valleywag. The anonymity makes him all the more dangerous.

Jason Calacanis, founder of Weblogs and arch blogosphere "frenemy" of both Nick Denton and Kevin Rose, is operating full steam ahead. He seems to be constantly on camera for someone's podcast. During a panel, he says with a straight face that after he sold his blogging network Weblogs to AOL, he became the samurai inside the East Coast media giant. He does a swordlike movement when he says this. A week or so later, he'd leave AOL and stun much of Silicon Valley when Sequoia gave him a coveted entrepreneur-in-residence slot. It's the same position held by Max

Levchin just after PayPal sold. Calacanis is often thought of as very "New York/LA," not of the same cloth as Silicon Valley entrepreneurs. But clearly the Valley's über-VC firm saw something they wanted.

And there's Michael Arrington, whose TechCrunch blog has been dubbed the reincarnation of the new economy publication *The Red Herring*. A mention of a start-up on TechCrunch and it has arrived, at least in this microcosm. You'll hear a lot of people dis Arrington when he's not around, but few start-up honchos would dare to say anything critical to his face. He's just that powerful. (Or is perceived to be.)

Indeed, the venue is so packed that conference organizers wouldn't let me in, sniffing that my book may never get published and they couldn't risk giving up a slot at the event. Nice. So I'm roaming the halls with a fake conference ID that James Hong of HotorNot.com made me in the hotel bar. While not the second coming of the bubble, the fact that anyone is making a fake ID to go to a conference is a sign of some kind of industry froth.

But, to Kevin's point, this is largely the Web 2.0 scene that everyone loves to hate. The people who decry all the hype but play their part in boosting it just the same. The people who aren't quite as tapped in as they pretend. The people who talk a lot about being entrepreneurs. It's the money guys, the opportunists, and the latecomers. There's no Chad Hurley and Steve Chen. No Mark Zuckerberg. At the end of the first day, Max stops in for a drink in the lobby, mostly because his office is nearby and James makes him.

"You actually paid to be here?" Max asks James. He did. He is the rare one among them who actually enjoys these things. Plus, he's relaunching HotorNot and for the moment needs to be seen. Ben and Mena Trott are there, some, but more often, other Six Apart folks are seen wearing their name tags. Big angel investors like Peter Thiel or Reid Hoffman haven't even bothered to attend.

They don't need to. They already know everyone in the scene and placed many of their bets before all this Web 2.0 hoopla started.

It's hard to imagine a place Marc Andreessen would hate to be more.

Yet here he is on day two, striding down the halls with a mini-entourage. He's staring straight ahead. No eye contact with anyone, which isn't hard because at six feet four, he towers above most people. This is a very rare appearance for Marc. Forget conferences or parties—he rarely even leaves downtown Palo Alto unless it's one of his regular trips to Los Angeles (mostly in his single days) or Las Vegas (it's an hour away, same time zone, and he loves the fights).

Marc doesn't even much like to go outside. He describes his new house, purchased after his summer 2006 wedding to Valley socialite Laura Arrillaga, as a "digital wonderland." It boasts a 10-gigabit internal network, 60 terabytes of storage, a new Vista media center PC, 1,080-pixel displays, high-definition DVD players, and blu-ray players. When the Nintendo Wii came out, Ning, Marc's latest start-up, got one of the first consoles. On the Wii, you use the controls to physically perform movements such as playing guitar or tennis that are then captured in the game. Marc's cofounder, Gina Bianchini, didn't get it.

"Why would you play Wii tennis when you can just go over to Stanford and do the real thing?" she asked.

"Because then you'd have to go outside!" Marc said. He and she were sitting in one of his usual haunts, the Peninsula Fountain & Grill, an old Palo Alto diner just below the Ning offices. "I should get credit for walking down the stairs!"

You can hardly blame him. At an L.A. party or a Vegas fight he's hardly the most important person in a room. Here he's *Marc Andreessen*, the guy who helped start the entire Internet revolution with Netscape. When Max goes to parties, he is constantly interrupted by entrepreneurs who want to pitch him on their new companies. It's exasperating, but he remembers what it's like to be where they are and feels bad just cutting them off. "Email me at Max@Levchin.com," he'll say. Little do they know it's a dummy email account set up just for such occasions. Ditto for Reid Hoffman. He decided to attend exactly one conference in 2006 in part because it was in Paris, not the Valley. He stopped to talk to a friend on the street and a queue of would-be entrepreneurs formed behind his friend to talk to him next. "I'm not a deli!" he wanted to scream. It reminded him why he avoids such things.

Back at the Web 2.0 conference, Marc's friend David Sze sees him coming and thinks he'll be funny. He turns and shrieks like a teenage fan, "Oh my God! It's Marc Andreessen!" He gets a glower from the entourage. He's pretty sure Marc didn't find it funny either.

Marc is here for one reason only: Gina Bianchini. She is launching Ning, the start-up the two of them cofounded back in 2004. Gina is the chief executive, and Marc, Ning's chief technology officer, is careful not to overshadow her. But Battelle would give them a prime Web 2.0 slot only if Andreessen showed up too. So he stands onstage stone-faced while Gina talks. If you didn't know better, you might think he was her bodyguard. He sums up with a few quick—and smart—statements. And that's that.

He sneaks backstage, where he hangs with a few select friends; then at Gina's suggestion they head to the dark, wood-paneled hotel bar for some drinks. He tries ordering guacamole, but in a California rarity, the bar doesn't have any, so he gets an assortment of fried appetizers for the table instead. This is just another thing that is annoying him about being here. In a few months he'd make a New Year's resolution: not a single trip to San Francisco in 2007. He gives me his Web 2.0 speaker's badge before he leaves.

"I'm not going to need it anymore," he says with a smile.

To say Marc is "here" because of Gina has a meaning beyond just the conference. Three years earlier Gina convinced Marc that the consumer Internet wasn't dead. It wasn't any single meeting where the lightbulb went off. For Marc to admit he's wrong, it takes far more than that. It was over the summer and fall of 2003. Marc had met Gina through her previous company, Harmonic Communications, funded by Sequoia Capital. Marc was on the board and Gina quickly impressed him, even as the company stalled after the bust.

Gina stands out in Silicon Valley, and not just because she has two X chromosomes. She's a tall, stylish, and scrappy brunette. She did the whole Valley shtick of going to Stanford undergrad and business school and getting funding from Sequoia. But she rails against entrepreneurial posers. She calls herself a self-hating MBA. She starts companies because she doesn't have another choice, she says. She doesn't do it to be cool or make a quick buck. She's obsessed. And like many entrepreneurs, she has found herself at home in Silicon Valley. She grew up in Cupertino just a few miles from Ning's headquarters, and although she doesn't elaborate, she says she "can never go home."

Andreessen is the same way. He hasn't talked to his family in years and hasn't been back to the Midwest in even longer. At his wedding, none of his relatives were present. He had in total about five people on his side of the aisle, including Ben Horowitz, a longtime friend, early Netscape coworker, and cofounder of Marc's second company, Loudcloud (later restarted as Opsware). Michael Ovitz, the Hollywood power broker, was there too. He reportedly gave a disastrous toast, but no one will divulge the details.

Perhaps this is the reason Gina and Marc just click. Harmonic Communications, however, did not click. Harmonic sold software for companies' marketing departments that aimed to help them do sophisticated advertising campaigns that would include Internet advertising for the first time. Then in 2000 the advertising recession hit, and "that was it for that business model," Marc says matter-of-factly. The company was sold for a lackluster amount in 2003 to Dentsu, a large Japanese advertising agency. Gina started to spend a lot of time doing consulting for Ovitz and other people Marc knew and hanging out with early believers in social media such as Reid Hoffman. She was tracking things like the convergence of media with high tech and overall Internet adoption trends. During the bleak years between 2001 and 2004 she noticed that all of the numbers were growing fast: Internet use, broadband adoption, social networking traffic, Internet advertising, revenues, even *profits*. Everything.

She'd meet with Marc regularly, showing him all the data and filling him in on very under-the-radar Web companies that were raking in hundreds of millions a year while conventional wisdom still said the industry was dead.

"Look! It's all working!" she told him.

The more they talked, the more Marc started to think, "She's right. She's absolutely right."

His second thought: "Very few people realize this."

This was a huge reversal for Marc. It took courage to believe again after living through the incredibly wild ride of 1995 to 2001. Simply put, Marc is brilliant: He taught himself his first programming language at age nine from a library book, then got bored by computers until he first glimpsed the Internet. But he's also highly emotional. He doesn't own any stocks of public companies, aside from his own companies, because he always buys high and sells low. Indeed, emotion caused him to sell many of his Netscape shares on the cheap. "I fall for it every time," he says. "My instincts are exactly wrong. I fall for the cover stories. I thought Enron was great! When everyone is pissed off or depressed, I'm the exact same way."

So back in late 2000 and 2001 when the story of the day was

the death of the Internet, Marc bought it. "I was just totally convinced the consumer Internet was over," he says. "It was tried and it failed. It's over. It's toast. I had lived through the whole thing with Netscape, then AOL, then also with Loudcloud. There was just vast fear and loathing (directed at the Internet) and I was like, 'That's it.'"

Marc says he was bummed. This is an understatement, given that Marc's entire fame, career, and wealth were all predicated on the power of the Internet. Marc describes it in academic terms: "I made the classic mistake of extrapolating from short-term trends. It's basic human psychology to keep us from being eaten by lions. If I see a lion over a hill, I'm going to assume five minutes later the same lion is still there. Because that's the only way to survive."

In this case, the lion wasn't still there.

At eighteen Marc helped build the first modern Web browser. The Internet was just a loose network of academics at this point, and it wasn't at all obvious that it'd ever be much more than that. It was nearly impossible for an everyday person to surf it. You had to memorize nonsensical text commands to navigate around. More hard to believe, the Web was text only. There was no way to put up images—let alone the kind of video and animation that dominates the Web today. What Xerox's Palo Alto Research Center and the Macintosh did for a computer's graphic interface, Mosaic, the Web browser Marc helped build at the University of Illinois, did for the Web. After acquiring the core of that code from the university, Netscape would build on top of it, making the Internet what we all take for granted today.

During the Mosaic days, Marc was getting plenty of attention. Nearly two million people were using it. And this was back in 1993. Only about a third of U.S. households even owned a computer, much less knew what a modem was. His university director of research told him, "Enjoy this while it lasts, because most things you do in life will not be this successful."

For most people, that's true.

Among the handful of job offers Marc got while he wrapped up his degree was one from a company named Enterprise Integration Technologies in Palo Alto. He picked it because he liked the warm weather of California and because he'd be working on Internet software, which he knew well from his Mosaic days. He also knew he wanted to work at a small company, thanks to a brief stint at IBM. And the horribly named start-up offered him stock options. He didn't really know what they were, but figured he wanted them. His starting salary was $80,000 a year—a testament to his Mosaic chops.

Marc didn't think much about his career at this point. He figured he'd just be a programmer. As long as he enjoyed what he was doing, was no longer in the Midwest, and was paid enough to be comfortable, he was content. He didn't really live or die by programming either. It was merely another thing he liked to do. He decided on a computer science degree only when he read a 1986 *U.S. News & World Report* story that ranked the average starting salaries for different degrees. "I figured the optimum thing to do was get an electrical engineering or computer science degree and go to work," he says. The report showed you didn't get much of a boost by getting a master's or a doctorate.

So in 1994, happy-go-lucky Marc was living in California, working at Enterprise Integration Technologies, and making a comfortable living. That's when he got the call that would change his life forever. Jim Clark introduced himself and said he'd heard about Marc from a friend. "I'm starting a company and I want to meet and see if you want to do something together," Clark said.

Marc was surprised, to say the least. He'd heard of Clark—who in high tech hadn't? The iconic firebrand of a Silicon Valley entrepreneur had started Silicon Graphics, one of the Valley's great success stories. But everyone knew he wasn't getting along with chief executive Ed McCracken. He was leaving, but legally he couldn't hire any of the Silicon Graphics folks, so he was casting about for other smart young people. Marc was one of a few on a list. "To my ongoing amazement, I'm the only one who bit," Marc says. "I've learned something about people. Most of them think they are risk takers, but you put the opportunity right in front of their face and they'll be attracted to it, flirt with it and, like, window-shop it a lot, but then go, 'Oh, no, I can't do that.' Most people will walk away. I had nothing to lose."

Well, except a few hours' sleep. Their first meeting was at Café Verona in Palo Alto at seven A.M.—the first time Marc had hauled his ass out of bed that early in as long as he could remember. He was still sleepy-eyed and yawning when Clark drove up in his Mercedes and parked right out in front. They talked for about an hour. Or Clark talked. Marc was still mostly asleep, listening. Over the next few months they wrote three business plans. Netscape was the last and the best. Marc was still working his day job at this point. He told Clark that if they were serious he needed to quit his job and Clark needed to pay him a salary. "Let's give it a shot," Clark said.

The browser is so taken for granted today, it's almost hard to conceive of how revolutionary this moment was. As Thomas Friedman describes in *The World Is Flat*, the now-ubiquitous browser was "one of the most important inventions in modern history." More than anything else, it took the Internet from the realm of geeks and academics to something anyone could use. Children. Your mom. Your *grandmother*. Before Netscape it wasn't clear at all that the Internet would be a mass phenomenon. It opened up a vast new territory of opportunity that resulted in the landgrab of the late 1990s. It wired the world together, skirting space and time, making e-commerce, online news, and social networking possible.

But hardly any of that was obvious at the time. Once Jim and Marc settled on the browser plan, they went on a tour of all the big telecommunications and media companies. Clark figured that for the Internet to take off, Netscape needed two things: content on it people would want to read and far more robust connections to the Net. They were counting on the old guard of East Coast media and telecommunications for both. They got a range of responses, but there was plenty of the "that's cute, now run along and let the adults roll out the broadband superhighway" attitude Marc had gotten back at the University of Illinois when he unveiled Mosaic. "I didn't realize at the time how much of what big companies say is just either flat-out untrue or they literally just don't know," he says.

Now that more than a billion people explore the Web via browsers, how often does he think "I told you so"? From time to time, he says with a smile that says it's more often than that. Especially when he walks into the Time Warner Building. They were by far the most negative. They told him they'd never do anything on the Internet and that ultimately the Internet didn't matter because it was "just for nerds." The cozy confines of America Online, aka the Internet with training wheels, was where the users were, and as far as Time Warner was concerned, that's where they'd stay, along with Time Warner's content. "Users aren't going to move," Marc remembers them saying. What's worse, he thought maybe they were right. Who was he, after all, to tell high-powered executives they were wrong?

Fast-forward to 1999 and Marc is sitting in a bar in Los Angeles next to funny man Norm MacDonald. They are surrounded by lights and TV cameras. It is more than 100 degrees outside, and there is no air conditioning. To create a smoky effect, a film crew was spraying vegetable oil everywhere. Marc and Norm were holding Miller Lites. Or Marc was. Norm was sort of wired to a Miller Lite. The ad agency wanted a light to shine through the bottle to make the logo pop, so they'd run the cord up through his pants and shirt and out the sleeve. So he was stuck in place the whole day. As Marc remembers it, Norm was cranky, from time to time spilling beers on people walking past.

Just then a bus full of gorgeous models pulled up—about eighty of them. They flooded the bar, surrounding Marc and Norm. Action! The two started making horrible dotcom puns, then began to hit on a stunning blonde standing next to them. ("Dot com here often?") They got shot down. Close on Norm saying one final, horrible pun.

The ad ran for about a week, and then Miller Lite fired the agency. Still, the fact that a Silicon Valley entrepreneur was put in a commercial he didn't pay for, a commercial aimed at the American consumer everyman, Joe Sixpack, shows just how big Netscape and Marc were. By the time he saw this commercial, he'd already appeared on the cover of *Time* sitting barefoot on a throne, seemingly laughing at all of us. The headline was "The Golden Geeks," and Andreessen was the king. A twenty-two-year-old king worth well over $60 million.

The entire Netscape years—the record-setting IPO, the commercials, the magazine covers, and the infamous battles with Microsoft's Internet Explorer—were all an exciting, stressful blur for Marc. Totally deadpan, he can describe it only as "very long workdays with a lot of shit going on all the time." He had no business experience and was learning everything on the fly. He was frequently described as an enfant terrible, and Silicon Valley is rife with anecdotes that back this up. Ben Horowitz loves to tell the story of Marc strolling into a meeting with a glass of milk and a bag of Chips Ahoy! cookies. "Not a small bag, one of those ones with three rows," Ben says. "And no one else got any." Marc left crumbs on the conference room table, his chair, and the floor around him.

Not everything about Marc's inexperience as a manager was so amusing, though. About the time Marc graced the cover of *Time*, Ben was frantically trying to put together a server product that customers would actually pay for, since the browser was free. The company was already public at this point, and the stock was soaring. Only a handful of people were working on the server product, and after some sleuthing Ben discovered Microsoft's upcoming server software was faster and better than Netscape's. He and a few others went into overdrive, acquiring various other technologies and cobbling together a suite of products for companies trying to connect to the Internet.

The company was planning on making a big media splash in New York to announce all this, when a few days before Marc decided to leak it to a geeky tech trade publication. Stunned, Ben sent him an email to the effect of "I guess we aren't going to wait for the press event next week." Marc wrote back, copying cofounder Jim Clark, Netscape CEO Jim Barksdale, and others, reaming Ben out for his crappy server division, which was going to cost Netscape $50 million in market value if it failed. He signed it:

> Next time do the fucking interview yourself. Fuck you.
> —Marc

Ben, seven years older than Marc and a Silicon Valley veteran, was stunned. He went home and showed the email to his wife. The *Time* magazine with Andreessen's bare feet and smug expression was on his coffee table. "You need to get a new job," she told him. But he didn't quit—how could anyone leave Netscape in 1995? It was the high-tech superstar. And it was a good thing he didn't. In the browser wars with Microsoft, Ben and Marc would become close. Ben developed a knack for tuning out—even sniggering at—Marc's frequent profanity-laced blowups. And Marc knew he needed someone like Ben. Someone who could manage people and had done this all before. They would leave Netscape together once AOL bought it. They'd start a new company, Loudcloud, together. And the two of them would steer it through the tumultuous post-bubble times, getting closer with each year. At Marc's wedding Ben was one of the few people on the groom's side.

The change underscores a few things about Marc's relationships with people. One is that his blowing up at someone doesn't necessarily mean he hates that person. Another is that once he befriends people, he's incredibly loyal to them. But getting into Marc's inner circle is hard. He has trust issues, and fame and fortune have only complicated that.

His inability to get along with people is one big reason Marc is never the chief executive of companies he starts even though he believes that founders usually make the best CEOs and counts as his personal heroes tech founder/CEOs such as Bill Gates, Steve Jobs, and Larry Ellison. "It wasn't an accident they were founders and CEOs and very successful," Marc says. "Generally speaking, there's a high correlation. You can have control you wouldn't otherwise." Control to make sure your vision doesn't get screwed up, that is.

But Marc just isn't wired for it. He says he's not good enough with people. "I manage like the Incredible Hulk," he told *BusinessWeek* in 2001. Ben says it's because Marc doesn't like to do things he doesn't want to do. Marc agrees, but adds that's especially true when people are involved. "Seriously, I don't like people," he says. "I really don't like people."

It's not that he hasn't tried. At Netscape he managed as many as 1,200 people at a time. It was enough to convince him of two things: It wasn't for him and he needed people like Ben who could

do it and love it. "If Ben can come in and spend all day with people, he's happy. He loves it. It energizes him. At the end of the day he feels great. I go home at the end of a day like that and I would be in the worst, foulest mood," he says. That's not a Marc Andreessen you want to see. It's not that he thinks people are stupid. They're just, well, people. Human. Unpredictable. With their own weird motivations. They're not machines. "Your lawn mower never argues with you," Marc says.

All that said, when Marc meets someone he clicks with, who he thinks is smart or doing something interesting, he has no trouble seeking them out, spending long hours with them, even mentoring them. His call to Josh Schachter in 2003; his insisting Ben quit AOL also to start Loudcloud; his investments in Jay with both Equinix and Digg; and of course his starting Ning with Gina. It's all very similar to that call from Clark he got as a young naive coder, the call that changed his life. This time he's just on the other end of the line.

And this time when he runs across people who tell him consumers won't adopt new technologies or change their habits, he doesn't believe them. Someone is always there, ready to tell Marc just how wrong he is. These statements almost always center on whether or not consumers adapt rapidly to change. Most people believe they don't—a misconception that enrages Marc. Think of all the things people have adopted in the last ten years, he says. Mobile phones, email, instant messages, the iPod, online auctions, voice over IP, TiVo—one thing after another. And of course the Internet: 1.2 billion people use it now, up from about 2 million when Marc built Mosaic thirteen years ago. Marc believes firmly that if you create something better, it doesn't matter if people are happy with what they're using now. They will switch.

This doomed his tenure at AOL from the start. When the company bought Netscape for $10 billion in 1998, Netscape's chief

executive Jim Barksdale told them above all they should make sure they kept Marc on staff. He was named AOL's chief technology officer and lavished with stock, pay, and perks galore. He personally made nearly $100 million off the deal and relocated to Washington, D.C., but never really felt at home. He holed up in a 7,000-square-foot house that friends say he hardly furnished other than one room with a huge TV, video game consoles, and a couch. It was almost like he was camping out in the cavernous living room.

Things weren't much better at work. He was constantly frustrated by executives' not listening to him—especially when it came to AOL's biggest blunder, underestimating how fast people would move from dial-up Internet connections to broadband. AOL owned the dial-up market, and again, like many of those big media and telecom companies in the mid-1990s who thought no one would use an Internet browser, AOL bought the myth that customers are slow to adopt new technologies.

By the time he left AOL to start Loudcloud, Marc had earned some benefit of the doubt. Loudcloud wasn't a consumer company like Netscape or AOL. It was a company that took everything Marc and Ben had learned at Netscape and used it to help companies adapt to the Web—fast. Before Loudcloud, companies had to hire an army of people in-house to build their Web site or store, or outsource it to someone like IBM. The Web was still so undeveloped in those days that few people knew how to do this well, and they were expensive. So by specializing and having Marc's star power, Loudcloud could fill a desperate need that wasn't being filled well by anyone at the moment.

It seemed brilliant in 1999. And even in 2001, as the company readied itself for an IPO, people were hopeful. Wall Street and the business press were still absolutely addicted to the IPO story, and by 2001 there were very few to talk about. Amid this void and high-

tech hand-wringing, how fitting, how poetic would it be if Marc Andreessen, the guy whose first company started the whole late 1990s IPO frenzy, could start it all again? "If anyone could do it, he could," people thought.

That was a lot of pressure on a young company that was losing money and trying to navigate its way through one of the worst public markets in modern time. With dotcoms going under, suddenly the old economy wasn't in such a rush to adapt to the Internet age. Companies who'd been sprinting to throw up Web sites now backed off. That crushed Loudcloud's pipeline of incoming business, making an initial public offering all the more crucial as Loudcloud came dangerously close to running out of cash. But the markets can smell desperation. When the IPO didn't go well, the press lashed out at Marc and Loudcloud.

BusinessWeek followed Marc throughout the road show and wrote a scathing tell-all, calling it the IPO from hell. Marc's antics had already started to rub people the wrong way. People accused him of taking too much credit for the birth of the Internet and overstating his own brilliance. Now, as *BusinessWeek* pointed out, his first venture without the mentorship of Jim Barksdale and Jim Clark was floundering. "The Internet wunderkind could be a has-been at the tender age of thirty."

Ultimately, Loudcloud couldn't handle the change in the market. But Marc and Ben weren't willing to give up. Instead, they relaunched the company as Opsware. They took the core software that ran the Web sites and made that the business, selling off the consulting division to the Electronic Data Systems Corporation. And all the while, they kept personally buying more of the stock to show they still believed in the company. About the time executives at Enron and WorldCom were getting sued for insider trading—or selling shares with inside knowledge that things were about to get a lot worse—Marc and company actually got hit with a shareholder suit alleging insider *buying*. Opposing attorneys argued that the Opsware board of directors was trying to signal some disingenuous optimism by buying up more shares; that this was an attempt to trick the market into believing that things were okay. It was a tenuous argument at best. "You gotta be kidding me," Marc said when he got served. Even when he was trying to do the right thing in a bad situation, someone was there to give him shit about it. (The case was ultimately settled for what Marc characterized as a paltry sum.)

Opsware did make it. And while it was hardly a second Netscape, by November 2006 it was closing in on a milestone: a $1 billion market capitalization. The number $1 billion is magic in the Valley, the number that separates the men from the boys. Just $4.5 million away, Marc was poised, ready to throw a huge party. It'd be a combination of a reward for all the Opsware troops who'd worked so hard through the bleak years and a big fat "told you so" to everyone who trashed the company. The next week, Opsware slipped back down, but not for long. It managed to cross the billion-dollar mark the following spring and stay there. Finally.

Then in July 2007, the news hit the wire: Hewlett-Packard was buying Opsware for $1.6 billion. As much of a runaway success as Netscape had been, Opsware had been an equally long, grueling slog. And that slog was finally over. Marc and Ben had refused to give up, no matter how they had to reinvent the company. And now Marc was $138 million richer.

Of course the purchase meant something else too. Marc is now in the elite category of having started two companies to cross the $1 billion milestone. Among all the storied entrepreneurs who've ever come through the Valley, you can count on two hands how many have done that. And only one guy has done it three times: Jim Clark. Once called a one-hit wonder, Marc was now in a race with his former mentor. It's too early to tell now, but he's hoping the third one could be Ning.

Once Gina convinced Marc that the consumer Internet was working after all, they came up with the idea behind Ning. This time Marc is the veteran with solid hits behind him and Gina is the sleep-deprived hardworking entrepreneur. There were several elements to Ning they loved. Gina had been obsessed with social behavior online, and the technologist in Marc wanted a company that would be an open platform, giving people total creativity to make it whatever they wanted.

Although Netscape came out roaring, Ning has been very under the radar for the first two years of its life. But differences in hype aside, there are a lot of parallels between the two. For one, Ning brings Marc back to the consumer Internet world. And once again people are telling him he's wrong. The site is a bit hard to grasp, but essentially it allows people to create their own mini-MySpaces. If you want to stay in touch with people you went to high school with, you create your own social networking site just for that. Like Facebook or MySpace it has profile pages, photos, videos and messaging. Name it whatever you like, pick the layout, and voilà, you have your own social network. At the core is a fundamental premise: People like people. "I don't," Marc says, smiling. "But most people do." (Jay Adelson nearly doubled over in laughter the first time he saw Marc give a Ning presentation complete with a huge PEOPLE LIKE PEOPLE slide. Words he never thought he'd hear Marc Andreessen utter. "Don't say it," Marc said to Jay once he got offstage.)

Everything about Ning is customizable. All the underlying code is open to being tinkered with, so if you know the Web languages like HTML, you can completely reconstruct the look and feel of the site. If you don't, you can just follow the easy-to-use templates: Put this column here, ask people these questions when they fill out a profile. The site is free if you want ads on your social network. If you don't want ads, you can pay a monthly fee to Ning. Want to sell your own ads? That's cool too.

The idea here is appealing to everyone by having virtually nothing locked in place. It's about getting to the mass market by filling every conceivable niche. Not too different from mass Web stores Amazon and eBay, which sell nearly any out-of-print book or any random flea market find someone might want. "You give people that level of freedom and flexibility and over time they make it into everything it could possibly be," Marc says. "That plays out in the long run, but it's not an immediate killer thing. We're keeping our heads down."

It's the exact opposite of MySpace, which is a one-size-fits-all approach that may appeal to millions but also turns off other people. People who want more privacy, people who don't want flashy ads with half-naked women, people who want a site that loads faster. People who want only their friends in their online world.

Marc and Gina were quietly building this for about two years, at one point operating under the code name "24 Hour Laundry." In February 2007, it was finally ready for prime time. They hit *BusinessWeek, Newsweek, The New York Times,* and of course all the bloggers. Where the influential blog TechCrunch had been critical of Ning a year earlier, Michael Arrington now raved about the company. "I have to hand it to Ning," he wrote. "It took them well over a year after their initial beta launch to fulfill their promise of allowing 'anyone' to create social applications, but they've done it.... After seeing a demo earlier this afternoon, I'm now willing to offer a full mea culpa." As Marc said, "the smarter members of the media were off the charts positive." To the rest, he just says smugly, "Okay, wait and see. Watch."

Before the February 2007 launch of Ning, thirty thousand mini social networking sites had been created. The week after, thirteen thousand more were added—a big jump. Of course those aren't the only metrics Marc studies. To illustrate his point, he pushes aside his cheeseburger and starts drawing charts on the paper tablecloth of one of several Palo Alto coffee shops he frequents. He points out that with every new mini-site created on the Ning network other numbers spike: registered users, page views, photos, and videos on the site too. "In the last week these shot up, which is what you'd expect because each of these applications brings in people and page views," he says, speaking rapidly.

But not everyone is a believer in Ning. There are plenty of critics who say people don't want to build their own social networks. They claim it's too hard to fight the early lead and fast growth of MySpace and Facebook. To Marc, this is no different than when people told him in the early Netscape days that all the users were already on CompuServe, AOL, or Prodigy, and he couldn't fight that momentum with a browser that could search the entire Web. The Web won because developers built cool sites on a space people found far more compelling than the narrower world of AOL or Prodigy. He believes if he gets creative people and a critical mass of developers to build better social applications on Ning, it too will become social networking's mainstream.

"Literally people have forgotten that this happened, and I love when I get the question [of how Ning competes with MySpace and Facebook] because now I have an answer for it," he says. Back in 1994 he thought, "Who the fuck am I to argue?" "Now I know. I've seen it happen before. I'm convinced this is an exact replay of that."

Marc's personal motto is "often wrong, never in doubt." Just as he was convinced back in 2000 that the Web was over, today he's unwaveringly bullish on all the companies he has started and backed. You'd almost never know he ever doubted. "Just because those companies didn't work at that time doesn't mean successors won't work now," he says. "Just through the simple virtue of the fact that time passed, a market developed."

In other words, all those dotcoms? Not so dumb. Just off in their timing by about four years. He's constantly annoyed at people who say 2006 is another Internet bubble. His key point: As of early 2007, no Web 2.0 companies had gone public. In a bubble, hundreds of companies go public, get astronomically high valuations, and soon afterward turn out to be worth nothing. Like anything else, Marc has studied this. "If you look at all the bubbles of the last five hundred years, very few are not associated with public stocks because they are mass psychologies, not insiders getting lathered up."

He doesn't stop there. Marc is starting to wonder whether there ever was a dotcom bubble at all. In the spring of 2006, he has just read a paper arguing there was no tulip bubble in the seventeenth-century Netherlands. It has gotten him thinking. "Don't get me wrong," he writes over instant message one day. "I do think people lost their heads and got silly for about eighteen months, so I'm not literally arguing that the whole period was rational." But a bubble is a different matter. Marc argues convincingly that for the bulk of the late 1990s things weren't so irrational. "There were a lot of very solid forecasts from very reputable people and a lot of data to support that a lot of NASDAQ companies were on incredibly fast growth trajectories, and some economists argue that NASDAQ stock prices simply and rationally reflected that," he writes.

What's more, a lot of forecasts, like Internet advertising revenue, turned out to be true in the long run—even understated. So what happened? The Internet's growth slowed, and it took longer to get there. A well-known statistic that Internet traffic was doubling every three months was driving a lot of the investment in telecommunications and networking. And it was true in 1995 and 1996, but by 1997, it was doubling every year. When metrics like these slowed, the stock prices, rather efficiently and rationally, corrected. Over the last ten years, the S&P 500, mid-cap stocks, and small-cap stocks all gained between 9 and 14 percent. So people who bought index stocks and held them weren't affected by the bubble *at all.* "Some bubble," he concludes triumphantly over instant message. This is a typical IM chat with Marc Andreessen—nary an LOL to be found, although you might get a few smiley face emoticons here or there when he makes a point.

To Marc, the concept behind Ning is so obvious that if the execution is right, Ning will be huge. He believes this fervently enough to invest $9 million of his own money in Ning, along with small investments from a host of friends. As of Ning's early 2007 launch, no venture capital money was involved. In fact, he capped how much his friends could invest at just a few thousand dollars each. If he can't have control as the CEO, he'll keep control as the only investor of any size. It has allowed Marc and Gina to move just as fast or slow as they want without any outside pressure from anyone. Not that funding would be a problem. People may have their doubts about Ning and Opsware, but not about Marc. By 2007, when they formally launched the product, he had a list of twenty of Ning's "closest friends" who were dying to invest. He promised to give them all a meeting once the company gets to that point.

Easier said than done, say those who know him. Actual preplanned meetings with Marc are hard to get. He decided he wouldn't keep a schedule in 2007. In other words, to meet with him, you have to be in his neck of the woods and just call and say, "Want to meet?" He loves this plan. People wanting to meet with him, on the other hand, do not. It's the ultimate statement that his time is more important than other people's time. But he doesn't care how he comes off. After more than a decade of being publicly dissected, Marc has simply gotten over what people think about him.

Nonetheless, when the time does come to raise money, he'll be ready. He keeps the list of would-be investors on his laptop. "It's triple encrypted," he says. Marc's a big fan of triple-encrypted lists.

The roster of potential investors is just one folder over from the Marc Andreessen shit list: a ranking of everyone who has pissed him off or betrayed his trust over his tumultuous twelve years in the Valley. For someone who's known to have a short fuse, it's amazingly short, about ten people. He has to feel that someone has deliberately tried to do him harm to make the list. And next to that list is one of all the different features and products he wants to add to Ning. That list is considerably longer than either of the other two: eighteen pages of double-column single-spaced text in a tiny font. Three layers of encryption, all different encryption algorithms, none of which have any known ways to crack them. It takes Marc five minutes just to log in. "I love it," he beams. "If anyone ever steals my laptop, they are going to be so frustrated."

It's not that Marc is forgetful, he just likes lists. If it's on a list, he doesn't have to worry about it or think about it. That brain power that would go toward, say, remembering the names of those he hates can be put toward something else. Of course he doesn't exactly want it getting out, hence the security measures.

"Not that I'm paranoid," he laughs. "Not a bit."

Thirteen years after he first arrived in Silicon Valley Marc hasn't changed at all in some ways. When he talks about his triple-encrypted files he beams like the kid from the University of Illinois who co-created Mosaic and set the world on fire. He still frequents the same places: the Peninsula Fountain & Grill and Cuppa Café in downtown Palo Alto. And of course Hobee's. He eats at Hobee's so much that they've discussed putting his much-customized usual on the menu and naming it after him. He eats there so much, two Hobee's employees once fought over which one of them could nominate him for customer of the year. Friends knew Marc had found the woman for him when they heard his wife, Laura, adored Hobee's just as much.

But it's also a very different Marc Andreessen than the one who moved to the Valley in 1994. He may not like meeting with people, but he can be charming when he does. He spends money on clothes. He's fit. He still loves cheeseburgers, but also eats sushi—something he once vowed he would never try. He no longer has to prove anything to anyone. That said, when Ning becomes a success, he'll be happy to take one hell of a victory lap before those who doubted that he could make it without Clark and Barksdale. All those investments in other hot start-ups are just more fodder to prove he is still Silicon Valley's "golden geek." Some early evidence: While people have been calling Marc a has-been, his net worth has grown nearly fivefold and is now well north of $600 million.

But in spite of Marc's confidence in the future, he is disturbed by one fact: Most of the fundamental breakthroughs in science, math, culture, music, or business came from people in their early twenties. He can't figure out why, but he has studied enough history to know there is some sort of correlation between young people and breakthroughs.

He also lived it.

"As far as I can tell, it's not because those people are particularly brilliant or unusual, it's because you know enough to be able to actually produce something...you have enough of an education and training," he says. "But you're so young, you know little about what's been done before. You've not bought into the assumptions that exist in any field. By the time you're thirty-five, you start to have a really good understanding of the things that are possible to do and not possible to do. To have a fundamental breakthrough, you have to look at things so differently—different from how they've been looked at for the last thirty years. Once you have all that stuff in your head, that's hard."

So while he's happy he has gained the experience to know that good times always come back in Silicon Valley, the confidence to tell doubters they're flat wrong, and the money to do whatever he wants, Marc knows this knowledge may be a hindrance if he wants to truly change the world again. "I'm not twenty-two anymore, I'm thirty-five," he says. "I think I'm having a lot more fun now than I did, because I feel much more comfortable.

"But I do worry about that. A lot."

At first he calls it the Mozart phenomenon. But soon he corrects himself, calling it by another name: the Mark Zuckerberg phenomenon.

7

THE MARK ZUCKERBERG PHENOMENON

Every society has its urban myths. Maybe you know the one about the college girl who goes drinking in Tijuana and finds a cute little Chihuahua. She decides to take him home and wakes up the next morning cuddled up to a Mexican street rat. The stories vary depending on who is telling them, but the punch line or kicker is always the same. And the person who tells you this always swears it happened to a friend of a friend. Really.

Silicon Valley has its own urban myths, and unsurprisingly they come in a slightly geekier flavor here. Typically they spring from the myths about the founders, like that one about eBay and the PEZ dispensers. But the details can frequently take on a life of their own. I once asked Marc Andreessen which table at the Peninsula Fountain & Grill was the "Netscape table"—the one where Marc and Jim Clark met and sketched out the business plan on the back of a napkin. He just laughed and said, "I don't know what you're talking about. This can be the Netscape table from now on, if you want."

But the most famous urban legend of late, one told and retold over breakfasts at Buck's and lunches at Il Fornaio, is the story of the controversial 2005 deal between Accel Partners and Facebook. Several versions float around the Valley, all from tapped-in people who *swear* this is what really happened. If entrepreneurs had pep rallies, it's the story they'd tell to pump one another up. If venture capitalists ever sat around a campfire, it's the tale they'd use to terrify one another.

> ***Version A:*** Jim Breyer, the sage elder statesmen to the young Zuckerberg, takes him to dinner. The twenty-year-old Zuck can't even legally order wine at that point. Zuck unspools his great Facebook vision. Breyer is struck by how brilliant Zuck is, and decides to invest in him on the spot.
>
> ***Version B:*** The tech downturn wasn't good to the beleaguered Accel, and the firm is desperate for a big hit. So desperate that Breyer, or in some versions younger partner Kevin Efrusy, comes down to the Facebook offices and camps out until Zuckerberg agrees to meet with them. They give Zuck whatever he wants.
>
> ***Version C:*** Accel, again beleaguered, begs Facebook for a meeting. Zuck doesn't really need the cash, but heads a few blocks down University Street to pitch them all the same. Efrusy and Breyer are in the room. Zuck is doing his dog and pony show when he looks over and sees Breyer more absorbed in his BlackBerry than in the presentation. Rude, yes, but incredibly common in the Valley. That doesn't mean Zuck is going to take it. He knows Accel needs him more than he needs them. He slams his laptop closed, says, "We're done here," and walks out. Efrusy chases him down the street, begging him to take Accel's cash. Zuck names the most outrageous terms he could come up with,

and the partner breathlessly says yes. And the deal is done. Many versions end with the deal being finalized in a strip club. "It's common knowledge," whispers one Web entrepreneur.

With so many versions and only a handful of people knowing the truth, it's hard to know the whole story. But repeat all the variations of the story to Zuck, and he's clearly stunned at the level of speculation over what seemed personal to him at the time. Of course parts of each version are true, and parts are simply bizarre. Accel had to court Zuck extensively in order to arrange a meeting with him. He was highly suspicious of venture capitalists and didn't want to take their money. He did have a dinner with Breyer where he couldn't order wine, and yes, he did outline some pretty outrageous terms, mostly in the hope Accel would leave him alone. But the slamming of the laptop and the strip club? No clue where that came from. "Maybe the Accel guys went to a strip club," he says. "But I wasn't with them." Says Breyer of the strip club rumor, "One hundred percent untrue. One hundred percent."

Indeed, strip clubs don't quite seem the ultra-shy Zuckerberg's style. Zuckerberg's hobbies in high school were fencing and Latin. Once he wrote an all-Latin version of the board game Risk so he could spend his spare time dominating the world in his favorite dead tongue. His bar mitzvah had a Star Wars theme. In other words, central geek casting.

To understand how and why the deal really went down, you have to understand the relationship between Zuck and a controversial Silicon Valley boy wonder named Sean Parker. Sean was Zuck's version of Jay Adelson—the older, wiser, and more burned friend advising Zuck on the pitfalls of the Valley. Sean may not have had a clever, derisive name for them, but he was no friend to venture capitalists. He had a pattern of blowups with them longer than Jay's.

Some venture capitalists have even called Sean "everything that's wrong with Silicon Valley."

In many ways he's like most successful Web entrepreneurs. Sean doesn't operate well by traditional business or social rules; he has deep scars inflicted by the bubble and bust. When you meet him, you're not sure if you like him or not. He can be abrasive and charming at the same time, not unlike Andreessen, Zuckerberg, or Levchin. He's incredibly smart, and not just in a mathematical or book-smart kind of way. He just viscerally gets the Web. He sees where it's going before a lot of people. He intuitively knows what makes a good site great. As a result, he experienced insane success at a very young age. Still under thirty, he has been in the vanguard of every Web movement—save e-commerce. But like many Valley guys, he has his demons. All that insight hasn't necessarily translated into monetary or business success. It has resulted in a lot of burned relationships.

For all his inward geekiness, paranoia, and insecurity, Sean has this not-afraid-to-be-subversive edge that many shyer entrepreneurs like Max lack, or don't display until they have more money and success. Sean can play the slick extrovert. Although he has spent much of his adulthood crashing on friends' couches, he's always managed to look more coiffed than your typical Web guy. Maybe that's because in his spare time he wines and dines women in Los Angeles and parties in the Hollywood Hills. (Or at least claims to.) It's as if he's two parts geek, one part frat boy. Gossip site Valleywag dubs him the bad boy of Silicon Valley, but sometimes his behavior seems put on. After all, Sean surrounds himself with geeky, goody-goody business partners. "He wants to play bad boy to the nerds," says one of them.

Sean can articulate what his company is doing and why it will change the world better than most. He can get people whipped into a frenzy about it. As Zuck says, "Sean can convince anyone of anything." This is part of what makes Sean so effective, and what makes him dangerous. When he was a junior in high school he convinced his school district to count the time he spent writing computer code as credits toward their computer science and foreign language requirements. He successfully argued that mastering computer languages was equivalent to taking French or Spanish. That gave him enough credits to spend the bulk of his senior year writing code for WorldCom instead of taking classes. It also gave him plenty of time to help start a revolution: Napster.

Lawsuits and questions of piracy aside, the peer-to-peer pioneer Napster sparked a new wave of indie bands who had been largely locked out of the mainstream music scene. They no longer needed big, powerful studios to get their music in stores or on the radio, where people could hear it; they just uploaded it to Napster's servers. Audio geeks uploaded out-of-print recordings, making them suddenly available again. It got people excited about music again.

And Napster was *cool*. It was one of the first ways the Internet became a world the popular kids were spending hours a day in, not simply the wonky playground of the geeks. The old idea of the mix tape was back with a twist, and everyone in their teens or twenties was ripping, burning, and swapping CDs like mad. When the Recording Industry Association of America came down on Napster, it publicized the situation even more, initiating a full-blown us-versus-them cultural war. Those who came of age in the 1990s viscerally remember when the injunction against Napster was filed on July 28, 2000. It was talked about every day on Howard Stern. People spent entire days downloading music before Napster was shut off—millions and millions of tracks. A young Mark Zuckerberg and his friends were in boarding school ripping and burning away too.

Coder Shawn Fanning perfected the product, leaving Sean

Parker in charge of all the business aspects. He didn't know what venture capital was or how to, say, dole out stock options, but chutzpah was never a problem for him. And Sean did actually have a legitimate business plan. Napster would show the record companies how powerful digital dissemination of music could be, how Napster could make music fun and accessible again.

Then Sean would have them right where he wanted them. The RIAA would have two choices: work out legal deals with Napster or fight them. Sean argued that in the process of suing Napster—and its users—into oblivion, the RIAA would get a public relations black eye, and for what? File sharing wouldn't end. It would simply be shattered into a million uncontrollable pieces, many operating offshore and outside the auspices of U.S. copyright law. The record companies chose to fight, and that's exactly what happened. Oh, and the recording industry became one of the most reviled on the planet as record companies dragged these "pirates"—also their potential customers—into court. Kicking and screaming aside, the labels were ultimately forced to bow to digital progress. Today Apple's iTunes isn't much different from what Napster had hoped to build. (Of course it took Steve Jobs to pull it off.)

Sean naturally clashed with his investors. He says they understood the company about as much as the RIAA did. Napster's staff was mostly a ragtag group of youngsters who stayed up late and dragged into the officc about noon. But they lived the company, feeling they were part of a movement, a revolution. Sean remembers his investor John Hummer giving the company a talk, saying they needed to get their butts out of bed early and go home at five P.M. because this wasn't a revolution. "This is a J-O-B, job," he barked at them. Sean bristled. It showed an utter lack of understanding of the passion that made Napster so powerful. The investors, on the other hand, saw Sean as a liability, particularly once emails of his were used as courtroom evidence that Napster was encouraging piracy. Sean was ousted just before Napster graced the cover of *Time* and was mostly written out of the official company history. It was just the beginning of the tension that would build between Sean and the venture set.

Napster is now just a tiny part of another company, but its outsize legacy continues. The Hummer Winblad partners only recently settled with the RIAA. Meanwhile, other groups like the Motion Picture Association of America are trying to do everything in their power not to repeat the RIAA's mistakes. Instead of suing BitTorrent or YouTube—two companies that enable the same kind of illegal file sharing, but for video—most big studios and television networks are trying to work out legal arrangements with them. And of course the rise in the coolness factor of the Internet and computers has helped give rise to the latest set of Web entrepreneurs.

Still, despite all of this, Sean doesn't consider Napster to be his most influential company. Digitization of media was inevitable; Napster was just the one who happened to spark much of it. The true power of the Web would come from digitization of identity. What does that mean? Basically getting a true picture of who you are as a person represented online. It includes tangibles like your favorite movies and music and who your friends are, but also all the fuzzy gray area in between that's harder to define. Your *essence*. If the Web could capture that, it could unlock all kinds of new, powerful applications from meeting the perfect mate to finding the perfect job. The Web would know *you*, and as a result what you would like.

There was also a big money-making opportunity here: If the Web knew what you liked, a site could carefully pick and choose what ads to show you. It was the ultimate holy grail for advertisers. Instead of wasting millions of dollars mass-broadcasting messages and hoping to find a few potential customers, messages would be so targeted that every one would be almost guaranteed to result in real interest. By 2001 or so, the Internet was crashing, but Sean was starting to think this was the next big wide-open opportunity to build a business online.

His first attempt at this was Plaxo, the least well known of his ventures. It was 2002 and Sean was twenty-two. He hadn't made any money off Napster, and he didn't come from money either. So he spent the post-Napster years sleeping on friends' couches and living out of a duffel bag. A couple of those friends were Cameron Ring, an old classmate from high school, and Cam's roommate at Stanford, Todd Masonis. Todd and Sean became fast friends as Sean unveiled his vision of the digitization of identity for Todd, who had always wanted to do a start-up. Sean assured Todd his Napster credentials would get them funding even in the harsh days of 2002—when no one in their right mind would fund a dotcom with no business plan.

It wasn't so easy. For six months they banged on doors, both penniless and crashing at Todd's girlfriend's apartment. Sean, who has severe asthma and allergies to peanuts, shellfish, green peas, and a good many other things, spent his nights on her couch with his inhaler, humidifier, and other equipment scattered around him. Finally they got a meeting with Sequoia's rock star partner Mike Moritz. To Todd's exasperation, Sean almost made them late, stopping for a latte at his favorite Palo Alto coffee shop. During the pitch, Sean had to constantly remind himself not to raise his left arm because there was a gaping hole in the underarm of his sweater. Amazingly, Moritz bit.

Plaxo attempted to digitize who people were through the most basic route: collecting contact information. The program scours your email looking for the contact info for everyone you know. It puts that together in a database and sends emails to those folks, asking them to add more information, such as their Web site, phone numbers, or birthdays, and subsequently updates that database. Then whenever someone moves or changes contact information, they'd ping Plaxo and everyone who knows that person would get the updated info. The idea was that once everyone got in this Plaxo "cloud," interactivity and keeping in touch would be almost automatic.

But the idea didn't really pan out, partially because it was ahead of its time. Plaxo was part of the first wave of social media companies like Friendster, and a lot of people didn't really get the point of them yet. And there were some flaws in execution. People got irritated by all Plaxo's requests for information flooding their in-boxes. There were also privacy concerns. What if this grand database got hacked?

It didn't help that inside the company a battle was brewing too. Sean was getting ousted again, and it was ugly. The details are sketchy and accounts are contradictory. But Sean wasn't reliable: missing meetings, coming in at noon, and always pushing new ideas long after the company had settled on a strategy and needed to focus. Todd and Cam, once Sean's best friends, realized that behavior that was funny or charming in your friends didn't play well in a start-up trying to distance itself from dotcom mania by looking serious. At one focus group in Atlanta, Sean started inexplicably barking from behind the two-way mirror. "We can hear you," one of the subjects said, looking into the mirror.

Ultimately Todd and Cam wanted him out, as did Plaxo's powerful investors Ram Shriram and Mike Moritz. Sean says he was willing to leave, but when he tried to sell his shares for some walking-around money, things got contentious. In a bid to prove he got fired for cause, they had a private investigator tail Sean and scanned all his email and phone records trying to dig up anything nefarious. The best they got was "a suggestion of impropriety" related to Sean's personal life, he says. Amid all this, word got out in the Valley that Sean loved drugs and the ladies a bit too much. Even Sean admits he is no saint, but he argues that this had nothing to do with his performance on the job.

This was a miserable period for Sean. He had no money and no job and his reputation was taking a beating in the professional world. And all his friends he'd hired at Plaxo were told they couldn't talk to him or they would be fired. Even so, Sean was still obsessed with this idea of digitizing identity. Amid helping his lawyers examine whether he had a case against the Plaxo board, he was trolling the Web for cool new stuff. That's when he came across a site called TheFacebook.com.

Other colleges had their own online directories, but TheFacebook was the first one to take what worked well at Harvard and expand it to other schools. In 2004, with the last money he had, Sean took a break from the Plaxo drama and flew to New York. He treated Zuckerberg and his friends who'd helped start the site to dinner at a fancy Manhattan Jean Georges restaurant. It overdrew Sean's checking account, but he came back to the Valley even more in love with the company. As the Plaxo drama continued to play itself out, he kept thinking about TheFacebook.

A few months later, Zuck and his small entourage of Harvard buddies moved out to Palo Alto for the summer. They rented a house off the leafy downtown strip, University Avenue. Walking back from dinner one night, they saw a skinny, curly-haired guy dragging some boxes into a house.

"Parker?" Zuck said excitedly.

Sean, still penniless, had been living at his girlfriend's apartment near Cal-Berkeley for months. But now the semester was up. When Liza moved back home to Palo Alto to live with her parents for the summer, Sean came with her to crash on their couch. He had nowhere else to go. As it turned out, that couch was five doors down from Zuckerberg's summer rental.

This odd coincidence is one that Sean and Zuck love to play up for the benefit of reporters. Founding mythology is always best when it involves chance and serendipity, as if this start-up was just destined to happen. In truth, the two were planning to get together again anyway. Still, it was a true Silicon Valley moment: that concentration of grizzled dotcom veterans and young hotshots packed into a small peninsula that makes the area what it is. Even if in this case the so-called veteran was still under the age of thirty.

Sean put his boxes away and joined the guys at their house. He was sitting on Zuckerberg's bed when his cell phone rang. He had to take it; it was his attorney. This was the final act in the whole Plaxo drama, which had now gone on for months. Sean, who usually punctuates his stories with a boisterous laugh, was suddenly serious, looking down, talking low. He hung up. That was it. It was over. For the second time, he'd been right about the Web but wrong about nearly everything else and had wound up with nothing.

That moment made a deep impression on Zuck, who was already distrustful of venture investors. Even if Sean's critics were right, even if he was so volatile that he deserved everything he got, Zuck could still see that Sean felt wronged, but that he was powerless to fight back. Even if he had a good case, suing a venture capitalist was Silicon Valley suicide. Sean had already been through months of separation hell, and now he just needed to suck it up and move on. Of course there was one comfort: Sean knew that in the room with him was his chance at a far bigger payout.

Sean helped Zuck, his cofounder Dustin Moscowitz, and a few others restructure Facebook as a proper company, reallocate the shares in a more standard Silicon Valley way (which included Sean getting a healthy chunk), and do all the other things start-ups need to do, such as setting up a data center and making sure that as the site's traffic grew, the company could handle it. Oh, and he got rid of that *the* in TheFacebook.com, which had always annoyed him.

Sean was a pivotal figure in the company's early days because he had real experience starting companies, but was only about five years older than Zuck and his friends. "You trust people you can relate to; I could relate to Sean," Zuck says. "And I was impressed he'd done something cool."

In other words: Napster. And overhearing Sean's end of the call with his attorneys that day, Zuck realized he couldn't trust everyone in Silicon Valley. Especially, he thought at the time, venture capitalists.

Zuck says he's not sure what contributions were Sean's and what were his because they spent so much time bouncing ideas off each other. Zuck has always had an innate sense of where Facebook was going, but thrown in the middle of a Silicon Valley still distrustful of Internet companies, he found it easy to doubt himself. Sean remembers one night Zuck was walking around the pool at a friend's apartment complex. Zuck stopped and asked Sean, "I've really got something here?"

"Yeah, Zuck, you do," Sean said. Digitization of identity, he thought.

Sean, never one to be humble, claims the company would have been sold for a paltry amount without his guidance, and that's probably true. But his biggest contribution by far were the two venture capital deals he brokered, one with Peter Thiel and the other, more famous one with Accel. "If he hadn't been there to be that bridge, we probably wouldn't have raised money," Zuck says. "By seeing Sean's experience with Plaxo, there are ways I think I learned from him that I don't even realize."

Here's how the real story of Facebook and venture capital went, according to Zuck at least. One of the first things Sean did was set Zuck up for a meeting with Peter Thiel. Peter and Sean had known each other since the Plaxo days but had never really worked directly together. Peter liked Sean. The rumors of drugs and other inappropriate behavior didn't necessarily put him off. Peter is a contrarian, and as such, he gives little credence to rumors coming out of the Silicon Valley clique. His offices are in San Francisco's Presidio, an old army base by the Golden Gate Bridge that has been reworked into a swanky space. It's far from Sand Hill Road and San Francisco's financial district, and Peter likes it that way.

Peter is used to aligning himself with difficult or controversial entrepreneurs, assuming they are brilliant, of course. Remember, he started PayPal with Max, not exactly the easiest guy to get along with. When he hired the young and inexperienced Roelof Botha to be PayPal's CFO just before its IPO, people were stunned. Today Roelof is a partner at Sequoia Capital, where he's better known as the guy who funded YouTube—a single deal that repaid investors' cash for Sequoia Capital's entire eleventh fund and then some—along with a few other promising start-ups.

Sean knew that two of the only people who thought differently about the Internet and social networking in the early 2000s were Peter Thiel and Reid Hoffman. They may have called it different things, but they, too, got this idea of digitizing identity and what it could mean for people and the future of business online. Once you had people's essences on your site, you could make your site into a hub of their work or social lives. Social networking sites weren't just a fun way of organizing your friends; the best ones became the next iteration of email, instant messaging, and text messaging—the conduits for staying in touch and organizing your life.

And social networks would grow on their own. Once a site had someone's identity, as defined by his or her likes and dislikes and the social graph surrounding him or her, the number of really useful new features the site could launch on top of that were practically limitless. All of the original dotcom ideas took on new meaning. For instance, selling your couch on Facebook, where you could advertise to other Harvard kids, meant no hassles with shipping and a greater likelihood you could trust the person you were dealing with. On LinkedIn, job seekers could see at a glance who they know who is acquainted with the hiring manager, and hiring managers could *really* check out any potential hires by seeing the complex Web of who they knew who knew or had even worked directly with that person. The Web had made interaction anonymous; Web 2.0 brought back in some of the social pressures that govern real world relationships.

While few of these social networking companies launched with a complex business plan in mind, revenues weren't a stretch if the site was built right. They could charge for some features while keeping most of the others free. Or better yet, they could use all that information they'd gleaned about people to target ads specifically at them and make money that way. After all, for years Google had had no idea how it would make money. But the site's founders knew if Google organized the Internet's information, that would be worth something—$195 billion and counting.

Amazingly, through this idea of digital identity, the Web was groping its way back to the early Internet idea of the portal—the one place you could come to every morning to get all the information that mattered to you. Only this time, it wasn't a merger between AOL and Time Warner bringing you this nexus of Web utilities and content. Nor was it Yahoo!'s content deals with Hollywood or Manhattan media empires. Corporate biz dev guys had nothing to do with it. You were creating your own portal. You were adding your friends, your photos, news feeds you were interested in, even content from other people's blogs and sites.

But at the time, almost everyone was thinking of social networking only as a handy tool to help singles meet. At best, they figured, maybe Facebook could be an offshoot of a site such as Match .com or Yahoo! Personals. Pundits and journalists said over and over again: Social networking is just a fun feature that can't really sustain an actual business. For a lot of people, this idea was too similar to the bubble thinking that a torrent of loyal users was somehow worth millions, even if you hadn't yet found how to make money off it. In 2002, Kleiner Perkins took a risk on the biggest one, giving Friendster a $50 million valuation. When Friendster failed, they looked foolish to have believed. For years the knock on MySpace and Facebook would be, "Yeah, they look good now, but just wait until the fad is over. Friendster looked good too, remember?"

But Kleiner Perkins hadn't been stupid: Friendster was a great idea and got a lot of social networking right. The management team just failed in the execution of the idea. Peter, Sean, and Reid—all of whom were investors or advisers to Friendster—were among the handful of people who knew that. They still saw the potential. Rather than being put off by the supposed failure of social networking, they simply took lessons from what had been done wrong. Reid applied them to LinkedIn, where Peter was one of the first investors.

So when Sean discovered Facebook and needed money to keep up with all the schools adding it month by month, he called Peter. Peter had just started a side venture fund called the Founders Fund. (Reid would also chip in as an angel.) Matt Cohler, another twenty-something East Coast transplant in the Reid/Peter crew, worked at LinkedIn at the time and happened to be at Founders Fund the day Sean and Zuck came to pitch. Having watched LinkedIn slog away to build membership within the professional set, he was amazed at the numbers Facebook already had, seemingly effortlessly. That day he decided he wanted a piece of the company, and within a few months he was the company's vice president of operations and one of its first five hires—complete with early stock options.

Peter was impressed too. Founders Fund invested, getting a 7 percent stake in the company and one of its five board seats. Peter would take over as a friend-tor where Sean left off. After all, Peter had been through it all himself with his tumultuous PayPal ride. Unlike Sean, he'd done things his own way and won at seemingly the bleakest time possible. Starting a new social network in the wake of Friendster's flameout and MySpace's seeming dominance didn't faze Peter. For the first year after the investment, Peter had just five words of advice for the cocksure twenty-year-old Zuck: "Just don't fuck it up."

If Sean did nothing else for the company, introducing Peter to Zuck was enough to earn his keep. But Sean was also behind the Accel funding round in April 2005. If the Founders Fund deal was about hooking Zuck up with someone who got what the company was trying to do, the Accel deal was about getting money and giving up as little control as possible in the process.

Word of the company's early success at universities around the country—particularly at Stanford, Sand Hill Road's home school—was getting out, and the company was fielding a rash of interested calls. But Facebook was profitable and Zuck was still leery of taking money from traditional venture capitalists. Then he got to know an atypical investor, Don Graham, who was CEO and chairman of the board for the Washington Post Company, or as Zuck puts it in his college kid vernacular, "I was introduced to this awesome guy, Don."

The father of one of Zuck's classmates at Harvard was a vice president at the *Post*. Zuck happened to be in Washington, D.C., and the classmate's father suggested that Don might want to meet Zuck. As Zuck described Facebook, Don was fascinated. While Don was in his sixties, he remembered vividly how obsessed he and his friends were with one another's lives when they were in college. In his day, his college newspaper had a comment book where people wrote their opinions or notes such as "Going to the racetrack. Anyone want me to place a $2 bet?" This was a digital version of that, and so much more. Don said to Zuck, "I think you have a wonderful business idea. In the end you won't do this, because it's much more normal to have VC investors or a wealthy person, but if you were looking for a company to invest in your start-up, we'd do it." This was the first time Don had ever made that kind of offer, and the two began to negotiate terms over the next few days.

Zuck was excited, mostly at the prospect of working more closely with Don. As much as he hates to be interviewed, Zuck has a deep reverence for journalism and has always seen Facebook as a site that can help you make sense of the world around you, not unlike a local daily newspaper. Still, Zuck has to be one of the few wide-eyed entrepreneurs to get a hot idea, make the pilgrimage to Silicon Valley to do it right, then eschew the West Coast venture capitalists for a newspaperman from the East Coast.

Meanwhile, in the Valley, one of Accel's associates had told the partners just how hot Facebook was at Stanford, and Kevin Efrusy really wanted a piece of the company. When word leaked that Facebook might be raising money, Accel started coming after them hard. They wouldn't leave the Facebook guys alone. Zuck flat-out refused to talk to them, so Sean was the one who took the calls. He was the bad cop. "A hundred million valuation or nothing," he would say, then hang up the phone.

Matt Cohler had recently been hired and had a more subdued approach, arguing that the company should raise a bigger war chest than what the *Post* was offering. Zuck and Sean finally went down to formally pitch Accel. As Jim Breyer saw "A Mark Zuckerberg Production" at the bottom of every page of the site, he realized there was one person he had to win over to do the deal, and it wasn't Sean. Also, the deal was going to cost far more than the average Web deal in 2005.

Zuck was about to finalize the deal with the *Post* and Accel was still trying to muscle its way in. It was willing to grant a near $100 million valuation as long as it could invest enough to take a 15 percent stake in the company. Breyer even wanted to invest his own money in the deal. Breyer knew Don Graham, and in the middle of an unrelated business lunch, decided to give him a courtesy call.

He stepped away, called him, and told him Accel was chasing Facebook too.

"I thought the deal was done," Don answered. But Breyer said he still sensed an opening.

Indeed, the amount Accel was offering was two and a half times what the *Post* was offering with far better terms. Zuck was stuck. He really wanted to go with Don and had given him his word. But these terms were too rich to be ignored. Although the Facebook project was still small, it wasn't just his project anymore. It was a company, and if he was serious about being chief executive, he needed to consider what was right for the company. He called Don and told him what was happening. Zuck hadn't signed anything, but he told Don he felt like he had a moral dilemma. Don was impressed that this twenty-year-old took his word so seriously. They had a long talk. Don asked if the money mattered to Facebook. Zuck said it did: The company could expand faster and wouldn't have to run at a loss. Don warned him that professional investors were going to be more impatient with him, more likely to force Facebook into an acquisition or IPO.

"I know," said Zuck. "But I think the money matters." And, he added, his other investors and founders felt the same way. Don knew that even if the *Post* bid higher, Accel would just top them. He wasn't a professional venture capitalist, and he wasn't going to pretend he was.

"Mark, I release you from your moral dilemma," Don said. Don knew that for the good of Zuck's business, he needed to go with Accel. It was, in business terms, a no-brainer. The average valuation for an early stage Web company at this point was more like $6 million. Getting a $100 million price tag ensured that Zuck could raise enough to keep Facebook flush with cash for a while and would still leave him with about one-third of the ownership.

That's when Zuck finally had dinner with Breyer at the Woodside Village Tavern, a white-tablecloth restaurant in tony Woodside,

Courtesy of Russel Simmons

The first company photo of PayPal ever taken, back in 1998. From left to right, Ken Howery (now at Founders Fund), Max Levchin (now at Slide), Yu Pan (now at YouTube), Russel Simmons (now at Yelp), Luke Nosek (also at Founders Fund) and (first row) Peter Thiel (head of Clarium Capital and Founders Fund).

Courtesy of Jeremy Stoppleman

Courtesy of Jeremy Stoppleman

Above left and above right: At the PayPal IPO after party, Max celebrates with a cigar and champagne and whacks at a dollar-sign piñata with a sword.

Courtesy of Jeremy Stoppleman

The celebration included a chess tournament. Max Levchin (seated with crown), David Sacks (standing), Roelof Botha (seated), and others challenged U.S. chess master Peter Thiel (standing with crown) to a simultaneous match. David Sacks pulled off the unimaginable: He beat Peter.

Courtesy of James Hong

Max (left); James Hong (right), founder of HotorNot.com; and another Valley entrepreneur, Maryse Thomas, celebrate at the Hollywood premiere of Thank You for Smoking, *produced by PayPal mafia members.*

Geoffrey Ellis

Scott Bannister (left), Max's friend and collaborator since his University of Illinois days, and Keith Rabois (right), a PayPal alum who worked at LinkedIn and now Slide.

Courtesy of Russel Simmons

At an early Yelp party, Jeremy Stoppleman (left) and Russel Simmons (right) take a turn behind the bar.

Geoffrey Ellis

Max with his constant companion, his Wheaton terrier Uma

Jay (top row, third from the right) and some of his early hires on Equinix IPO day

Courtesy of Jay Adelson

Scott Beale

Jay Adelson and Kevin Rose at a Digg party, just before Digg became one of the most high-profile Valley start-ups

Scott Beale

Revision3's most popular show by far was Diggnation, hosted by Kevin (right) and his former TechTV cohost Alex Albrecht (left).

Scott Beale

Jay takes the stage to formally debut the existence of Revision3.

Jay stands in Revision3's new state-of-the-art studio under construction.

Geoffrey Ellis

Courtesy of Marc Andreesen

A young Marc Andreesen (standing) in a meeting at Netscape

James Duncan Davidson

Andreesen on stage at the November 2006 Web 2.0 conference to formally debut Ning to thousands of attendees

Courtesy of Facebook

Nineteen-year-old Mark Zuckerberg coding away at Harvard

Courtesy of Facebook

Zuck and his cofounders in Palo Alto, where they spent a summer trying to figure out how to make Facebook into a real company

Courtesy of Facebook

Zuck looks nervous during one of his first keynotes, announcing Facebook's application platform in May 2007.

Zuckerberg (below, right) is a reluctant Web 2.0 poster child. Matt Cohler (below, left), an early Facebook hire, describes this photo as one of Zuck's most "representative."

Courtesy of Matt Cohler

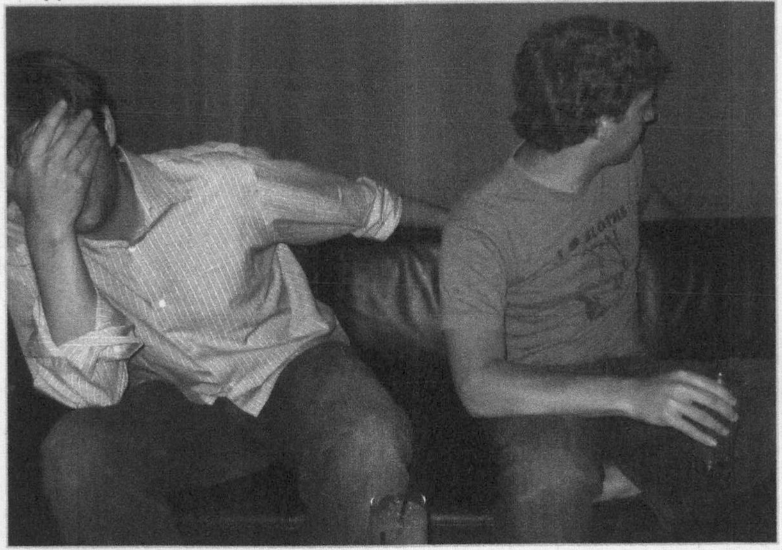

Dave Getzschman

Reid Hoffman (right), founder of LinkedIn, with the company's CEO, Dan Nye (left), in 2007

Evan Williams, the famed "nontrepreneur"

Sara Morishige

Six Apart was started as a hobby back in 2002 by husband and wife Ben and Mena Trott. Here they are in high school (left) and today (below).

Courtesy of Mena Trott

Courtesy of Mena Trott

a town on the peninsula where many of the richest and most powerful venture capitalists live alongside some of the area's oldest farmers and cowboys. Throughout this sleepy Western-themed town, BMWs are often parked next to rusty pickups. During dinner, the reality of just how much Accel was offering sunk in. In addition to the steep valuation, Zuck, Sean, and Dustin would get $1 million each, cash: a million each for about a year's work, or in Sean's case a few months' work. (Sean wasn't going to leave empty-handed this time, no matter what.) A million each just for the privilege of letting Accel invest.

And Zuck would get two board seats that could never be taken away from him. Sean would get one too, with Thiel and Breyer getting the other two. Much like Jay and Kevin at Digg, Zuck and Sean could together veto the investors. (Sean was ousted from Facebook months later, amid rumors of a run-in with the law, although there's no arrest on record. Neither party will comment, aside from saying it was time for Zuck to take greater responsibility as head of the company. Sean held on to 5 percent ownership in the company although he had to leave 5 percent on the table. But he left Zuck his seat, giving Zuck the ultimate say-so in anything the company did.) Zuck was protected from what Sean went through, and by traditional standards, he was rich. (Valley standards were more like $50 million plus; $500 million if you wanted to have jets and yachts. Even then, people have been known to mope, "I'm not a *billionaire* like some of my friends.")

Somehow twenty-year-old Zuck had it all. He'd founded what could be the next great Silicon Valley company. He was the latest boy wonder who saw something simple that the older Silicon Valley set had missed and was smart enough to act on that insight. Since he'd missed the bust, he still thought he could change the world. But via Sean and Peter he was also warned off from making mistakes of the past. So far, at least.

Still, the whole thing stung on a personal level. He picked

Dustin as a cofounder because they were roommates. He picked Sean as his mentor because he could relate to him and he was cool. Peter was the ideal investor because he was a maverick who'd lived through the whole dotcom morass and made money off it even during the bust. And Peter—with chessboards and books all over his home and office—is just the kind of guy who might play Risk in Latin.

Up until now Zuck picked people he liked to own part of Facebook, but in this case he had to pick the person offering the best deal, while the guy he liked missed out. Zuck's early business cards had cheekily read: "It's CEO, bitch." But that dinner was his first lesson in what being CEO of a scorching hot start-up was really all about. The next day he walked down University Avenue to Accel's offices and shook hands with Breyer.

"It's done," he said.

"*Done* done?" asked Breyer.

"*Done* done," said Zuck. Breyer smiled. He'd told his partners he thought Facebook could one day be worth $750 million, and even *that* seemed outrageous. Even Breyer had no idea just how big a coup Accel had narrowly pulled off.

It was July 2007, and Zuck was taking a much-needed break from Silicon Valley. He spent some time in his favorite city, New York, on vacation—not doing the *Today* show, not meeting with East Coast media moguls. He was just chilling with friends. He'd always loved New York because it was so anonymous. Even his friends had little idea that Facebook was now being hyped up to be the next Google.

That's when it happened. He was having drinks with a friend and a guy wandered over with his girlfriend, nervously.

"Are you Mark Zuckerberg?" he asked.

"Yes." Zuck was cold and deadpan; any levity from the conversation was gone as soon as this guy walked up.

"Great job on Facebook—I love that site!" the fan gushed.

"Ok. Thanks." The guy left, but not before he pulled Zuck's waiter aside and gave him a wad of cash for Zuck and his friend's drinks. This lack of anonymity may be the only thing Zuck hates about Facebook, and if he was being recognized now in New York, he knew it was getting worse.

He blames the flip-flops. Zuck wears his trademark black-and-white Adidas flip-flops every single day, usually slipping them off when he sits down, coiling his legs up underneath him or putting his bare feet up on a table in front of him. He loves the flip-flops and is terrified he'll run out because Adidas has stopped making them. His stockpile is down to a measly four pairs. But now he realized this might be a blessing: Every single reporter who has ever written about Zuck has mentioned these flip-flops, and they have become the most recognizable thing about him.

In many ways, Zuck is a reluctant phenomenon. Whereas Tom from MySpace is automatically everyone's friend on his site, Zuck hardly adds anyone he doesn't know well. The bulk of his Facebook friends are still people from Harvard. While Kevin Rose will work a party for hours, graciously signing autographs, mugging for photos, or, on occasion, signing a girl's cleavage, Zuck doesn't even go to parties. The first time I interviewed him, I was expecting the brash, cocky, self-assured kid of all the urban myths. After all, there were those business cards. And every Facebook page had a drawing of a guy in the top left corner that everyone assumed was supposed to be Zuck; the bottom of every page read: "A Mark Zuckerberg Production." Not exactly a humble fellow.

Instead, I met a shy kid with a slight build who gave one-word answers, refused to talk about his background or family, and by the end of the interview had sweated through his white T-shirt. "It has nothing to do with temperature," he explained. "I only sweat when I'm nervous."

This was the most awkward interview I've ever done. Zuck couldn't just answer questions or have a conversation. He'd constantly speculate about why I was asking them. If he didn't deem a question relevant, he just wouldn't answer it. It was as if he was writing code. The best coders are ultraefficient. They want to write only the minimum instructions necessary for the program to work. That was how Zuckerberg navigated his way through an interview.

Midway through the interview I asked an open-ended question, hoping it would trigger something—anything—and he would just start talking. He cocked his head, furrowed his brow, and looked askance at me. "That's a really broad question. I don't know how you want me to answer that," he said, almost as if he were a robot and it simply didn't "compute." Later he told his PR person he felt it was one of the best press interviews he'd ever done.

David Sze, who invested in the company after the Accel deal, says of his first meeting with Zuck, "I thought he hated me." And bear in mind that David is the venture capitalist even guys such as Jay "I hate the sweater-vests" Adelson love. If David can't put an entrepreneur at ease, no venture capitalist can.

Zuck does open up, though, the more you get to know him, and he's not the cocky jerk people expect. He says obnoxious things, but it's almost in a playful way. As Max once described Zuck, he's the kid standing awkwardly in a corner at a party, and when you go talk to him to make him feel better, he says something like, "Why is it that my company is so much better than yours?"

Not too surprising, he can play the role of impish younger brother. Zuck's older sister Randi was two years ahead of him at Harvard. She had graduated and was working in the Manhattan advertising world by the time he dropped out to do Facebook full-time. Randi and Zuck couldn't be more different or look more alike. They talk alike and use the same phrases and mannerisms, but unlike her brother, Randi loves people, enjoys having fun, and considers work just one part of her life. She puts you at ease just as fast as Zuck can make you feel uncomfortable.

Still, the two are close. She even tried setting him up with some of her girlfriends when he went to Harvard. (Didn't go over so well.) One night during the early Facebook days while he was crashing on her floor, Zuck informed his sister that she should get a new job because she was in a dead-end industry. A few months later, over instant message he indirectly asked her to come work for him. The gist of his message was, "I think we need some marketing people or something. We could probably find people worse than you." Later on, he added this, "I really asked because I wanted to hire Brent." Brent was Randi's boyfriend and an upperclassman engineer Zuck had looked up to at Harvard. Randi is the one person within the walls of Facebook that will strike back. One day in the elevator at Facebook, she lifted her hand to move some hair out of her face and Zuck flinched. "You see that?" she said to the toast of Silicon Valley, laughing. "That's power." Having his big sister work with him may be one of the few things that keeps him humble these days.

People frequently describe Zuck in the form of anecdotes about him, and there's a reason for that. He's got a very hard-to-define personality. He doesn't show emotions, and it's nearly impossible to get him to talk about his life, his family, or Mark Zuckerberg the entrepreneur. He's friends with someone only if he thinks that person is smarter than he is in some way. Otherwise, he feels friendship is a waste of his time. You only really get Zuck by hanging out with him. He's shy. He's funny. He's playful. He has a great deal of confidence in Facebook as a company; he believes that it's truly making the world better. He's always had an instinctive feel for where the company was going even if he couldn't articulate it.

He's convinced he's the only one to lead the company, but at the same time he's well aware of his inadequacies as a CEO. He's willing to listen to people older than he is who have more experience. But he questions them, and when they fail him, he's quick to go another way. After the unconventional Sean Parker was ousted from the company, Zuck hired a more experienced slate of managers, who taught him to talk on message to the press and stocked the office with fancy Design Within Reach furniture. He hated it. He fired many of them and still bitches about the furniture. "This was a mistake," he says. "These couches aren't even comfortable! You can't sleep on them." He brought in the graffiti artist who had decorated their first office to mess up the walls again.

He has had a lot of blowups with onetime Facebook advisers and managers, sometimes screaming threats at them in front of dozens of employees. Facebook is personal. Ask him if he misses being in college or is sad about being so far from his family and he'll look at you almost confused and say, "I'm doing this now." As if it's incomprehensible there could be anything but Facebook in his life. When his girlfriend Priscilla graduated from Harvard and moved to Palo Alto, they didn't move in together. And they had a series of "negotiations" over how much she'd get to see him. The final treaty: one date per week, a minimum of a hundred minutes of alone time, not in his apartment and definitely not at Facebook. "I figure she must love my brother," Randi says.

He does, however, have a few distractions. He likes driving up and down the pastoral Highway 280 when he needs to think. He likes being among his friends at the Facebook offices, although he usually works through the weekly poker games. And of course he is fond of Priscilla. He met her just before he moved to Silicon Valley. They were both in line for the bathroom at a Harvard party. Zuck was facing expulsion for an early version of Facebook that ranked students based on how attractive they were, so he was feeling ballsier than usual when he struck up a conversation with her. Unlike Zuck, she's charming and chatty, and she remembers people's faces and names even after a quick meeting. Still, she hates Facebook, the thing that has taken over her boyfriend's entire life. It took her a while to sign up for an account. Zuck goes through most of this scene as Web 2.0 wunderkind simply feeling uncomfortable. "People think I'm rude, and maybe I am, but it's not intentional," he says. "I just don't like to leave the house." (When he uses the word *house,* he really means Facebook's offices.)

He's more than ten years younger than Andreessen, but already Zuck hates going to parties and events, and similar to Andreessen, he almost never goes to San Francisco, where much of the Web 2.0 scene takes place. He says it's because he's deeply afraid of seeing people do drugs. "I can't talk about this anymore or I'll pass out." But he's increasingly fearful of just getting harassed by well-wishers and opportunists. Like Andreessen, Zuck has a deep reverence for the press; he just hates being the one poked and prodded and dissected by it.

Zuck doesn't even drop names for his parents. In 2007, he stopped by to see them in New York on his way to Davos for the World Economic Forum. He didn't call his parents for three weeks after he got back. His dad was dying to know which world leaders and celebrities his twenty-three-year-old son was rubbing elbows with. Zuck finally called, and upon grilling, said he didn't meet Bill Clinton or Bono or Angelina Jolie but he did "chill with the Google guys some." His dad found out later, almost by accident, that *chilling* meant he'd hitched a ride with them back to Silicon Valley on the lush Google jet.

The Zuckerbergs have become reluctant celebrities in their hometown in Westchester County. People wander into Edward Zuckerberg's dental office with quips like, "Why aren't you retired yet?" When new acquaintances ask what the Zuckerbergs' son does for a living, they demur by saying that he dropped out of Harvard and moved to Silicon Valley, hoping for no follow-up questions.

Because he's such an enigma and a hermit, people always get Zuck wrong. He's called arrogant and unwilling to listen to others; others say he's in it for the money. That concept doesn't make sense to him. If you're motivated by money, what do you do after you make it? As he told *Rolling Stone* in 2006, "What people don't get is that I've already turned down more money than I could ever spend." This is not an exaggeration: Zuck leads a spartan life. He doesn't have an alarm clock or much furniture, and only recently got high-speed Internet in his Palo Alto rental. He was so sick one day that he couldn't make it into work and the dial-up connection drove him insane. And as the owner of approximately a third of Facebook, Zuckerberg has already turned down hundreds of millions of dollars.

A pivotal moment was June 2006, when Yahoo! offered to buy Facebook for $1 billion. One *billion* dollars? At the time this seemed exorbitant for what most people thought of as just a college social networking site. Yahoo! needed something radical. It had weathered the bust and was one of the largest dotcom survivors. But Google was killing Yahoo! in the most lucrative form of online advertising: paid search ads. While Google's stock soared past $400 a share, Yahoo! was in Wall Street's doghouse. There was pressure on the company to do something big, and acquiring Facebook was as big as it got.

As a founder, Mark is an odd combination of heart and mind. He navigates product strategy by his gut, but he navigates business strategy via a highly analytical measurement of users, growth, engagement, and other stats. Both argued against the deal. His gut was telling him he wasn't finished creating the site, his ultimate vision. His analytical mind was telling him that $1 billion was simply not enough. He saw how many people were using the site and how obsessively they were using it. He knew the company was worth more. He convened the board meeting to talk about the deal by glancing at his watch, looking at Peter and Jim, and saying, "Eight-thirty seems about as good a time as any to turn down $1 billion." He wasn't going to be some has-been Web 1.0 company's life raft. It wasn't part of his plan.

Was he stupid? At the time most everyone thought so. One billion dollars is a lot of money; MySpace had sold for about half of that, and at that time most people thought Fox had grossly overpaid. Google's $1.65 billion had reduced Chad and Steve to giggling teens. His board members were agog—this was $1 billion Yahoo! was talking about. Zuck and Peter spent six long hours debating about whether Facebook should even consider the deal. After all, Peter had sold his company to eBay. This was a dilemma he was familiar with, and while he wasn't pushing Zuck to sell, he wanted him to consider it. In the PayPal case, selling had been for the best. PayPal's future had been uncertain for a variety of legal reasons, and it was uncomfortably dependent on eBay for much of its customer base. Beyond that, everyone at the company made money and got to stay friends. And considering all the innovation that has emerged from the gang, in Slide, Yelp, YouTube, LinkedIn, Geni, and others, selling was probably best for the Valley too.

By the end of the conversation, Zuck was at least open to exploring a sale, which was all Peter asked. Then a few days later, Yahoo!'s stock fell by 20 percent, and it tried to discount the deal. That was it. No sale. This time Peter and Zuck agreed. Even Breyer agreed. "If it had been a clean $1 billion offer, I probably would have wanted to consider it seriously," he says. After all, his goal for Facebook had been $750 million. "But that offer never came."

Ultimately they were wise to hold out. Yahoo! had blown it, much like it blew the chance to buy Google for some $3 billion back before its IPO. It would soon become obvious that $1 billion would have been a *bargain* for Facebook. By December 2006, just a few months later, the company was valuing itself at $8 billion, based on the ad rates and the valuation of MTV, which boasted a similar demographic to Facebook. Valuations of private companies are always open to interpretation. In practical terms, it's the price a company would sell at. And by the end of 2006, Facebook wasn't selling for anything less than $6 billion. Yahoo!, or anyone else interested, had missed its window.

8

WORLD DOMINATION

It may be hard to understand why Facebook could be worth billions unless you're in high school or college. Facebook started as an online directory of pictures and contact information for a school's student body, but as it has grown, it has become much more. People have uploaded so many photos to their profile pages that Facebook is now the largest photo-sharing site on the Web, far outpacing Slide or Flickr. People upload video too. It's no stretch to imagine a day when Facebook displays more daily videos than YouTube. People blog on the site. They message one another through the site. They even plan events on the site, rather than using another Web site such as Evite. Need to buy a new TV? Facebook has classifieds too. For people in college and to a lesser extent in high school, Facebook is like an Internet within the Internet. They log on in the morning, check their email, and open Facebook. A full two-thirds of the users come to the site every single day.

Facebook allows teens to effortlessly stay in touch with older siblings or friends who've gone away to college and other friends who've moved out of town. The site warns you when a friend's

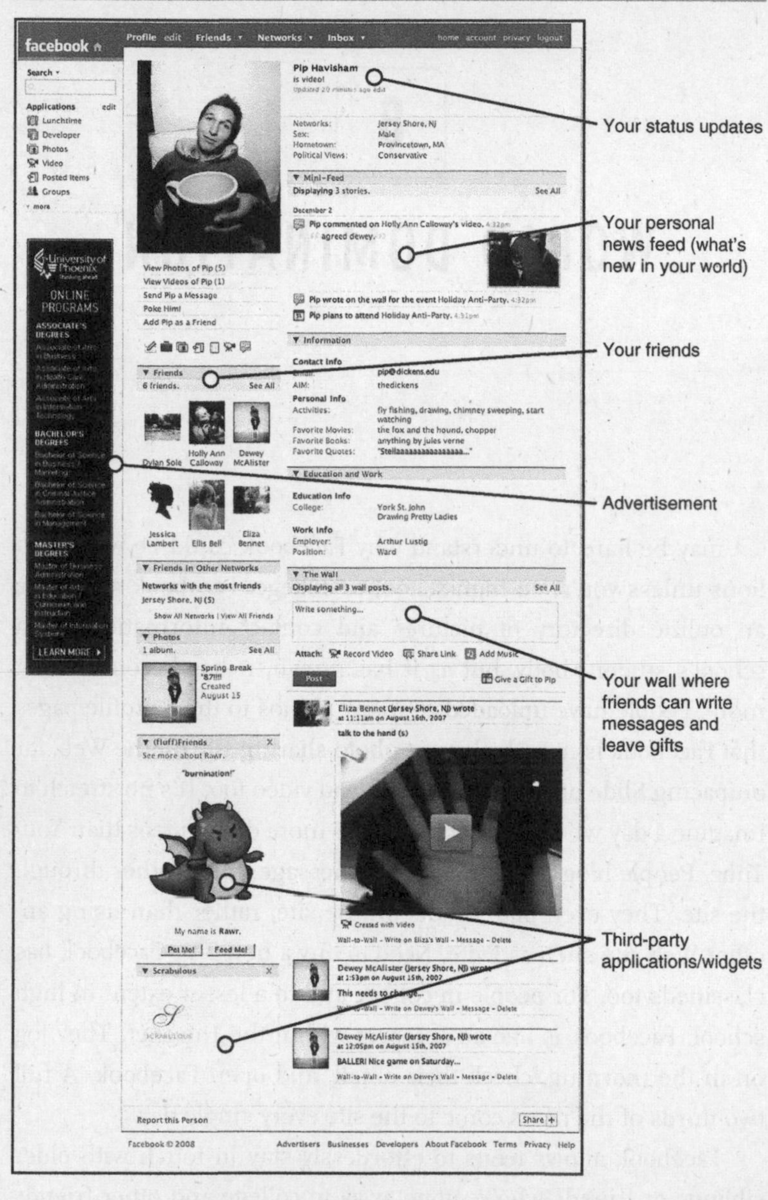
facebook
Profile edit Friends Networks Inbox
home account privacy logout
Pip Havisham
is video!
Your status updates
Your personal news feed (what's new in your world)
Your friends
Advertisement
Your wall where friends can write messages and leave gifts
Third-party applications/widgets

birthday is approaching. You get updates on the lives of others, such as who got accepted into college, or who got a new boyfriend, just by looking at their profile page. Parties are planned on Facebook, and photos from those parties are posted on the site—to such an extent that some schools have to specify in invitations, "No photos posted on Facebook, please."

This college demographic is key. It gives Facebook an insurance policy against being just a fad. For college students, having a Facebook profile is as essential as having a campus mailbox, a dorm room extension, or an ".edu" email address. Even if Facebook can't beat MySpace among high school students, or LinkedIn in the professional world. At the very least, the fact that Facebook is considered essential on the campuses of most U.S. universities guarantees it a new crop of users every fall. That's a safety net no other social network has. And surprisingly, 60 percent of college grads continue using the site after they graduate. Facebook doesn't have to convince people in their thirties and forties they're not just a college site; over time the Facebook-loyal will become the thirty- and forty-year-olds.

And for the Facebook loyal, Facebook is simply their life.

Max Levchin puts it in starker (and geekier) terms: Social networks are the new operating system, particularly for young people. They check MySpace or Facebook more than they check their email. It is the hub of their online world, particularly thanks to something called the widget economy.

Widgets are mini-applications you bolt onto a site. A YouTube video you add to your MySpace page is a widget. A Slide slide show you may add to a blog is a widget. By 2007 there were dozens of widget companies emerging from the Silicon Valley start-up machine, which by now was running at full strength. It was amazing. Just a little more than ten years after Marc Andreessen and Jim Clark released Netscape, people weren't just using the Web, they were assembling their own pages by using these easy-to-install widgets—like snapping together LEGOs to make the site of your dreams.

In business terms, no one really knew what it all meant yet. Maybe it was just a fad. But Max, whose company was enabling people to build hundreds of thousands of widgets every day, saw the Web browser as the new computer, Facebook or MySpace as the new operating system, and companies like Slide as developers of the new programs and applications. "In this world, Zuckerberg may well have played his cards the best," Max said in early 2007.

In May 2007, in a vast conference center in San Francisco, thousands of geeky developers waited, eyes fixed on a huge stage. Many of them were clad in T-shirts with start-up names like iLike or Picks-Pal splayed across their chests in bright colors; most of them displayed the dark circles under their eyes that betray all-night coding sessions.

It wasn't just the Valley's foot soldiers in the room—it was the Web 2.0 elite. Money men like Peter Thiel and David Sze were there. Iconic Web figures like Evan Williams, who started Blogger and was now on his third start-up, Twitter, were there. Bram Cohen, the guy who came up with ways to send large files over the net when he created BitTorrent, was there. Brad Fitzpatrick of LiveJournal and Six Apart, Kevin Rose of Digg, James Hong of HotorNot, Sean Parker with his new company code-named Agape. Max was there too. But he was backstage with the man everyone was waiting to see—Mark Zuckerberg, wearing his usual jeans, T-shirt, Adidas flip-flops, and black, lived-in North Face fleece. This was the same outfit he might have worn to grab a slice of pizza, except in a sign that summer had come to Palo Alto, he had just switched from the heavier black Patagonia fleece to the North Face one. "It's my summer fleece," he explains.

Zuck steps out onstage and tries to do the whole Steve Jobs

pump-up-the-crowd bit, but the applause is sporadic and awkward. Maybe it's because the room is more developers than marketing folks and fanboys. After all, most of the people in this room were up all night coding, and like Zuck, they are socially awkward. Or maybe it was Zuck himself. This was his first big keynote address and he looked tiny on the cavernous stage, surrounded by floor-to-ceiling screens displaying his PowerPoint presentation.

He was clearly nervous, continually wiping his sweaty palms on the thighs of his jeans. And thanks to a bevy of last-minute changes, the presentation hardly went smoothly. Slides didn't work, and even the demo had problems, when Facebook's much-touted privacy settings kicked in and the site banned Zuck from getting a preplanted message from his cofounder Dustin. "Well, that's a bummer," he deadpanned. He paused after that section of the keynote, smiling awkwardly. "This has been fun. It's working exactly how I thought it would."

The miscues were actually a blessing. Zuckerberg was able to think on his feet and loosen up a little. Still, it was like watching your younger brother do his first major presentation. In fact, Zuck's older sister Randi was watching. His parents and his girlfriend, Priscilla, were there too. The Zuckerberg family was having quite a month. One sister was graduating from high school and another was graduating from college, all during the same month Priscilla was graduating from Harvard. Randi and Brent were having an engagement party, Randi becoming the first Zuckerberg to tie the knot. And twenty-three-year-old Harvard dropout Zuck was announcing to the world that Facebook is the new operating system. The new Microsoft and Google in training. The next new dominant Silicon Valley powerhouse. That or the company will go under trying.

The event was dubbed F8. And it was not just a normal software update. In the parlance of Silicon Valley, Facebook was boldly announcing it was what every Web start-up says it wants to be: a platform. Three words are constantly bandied about in the Valley's start-up scene: application, feature, and platform. An application is a specific program that's part of something bigger. In the world of traditional computer software, Microsoft Word or Excel is an example of an application, part of the bigger Microsoft desktop collection of software. For the Internet as a whole, email has been called the killer app. A feature is usually a subset of an application. For instance, stock charts are a feature of Yahoo!'s finance page.

Then there are platforms. Platforms are broad, powerful sites or programs that many different applications and features plug into. For Microsoft, its ubiquitous operating system is the platform that all its other programs run on. For Google, its superior search engine is the platform. Google News and Google Images, for instance, are applications made possible by the search platform. Feature companies are typically sold for a small amount. Applications, if they become really huge, can be sold for more, or maybe turn into a larger stand-alone company eventually. But what start-ups really want to be is a platform.

The terms are agonizingly fuzzy and hard to pin down. No one will admit his company is just a feature. One entrepreneur's potential platform may seem merely a feature to a snooty investor. All of this is important when it comes to social networking because in the immediate aftermath of the bubble's burst, the conventional wisdom was that social networking was a feature, or at best an application to be run off a larger, more profitable site. But the reality was, once a start-up had someone's entire social Web captive on its site, it could roll out a number of applications that had never really worked before. This was similar to what LinkedIn already had with job searching.

By 2007, the Web scene had broken out in a raging case of platform disease. Every Web site that was doing well and had done any sort of job digitizing people's identities was calling itself a platform and brainstorming about all the ways it could use this new element called social media to become more and more core to its users' lives. Yelp didn't want to be just about restaurant reviews, but about reviews of all kinds. And not only that, it wanted to indirectly be a site for making friends, dating, hanging out. Yelpers organized regular get-togethers on the site and would hang out in its chat rooms.

Kevin wanted Digg to be about more than just collecting the headlines and ranking them; he thought it should be a way to find people who were like-minded. Digg could know the kinds of things you liked by the stories you voted on and could match you with someone who thought the same kinds of stories were cool. It could even compete with Yelp ultimately. If you are planning a trip to Fiji, for instance, you could certainly search Yelp for hotel reviews, or you could ask Digg. Digg would know like-minded people and could even poll them for you.

Ning was also trying to build a platform. You could build mini social networks on your Ning site, but also add photos and videos and build mini Flickrs and YouTubes for your friends. And at LinkedIn, job searching was just the beginning. Reid had pages of new features and applications he'd been dreaming up over the last few years during the period the site had been generating a critical mass of users and getting to profitability.

These guys all had the same vision, just through different lenses. They had an endless flow of ideas for new applications they could build; it was just a matter of prioritizing which were the most important. And they were right; the digitization of identity was that powerful and each of these sites had a piece of it. No matter how you sliced it, at this point Zuck had a lead on all of them.

But this event was more than just a keynote. All those geeks and coders in the audience had spent the night before building new applications for Facebook's platform. Slide shows to run on the site, mini-versions of Digg and HotorNot, or even more random applications, such as one that would serve up daily facts about cult actor Chuck Norris. Engineers could write whatever applications they wanted, and the best ones would take off. They'd all be listed on the site in the same directory—Facebook's own applications and ones written by others side by side. People could arrange them however they wanted on their page.

The only thing you couldn't move or delete was the News Feed—that was key to everything Zuck held dear about the site and crucial to the adoption of applications. As you saw several of your friends add something like a horoscope application, you were more likely to add it too. On the flip side, if you saw your friends deleting that same application weeks later, you might figure there was something wrong with it and take it off.

It was a bold move, and one that would change the company forever. If third-party applications were more popular than Facebook's own versions, the company would have to support that. Zuck couldn't have the same control over the site he'd long enjoyed. It was a 180-degree difference from MySpace, who tried to block sites like YouTube that got too popular on MySpace or to launch their own copycat versions of applications, as they did when Slide got too popular. Sure, you could still add a Slide slide show, but the MySpace version was pushed at you as soon as you signed up. True to Thiel's libertarian beliefs, Facebook would be a totally open application meritocracy. Companies could even make money running an application on Facebook, either getting a split of the ad revenues or using Facebook's existing micropayments system if they wanted to sell things through their application. The only rule was the applications had to be written in Facebook's scripting language so the pages would still look uniform and clean—not the garish loud, flashing, ad-heavy pages you'd get on MySpace.

The idea was brilliant. MySpace had always been more of a media company than a tech start-up; it was having even more problems innovating inside slow-moving News Corp. Now with one masterstroke, Zuck had mobilized all of Silicon Valley to innovate *for* him. It would free Facebook up to focus on the site as a whole, and of course on building the business.

And the Valley was only too happy to oblige. In many ways, MySpace represented everything they hated in a Web company. It was a media company from Los Angeles with an ugly site based on shitty coding practically held together with duct tape and rubber bands, at least according to Valley insiders. In the Valley, it's common to have two businesses compete intensely and have the founders still be friends. People will even root for both of them, saying, "This isn't a zero-sum game," or "This is a big enough market, we can both do well." But introduce an East Coast or Los Angeles–based company into the mix and the Valley gets vicious. Everyone was still pissed the biggest Web 2.0 success to date was a Los Angeles company who foolishly sold too soon. It was high time to take them down, and at the May conference everyone realized that Mark Zuckerberg actually had a shot at doing it.

This grand platform was launching at midnight. Once the keynote was done, members of the press and other folks would mill around various developer stations and check out whatever everyone had been working on, and by nightfall one big eight hour "hackathon" would begin hence the event's name "F8." The hackathon is a hallowed tradition at Facebook. It starts when someone in the course of any workday calls for a hackathon. This usually happens about once a month. Anyone except Zuck can call for one. They settle on a night, and over junk food, beer, and Red Bull, Facebook's corps of engineers stays up all night coding. A hackathon has only two rules: the project has to be something cool and it couldn't be something they'd normally work on. Once the sun comes up, they all go to breakfast somewhere together and then they crash the entire next day. All meetings on that day are canceled.

On May 24, Facebook was hosting a hackathon for all of Silicon Valley. That meant bigger tubs of Chinese food and more boxes of pizza, a full bar of Red Bull, bottled water, and soda, a whole area of beanbag chairs, and for some reason, blaring techno music. Even by Valley standards, this was a night when a geek could be a total geek. The Valley's best minds all working together, for their own companies sure, but also for Facebook. By eight P.M. or so almost everyone except the hackers were long gone and the mood was becoming euphoric.

Scott Banister, wearing a Slide T-shirt, came up to Matt Cohler as the hackathon was getting under way. Banister was Max's first business partner back when the two were starting half-baked companies in Illinois, and he had supplied the floor that Max and several other University of Illinois transplants crashed on back in the late 1990s. He had just sold his most recent company, IronPort, to Cisco for $800 million and was spending most of his time these days helping Max with Slide. In the ten years between those events, Banister had seen a lot in the Valley, but this was something new.

"The world just changed," Banister said to Cohler, giving him sort of a slapping sideways high five and glancing over at Zuck, who was pacing in front of the catering setup, anxious for the trough of Chinese food to arrive. "You guys rock." The rest of the Web 2.0 crew may still dream of their own platforms, but they've got to nod to Zuck on this one. With his 30 million regular users, more than half of whom come to the site every day, he has won. "Our plan is to go big or go under," Cohler says, smiling, damn glad he jumped to Facebook when he did.

It's hard to imagine this army has been mobilized by a twenty-three-year-old. When Zuck first met all of them he had to battle for respect. But Zuck is a different person from when he came to the Valley just four years ago. Facebook has been a runaway success, but one that has put Zuck through an intense bout of management training. Figuring out who is trustworthy, hiring people, firing them, digging deep within himself to find the confidence to tell his investors he won't take a $1 billion payout for what he had built. It has all been a surreal blur, and when Zuck steps back to think about it, even he isn't sure how he got here. Neither are those who know him best. Zuck's dad may have always known his late-bloomer son was special, but he certainly never thought he would see him doing a keynote address in front of hundreds of people.

Long after the keynote was done and everyone left was hacking away, Zuck and Priscilla were walking hand in hand, amidst a floor of empty chairs, locked in quiet conversation. The scene was more like a moment from a John Hughes movie than the pivotal point that would rock Silicon Valley's start-up world. As if they were going to start to slow-dance any moment. It's then you remember that he is just twenty-three.

The only thing that may be more astounding is how many times this scene has already played out in the Valley. It's not that kids build billion-dollar empires here every day. But the precedent is strong. Steve Jobs. Marc Andreessen. Larry Page and Sergey Brin. And almost all of them have truly changed the world. Still, lots of them get this far and flame out. As unbelievable as his success has been so far, Zuck has to realize that it will only get harder from here.

Of course, if you believe that Facebook has the potential to become the next Google, this raises another question: Is a young man with no business experience the guy to run it? In the company's early days, the answer to this question was unequivocally yes. Like Napster, Facebook is a revolution on college campuses. For it to be authentic, it needed someone of that texting, instant-messaging, always connected generation at its helm. The company has grown out of Zuck's experience, an innate instinct or gut feeling about what Facebook should be. For years, he couldn't explain or defend it. Fortunately he had enough control he didn't need to.

But there's also the issue of trust. Facebook is intensely personal for these people. It's a focal point for their lives. It was one of the first sites where people used their real names instead of made-up user names, and most people even list their cell phone numbers on their pages. Just as Zuck trusted Sean Parker because he could relate to him, college kids and postgrads trust Zuck because he's like them, only running a company. And the single coolest company to work for when you graduate is Facebook. That gives him the pick of the best up-and-coming talent, in a way Microsoft and Google did in years past.

Facebook is almost an extension of college. The average age of its employees is twenty-five. The bulk of them share rental houses in Palo Alto. The company even gives them a housing allowance if they live within walking distance. Facebook's offices look a lot like a dorm room—a *dream* dorm room. Top-of-the-line computers, a poker table, and Nintendo Wiis everywhere you look. There's always food around, laid out in big stainless-steel catering dishes.

And of course there is a copious amount of caffeine on hand. Each building's kitchens have cafeteria-style beverage racks with anything you could imagine inside. There's also a way-too-complex machine they've dubbed "coffeebot" that will grind up and dispense whatever you want. The original coffeebot couldn't handle the round-the-clock grinding, brewing, and frothing. When it died, the company immediately invested in a newer and better model: Son of Coffeebot. And on Tuesdays, there's a massive pile of laundry bags on the second floor where all the engineers work. A service comes and takes it away and, like Mom, does all the kids' laundry for them.

On hackathon nights the place looks even more like a dorm—a dorm the weekend before finals when everyone is geared up to pull the big all-nighter, cramming a semester's worth of information into their brains and hoping to retain it for at least twenty-four hours. Junk food is everywhere you look. People sit at their spartan desks or lounge around on huge red beanbags. The coding has gotten so intense at times that some engineers have suffered leg burns from laptops. Rather than rethink the tradition, the company just bought scores of Apple laptop protectors. Before a spring 2007 hackathon, engineers had torn into them, leaving the boxes strewn all over a couch and the floor. Zuck shoves them aside and sits down to soak it all in. This never gets old for him. Logically, he knows they could get the same production just working a normal day, and it wouldn't screw up everyone's sleep schedules. But he could never replicate this esprit de corps.

The next day the place is wrecked and those engineers who show up at work are groggy and nodding off between sentences. Empty cans of Red Bull are all over the room. Half-eaten slices of pizza are on the floor, as if someone was chowing down when a genius idea hit him, so he tossed his pizza on the floor and ran off to code it. Nearly eighteen hours later, the slice is still there. There are about ten sets of Wii bongo drums lying around. "You know, engineers like the bongos," Zuck says.

He adores the mess. "Creative chaos" is Jim Breyer's euphemism for it. Facebook's second building in downtown Palo Alto has a big cafeteria, and the day it opened everyone went over for lunch. It was just like high school, with people shyly picking out their table and those people they'd sit with for the first time. But it was too clean. Too nice. When the gang of engineers wandered back to the original Facebook building after lunch they opened the stairwell to a musty smell and fruit flies and smiled. "It felt like...home," Zuck says.

Anything to do with engineering and the culture he has built around it is the part of his job Zuck loves. As Facebook grows bigger, there are more and more parts of his job he doesn't love. Giving interviews. Going to events. And managing and all the politics. Zuck has had a hard time filling out his management team with people he trusts, and the result has been a lot of turnover in some key slots. The only other programmers of any real rank are still mostly his college friends. When a company grows this fast, there are inevitable cracks that don't usually reveal themselves until things start to get hard.

One of those moments of strain was the debacle over the News Feed. It was a pivotal moment for Zuckerberg as the leader of both his company and the Facebook community. He had to figure out his priorities fast. Who did this company belong to anyway? Zuck? His employees? The venture capitalists who invested in it? Or the millions of kids who made it so successful? Zuck was caught in the middle. He felt the News Feed was best for the company, central to his vision of making sense of the world around you. That was in the best interests of the employees and shareholders, right? The community was another matter. A lot of the college kids were outraged, feeling that Zuck had turned against them. The harshest criticism they could level: Facebook has gone corporate.

Zuck had been put in the middle of all these groups before. His decision not to sell Facebook didn't play well with many of the stock-option-holding employees who would have become instant millionaires. But that disagreement was behind closed doors; this time it was erupting on a national stage. All the major press outlets were covering it, quoting outraged students. College papers were covering it. Students were planning a boycott of the site. (Although this boycott was only for a day, and a lot of people couldn't be enlisted. Facebook was just that integral to their lives.)

As the controversy erupted, Zuck's first blog to the community came off a little flippant, starting out, "Calm down. Breathe. We hear you." His second one, posted a few days later, was better. It began, "We really messed this one up." It reiterated the point of the News Feed and introduced more privacy controls. Zuck humbly signed off: "Even though I wish I hadn't made so many of you angry, I am glad we got to hear you. Thanks for taking the time to read this, Mark."

There was still some rumbling, but largely the community was satisfied. Zuck managed to make the community feel like they'd won a victory while really changing very little about his original plan. And he learned from it: Never again would he toil away on a product for months, then do a grand unveiling. People hate change; better to prep them, keep them posted, and make them feel like they're a part of it.

That victory aside, college kids were right when they said Facebook was getting more corporate. It's a company, and as it grows, it has to. Processes have to be put into place. Rules need to be written and enforced. Still, the company is wise to gamble that Zuck's gut, his deep connection with his users, and whatever on-the-job training he gets will be better for the company than a traditional CEO. After all, the Valley is peppered with iconic founders who had never run a company but built empires like Apple Computer and Hewlett-Packard nonetheless. It's also chockablock with examples of so-called grown-up CEOs who killed the very innovation and uniqueness that had made the company a hot start-up to begin with. At least with Zuck, it's obvious what he's good at and where he needs work.

There's another somewhat counterintuitive argument for Zuck staying CEO: As the company inevitably gets more corporate, Zuck's presence softens the blow. Say the company has to add more advertising to the pages. If Zuck does it and explains it on his blog, it goes down much easier than if some stodgy guy in a suit announces it. Even though he's out of college, he can still speak for his generation. And as Facebook increasingly tries to keep college grads using the site every day, Zuck has a new group he can relate to. The very things that make Zuck so ill-suited for the job make him the perfect ambassador to the company's core users. In that vein, even his awkward keynote works. Facebook can't have it both ways. They can't have a highly polished CEO and someone who comes across as authentic.

Of course, thanks to Sean Parker, whether Zuck should stay CEO is purely an academic argument. With three board seats, Zuck is the only person who can vote himself out. In the short term, that gives Zuck a lot of leash. In the long term, it puts the pressure of whether Facebook succeeds or fails on Zuck and his gut. And as the company grows, employing hundreds of people and boasting a valuation of $15 billion, that's a *lot* of pressure.

One night in the spring of 2007, there was some sort of mini-crisis at the company and Zuck drove up to San Francisco to talk it through with Sean. He still trusts Sean. Zuck looked weary. When asked if he was having fun as CEO, he said, "Not really. People don't understand, I didn't really set out to start a company." He looked at Parker, smiled, and said, "It was more fun when you were there." Those were the good ol' days, and despite Facebook's loose, dormlike atmosphere, they are over.

Peter has always had one central piece of advice for Zuck: Typically only one or two elements truly matter when you're the CEO. The trick is finding out what those elements are. To Zuck, it's clear that one of them is not selling Facebook on the cheap. "I fuck up all the time," he says. "I fuck up all day long. But as long as I don't fuck up the big things, it's okay. Let's say Facebook could be worth $20 billion one day. If I had sold Facebook for $1 billion I would have eroded a lot of value. That'd be a pretty big fuckup." Zuck has even told Peter he shouldn't have sold PayPal. "It's going to do $2 billion in revenue this year and he sold it for $1.5 billion!" he says.

This may be the most important reason for Zuck to run Facebook, for his own good, for the company's good, for his investors' good, and for the good of Silicon Valley. He won't sell. Is it because he's cocky enough to believe Facebook can't possibly stumble? Naive enough to think markets and external forces can be controlled? Ego-driven enough to think he can build the next Google? Or is he just doing something so useful, so cool that anything else would pale in comparison?

It's likely a combination of all of them. It's the same ludicrous cocktail of ambition, delusion, and emotion that has resulted in most of the giants of the high-tech world, not to mention the technology that runs our everyday lives. The giants of Silicon Valley all had a chance to sell out at some point for what seemed a huge amount of money, an amount that would be stupid to turn down, but they turned it down anyway.

Every decade a handful of truly great companies come out of the Valley. If people did the rational thing—taking the money—that wouldn't happen. Someone has to believe. Someone has to say no. Maybe that's the key to the so-called Mark Zuckerberg phenomenon, why so many of the largest Silicon Valley companies come from young guys in their twenties. They haven't yet learned that when someone offers you a billion dollars, you should probably say yes.

9

MIDTOWN DOORNAIL

Max thinks he has a way around this Mark Zuckerberg phenomenon, the idea that at thirty-one he may find his best days behind him. He has recently read a research paper advancing the thesis that only certain inventors have that big breakthrough early in their twenties. Others were just wired differently. Some had their big breakthroughs late in their careers. The Grandma Moses argument, if you will. She started painting at seventy, when thanks to arthritis she could no longer do needlepoint. She became one of the best-known and most-celebrated American artists.

"It was a little self-serving," Max admits of the paper, since the guy writing it was middle-aged and had yet to have such a breakthrough. Still, Max mostly buys the theory. Because he doesn't think he has had his huge breakthrough yet. Or that's what he tells himself.

PayPal wasn't it.

As he explains this, he's sitting in Slide's conference room in early January 2007, easily distracted by his fluffy terrier Uma, who wants to come in the room and then leave the room, then come in again and then leave again. "Uuuuummmmaaaa," he says in his deep scolding voice. She playfully taunts him like a willful child. It's surprising that Max dotes on Uma so completely. He seems to have no control over her, and for Max most of his life is about control. That's why he was drawn to computers and why he has stayed CEO of Slide. That's why he is the company's largest shareholder even after raising nearly $40 million.

Max is wearing a shirt today that reads "I don't speak Japanese"—in Japanese. He made it himself. He made a whole series of these during the PayPal days. "I was fed up with wearing just PayPal shirts," he says. He has one that reads "I don't speak Spanish" in Spanish and one that reads "I don't speak Chinese" in Chinese. He loves two things about these shirts. One, cute Japanese girls find the Japanese shirt hilarious. Two, when someone asks him "What does your shirt say?" and he answers nonchalantly, "I don't speak Japanese" (or Spanish or Chinese), it's like an inkblot test. Smart people get the joke; dumb people think he's saying he doesn't know what his shirt says because he doesn't speak Japanese. Anyone who would think Max would wear a shirt and not know what the slogan on it means doesn't know Max very well.

Bloggers chronicling the Web 2.0 scene didn't seem to know Max too well either. By early 2007, just as Max was hoping to be the YouTube of 2007, Slide was the subject of several snarky blog posts. People didn't *get* it. Slide shows? Nice, but one of the largest photo-sharing sites, Flickr, had already sold to Yahoo! for a mere $30 million. How are you going to build a huge business on slide shows? It seemed the least exciting of all of the PayPal mafia's companies. Weird, since Max was the one who hired guys like Chad, Steve, Russ, and Jeremy. How could Max have come up with such a lame second act? Maybe he was just lucky the first time.

Part of the reason people don't get it is they don't get Max. They underestimate how obsessive he is. All his money and time are focused on one goal: making Slide into a big success. It's all he thinks about day and night. Max doesn't need snarky bloggers; he is more aware of the company's shortcomings than anyone. He watches graphs and traffic charts all day long. And since normal Web metrics aren't enough, he has actually written programs to track every aspect of how the company is doing. When the current strategy isn't working, Max is the first to suggest changing course. That's why PayPal had been successful, after all. It started out as Confinity, a company that allowed people to beam money over Palm Pilots.

Max isn't simply the wunderkind who hits on a great idea; he's the guy who figures out what the great idea is through painstaking trial and error. He's not so much visionary as he is relentless. Max simply does not get burned out and quit. Mid-2007, MySpace was making up about 40 percent of Slide's audience. The worst-case scenario would be for MySpace to ban Slide. If that happened, Max says calmly, his traffic would drop by 50 percent overnight. But it wouldn't be the end. In fact, every social network could ban Slide and there would be three guys left at the office picking up the pieces, still trying to build a $1 billion plus company. "I'll be one of them," Max says. "And I know who the other two are."

Of course, the other thing snarky bloggers and industry watchers don't know is just how coy Max is being about how well Slide is doing. By January, 120 million Slide slide shows are being watched on any given day. Most of these are running on people's MySpace pages, but also on other social networking sites, blogs, and home pages. Estimates are that some 50 million people are viewing these slide shows every day. And about 200 million new slide shows are made every day. Those numbers are all growing fast. From January 2006 to September 2006, Slide streamed just under 10 billion images across people's Web browsers. From October to December it exceeded that. "It better than doubled, and it certainly hasn't flattened out yet," Max says.

Hardly satisfied, Max is driving the team hard to make those numbers double *every quarter*. At the 2006 holiday party just weeks earlier, Max gave what he thought was an inspirational talk to the troops, telling them they'd worked hard but they needed to work a lot harder in 2007. This wasn't exactly what the exhausted corps wanted to hear. Max covers his head and groans when asked about it. "Awwww, I thought I was being warm and fuzzy." It's hard enough to build another PayPal-like success story, but this time Max is doing it as CEO, not chief technology officer. He's doing it without Peter Thiel, and he's having to learn a lot about people. But Max's number one concern was keeping those numbers growing while making sure competitors and potential competitors had no idea just how gaudy the numbers were.

Even Max's friends were surprised at how well the quiet company was doing. One night he was having dinner with Allen Morgan, a partner at venture capital firm the Mayfield Fund. They were eating at Kokkari, a Greek restaurant in San Francisco. It's the sister restaurant to Evvia, a spot in Palo Alto where every venture capitalist seems to have lunch at least once a week. It's a Valley equivalent to, say, The Ivy in Los Angeles, where who is eating with whom is as good an indicator of what people are working on as anything else. During a single lunch, the right entrepreneur could put together a syndicate of funding, find an attorney to do the paperwork, and probably wander around and make a few early hires. People go to Kokkari to eat good Greek food; they go to Evvia to be seen.

This dinner started out as a purely social get-together. Perhaps due to his good fortune with PayPal, Max doesn't seem to have the same general disdain for venture capitalists as some of the rest of the Web set. In fact, he was about to be spending some quality time with them. Slide was starting to run low on cash, and Max had made a short list of ten venture capital investors he was going to pitch in the near future. So far, he'd mostly taken money from his own bank account and the bank accounts of the PayPal gang: Peter, Scott Banister, and John Malloy of the little-known firm BlueRun Ventures, who'd been one of the first investors in "the Pal."

Allen Morgan had not been part of that gang, but he had wanted to be. He first met Peter back in the mid-1990s when Peter was a Stanford law school student and Allen was a partner at Wilson Sonsini Goodrich & Rosati, the legal kingpins of Silicon Valley. Allen had tried to convince Peter to come work for Wilson Sonsini, but Peter picked Sullivan & Cromwell in New York instead. And in six months Peter was bored. He moved back to the Valley, but to Allen's chagrin, Peter was done with law. Instead, he started investing a small fund he cobbled together from family and friends, and that's about the time he met Max. As luck would have it, Allen was also getting bored with the legal profession, and had just been hired by Mayfield.

Peter and Max pitched Allen early on to invest in what was then Confinity. He wasn't sure this idea of beaming money between Palm Pilots was going to take off. (It didn't.) But he was positive he wanted a piece of whatever Peter and Max were doing. Only, Allen was new to venture capital and he couldn't convince his partners fast enough. Meanwhile John Malloy swooped in, funded PayPal, and made hundreds of millions. Still, Peter, Max, and Allen had stayed friends. Allen didn't completely get Slide when Max was starting it either, but he still wanted to back this crazy Ukrainian if the timing and terms were ever right.

Max assumed this time wouldn't be right either. Mayfield typically invests in very early stage companies, and although Slide was revenue-light, it was pretty mature for a start-up. In fact, Max wasn't pitching any of his venture friends this round. Peter and John had already invested, and Sequoia had already invested in a Slide competitor called RockYou. This was particularly awkward because one of Max's closest friends is Sequoia's Roelof Botha, once PayPal's CFO. That meant Max couldn't even discuss business—that is, his life—with one of his closest friends. "It's not pleasant," Max says, grimacing. Knowing Max, Roelof has a feeling it's a decision Sequoia will come to regret. The same thing happened with Yelp when Sequoia invested in its competitor InsiderPages. While Yelp continues to grow, InsiderPages is no longer in business.

Mayfield didn't have any of these conflicts, so over dinner Max asked if he could casually run the pitch by Allen to get his thoughts. "We're probably too late stage for you, but here it is," Max said. He went through a fifteen-minute spiel about what Slide had accomplished so far and what he still hoped to do. Allen thought for a minute, then said, "I think you should come pitch us. I think this could work."

Surprised, Max did, and the Mayfield guys were interested. But there was a downside to the meeting: Max was forced to start the whole fund-raising process sooner than he'd wanted. Raising money is a time-sensitive thing in the Valley. Word gets out that someone is pitching and suddenly he or she has to close the deal quickly or the company seems stale. This is similar to listing a house on a market; you want your deal to have the appearance of being the hot commodity everyone wants. "You smell shopped, and no one wants to buy a shopped good," Max says.

Knowing word would leak of the Mayfield meeting, Max hustled to set up meetings with the three top firms on his list. He worked even later into the evenings to be prepared. He still beams as he talks about his artful PowerPoint presentation. He would start out talking about Slide as if it were pie-in-the-sky thinking. Step one was get millions of widgets. Step two, get millions of downloads on people's desktops pushing different Web content out to them. Step three, sell ads on the desktop, so far virgin advertising territory. Then once the investors bought into the idea, he would spring on them that Slide was already showing 100 million widgets a day and getting thousands of desktop downloads an hour. The inevitable response was, "You're already on step three?" To which a cocky Max would sit back and say, "Oh, yeah. Give us the money."

It was a strong pitch. While no one is quite sure how this whole widget economy will pan out and whether the desktop part of Slide's business would ever be as big, the adoption numbers and continued growth were just staggering. At a time when sites like Digg and Yelp were focused on powerful niches, Slide was a play to a mass market. As Allen put it, even if Slide could get just a penny from a fraction of the people building these slide shows, either through advertising or some other route, that would make up a lot of pennies.

Two of the other investors Max met with agreed with him and were hungry for another meeting. The third meeting was a disaster. The investor was forty minutes late and could give Max only ten minutes—twenty, tops—for his forty-minute pitch. Creating more chaos, the partners' secretary came in every few minutes to remind him of his four P.M. meeting. And the conference room was being repaired, with a jackhammer running just outside the room. Max was less than stellar. It still bothers him. "I can only think about him," Max blurts out. "Why weren't you transfixed?"

But at that point, he didn't have much time to dwell on this failed encounter. One of two things were happening: Either Slide was a very hot deal or else everyone was desperate for a piece of the Web, because things started to go very fast. That same day he'd failed to wow the partner with the jackhammer, Allen called to ask Max to come back for a meeting with all the partners—the last audition a start-up goes through before the negotiations begin. It's like a callback. Max was sure to tell Allen he'd met with some other firms, sending the message that the clock was ticking. Allen understood. "Slow down a little," he told Max. "But I'll commit to you that we'll be very quick." He was not going to let his partners slow him down again, as they did with PayPal.

A few days later, Max and his chief operating officer Kevin Freedman were driving down to meet with Mayfield. He'd already gotten calls from the other two "transfixed" investors asking for him to come back for meetings with their partners and he was feeling pretty good about things. That's when he got a text message from Dave Weiden, a close friend of Scott Banister and John Malloy's who had started a new investing firm with Vinod Khosla. Vinod had been one of the two superstar investors at the famed venture capitalist firm Kleiner Perkins Caufield & Byers. But at the peak of his influence, Khosla stepped away to start his own firm, a mix between angel investing and venture capital, much like Peter's Founders Fund. Thanks to the incestuous nature of Silicon Valley's business and social scenes, Dave had heard through Scott and John that Max was out raising some money. He wanted Max to come in and talk to Vinod.

Max had met Vinod once, at a lunch with James Hong. He says he found him a bit annoying, and then quickly backpedals. There are a few unwritten rules in the Valley, and one of them is not to call Vinod Khosla annoying. "He wasn't *annoying*. Just like, oh, there's Vinod in the ivory tower. 'Hey, Max, I'm Vinod, I'm very smart,'" he says in his best Vinod Khosla impression.

It hadn't even occurred to Max to put Vinod on the list. His impression was Vinod was doing stuff at an even earlier stage than Mayfield, and hardly any Web deals—mostly green technology, save-the-planet stuff. To Max, that didn't exactly sound like a match, but Dave didn't care. Thanks to his friendships with Scott and John he had a better idea of how Slide was doing than most. And he saw in Vinod and Max a similar quality: two engineers who could be very technical, but who also could think big—huge, even. "Changing the entire Internet one widget at a time" kind of big. "They are first and foremost engineers, but they are engineers trying to change the world," Dave says. "There are probably about ten people in the Valley who have that combination, but no one thinks bigger than the two of them."

Back then, he simply told Max, "Listen, you're smart, and Vinod likes smart people, so maybe it'll work out." Max was dubious, but told Dave he was in Palo Alto and could stop by.

"Yeah, show up right now," Dave said.

Max was nervous about meeting Vinod again, but he was also feeling cocky. As they were walking over, he told Kevin, "We just scored three full partnership meetings in two days of pitching. We obviously don't suck. Someone's going to pay up for this stock."

Max and Kevin pitched Dave for about fifteen minutes. Dave was ruining Max's PowerPoint dramatics by telling him to skip certain warmup slides and just get to the numbers. "Yeah, that's big," he said casually. He paused, and added, "We should get Vinod in here."

Max started to pitch Vinod, who got it immediately. Vinod was finishing Max's sentences. This time Max was the one transfixed, not unlike when he first met Peter. "You want to tell me more about my own business?" he thought, listening to Vinod. Max left with part of him almost hoping it didn't work out with Mayfield. Dave texted him ten minutes later: "Good job. Can you come back early next week?"

This was a Friday. The Mayfield partnership meeting was on Monday. Max was already stalling the other two firms because it was likely he'd have a deal by Monday night if the meeting with Mayfield went well. They'd promised to move that fast if they could agree on terms. Now Vinod might want a piece, too? Was it possible Slide was doing even better than he thought? Maybe he was the next hot Web property, the next YouTube. He couldn't help but smile. He was doing it again. And this time he was CEO, so it was all his.

He thought back to a time when Slide had just come out of the Maxcubator and he and a small team were working day and night to get Slideshow up and running. Back then, he was hardly thinking about pimping out MySpace pages. The word *widget* didn't exist, let alone the idea of taking this piece of a Web site and putting it on another Web site without knowing how to code. So when Slide launched, the idea was people would download it to their desktop, like a screensaver. Max took a deep breath and released it into the Internet wild. And then heard nothing.

No one was downloading it! Max couldn't believe it. For years he'd been so focused on bringing a new idea to life, it had never occurred to him that maybe people just wouldn't want it. As he watched the stats go nowhere, he realized that it didn't matter he was Max Levchin, millionaire, dotcom success, founder of PayPal. All at once it hit him: No matter how hard he worked, he simply couldn't will people to use his product. They didn't care who the great Max Levchin was or what he'd done. Even worse, they didn't care about his Slideshow. It was crushing.

Max bargained with himself: If we can take off just a little, I'll be satisfied. It doesn't have to be a $1 billion company. As long as it's some kind of success. As long as someone—anyone, please?—wants to use it. He did some surveys of college kids and started to figure out putting a slide show in a browser could evangelize the whole desktop idea. And he realized that MySpace was the perfect place to start. He tweaked the product fast and it started to grow. Then just as he was breathing easier, it started to grow faster. The bargain was off. Sorry, other Max.

And good thing: Monday came and with it the full partner meeting with Mayfield. True to Allen's word, the firm *was* moving quickly. The two had a follow-up call the next day, and Allen spelled out the terms. Max grimaced. They weren't as rich as he'd wanted. Allen cut through all the normal negotiating protocol. "I think we're both interested in making this happen very quickly," he said. "Let's lay down our cards and figure out what would work."

Max told him the valuation and other specific terms he wanted.

"Wow, you're ambitious," Allen said in his usual deadpan manner.

Max didn't deny it. He admitted he had no idea how much he could realistically expect, since he hadn't gotten this far with anyone else. This might be the best deal he was going to get. Still, he told Allen, he had to try. If Mayfield didn't want to be the one to pay up, no hard feelings, but he was going to try the other guys. Allen said he needed to think about it and talk to his partners, but they agreed that if they could make the numbers work, they'd have a deal.

Fair enough. Max hung up the phone and it rang again: Weiden.

"Are you going to come back and pitch Vinod or what?" Dave asked.

"How about today?" Max said and again started the drive down to Palo Alto. He'd been sneaking in time with Vinod whenever he could, even chilling at his Woodside mansion over the weekend. Max called Allen on the drive. "I'm going to be down in Palo Alto. If you guys are game and want to talk more, we can just do it in person."

He added tellingly: "I'll be really close." In Valley parlance, that means: I'm meeting with another potential investor. Indeed, Vinod's office was just a few doors down from Mayfield.

"Are you pitching someone else?" Allen asked.

"Yeah, I kind of made a promise," Max said awkwardly.

"Okay, well, just don't give away the kingdom," Allen said, exasperated.

Max met with Vinod again. Same old magic. Max walked out in a haze just as Allen was calling to say: "Fine, I think we can do this." Although it wasn't written up in a contract yet, they'd made that verbal agreement that if they could meet on terms, they'd have a deal. In the clubby world of Silicon Valley, conversations like these are as binding as any legal document. So in essence the deal was done.

It should have been great news. But venture capital isn't a grant or a loan, it's an investment. Every dollar an entrepreneur takes means giving up shares, and that means giving up control and potential spoils if the start-up is a big hit. In each round of funding, there's a natural tension between existing shareholders, who want to hold on to their stakes, and new investors, who want to get as much as they can. So once Mayfield, Scott, Max, Peter, and John all agreed to invest in this round, Max couldn't let Vinod in too. There was simply no room left. And that was a problem, because Vinod was increasingly falling in love with the deal and Max was increasingly falling in love with Vinod. "Vinod really gets it," he kept thinking.

Dave called Max soon after he hung up with Allen. He and Vinod had just chatted about the meeting. "We definitely want to give you a term sheet. We just want to get a better sense of what you guys are trying to do," Dave said.

"I have good news and I have bad news," Max told him. "I know exactly what I want and I already got it."

"Already?" Dave asked. He knew Khosla Ventures had come into the bidding late, but he thought they'd have more time. "Is there any room in the round?"

"Sorry," Max said.

"This is going to be such a disappointment to Vinod," Dave mumbled.

They haggled a bit longer. Any time a company raises money, the existing investors get the right to buy a certain percentage of shares to make sure their ownership doesn't get too diluted. So far, Max, Peter, Scott, and John were all planning to buy their allocated shares. Dave pointed out that as an investor as well as the founder, Max was a pretty large shareholder. He asked if he could let Vinod buy his shares in this round instead.

"Can some of you guys—you, Peter, or Banister—give up something?" Dave asked.

"You don't even know the terms yet," Max said. "You may not want to invest at this price."

"Just find out if it's possible," Dave said.

Max called everyone to ask if he could give up a few hundred thousand dollars' worth of their piece of the deal. Just a little stock here or there for one of the greatest Valley investors of all time? It was awkward, especially the call to Mayfield before the ink on their agreement had even dried. Max himself offered to give up all of his allocated stock in the round, even though it'd wind up diluting his ownership in Slide by 5 percent. "I think Vinod is worth it," he says.

Max had invested so much of his own money in previous rounds that he'd still own more of Slide than anyone else, a rarity in Silicon Valley when a company raises this much cash. Still, as the deal was closing, he started to rethink it. He couldn't stomach the idea of missing out on this round, especially given all the positive feedback he was getting. He called Peter and asked if he could buy some of Peter's shares. Peter seemed amenable, noting that the valuation for this round was high. He wasn't sure he wanted all of them anyway.

"It's pretty expensive. You can have my piece," Peter said.

"Okay, I'll take all of it," Max said.

"No, let's split it half and half," Peter said. After some haggling,

Peter ended up giving Max only a third of his allocation. Slide may have had a high valuation, but all investors know one thing: The signs are good when a founder begs to buy shares in his own company, no matter the price. If Slide turned out to be as big as Max hopes it will be, he was determined to make far more than $30 million this time.

At the end of this frenzied week or so of deal-making, Slide had raised about $20 million—a large round, in Web 2.0 terms. More than the entire amount raised by its competitor RockYou. Max won't divulge what that pricey valuation was. "Once you release information you can't retrieve it," he says. As open and collegial as Silicon Valley can be, paranoia runs high here too.

It was probably nearly $80 million. Yelp had raised a round just before, valuing the company at a rumored $60 million, something Max would be privy to as the largest Yelp shareholder. It's doubtful the competitive Max would ask for less. Valuations are so subjective for private companies that half of the point is simply having a way to keep score. And at the end of the day, only one thing mattered: Slide got a better valuation than PayPal did at this stage.

Of course, beating PayPal's venture capital valuation in this particular round was merely one battle in the larger war. And Max couldn't feel cocky for long—he's too paranoid and obsessive, and with good reason. The biggest success for Slide to date was on MySpace, and the competition was fierce. Sequoia's RockYou was nipping at Slide's heels, and MySpace had finally launched its own slide show. The MySpace win had been enough to prove Slide had something, but it needed a new market fast. The one thing Max didn't want to replicate from PayPal was the company's overreliance on eBay, and the linkage between Slide and MySpace was dangerously similar.

Besides, when he'd first conceived of Slide he had wanted it to be something much grander. He wanted Slide to be a vehicle for breaking chunks of news or e-commerce out of sites and delivering them to your desktop. Interested in little black dresses? Slide could go find them for you and parade them in front of you. Ditto news on, say, Paris Hilton. The plan had a decent business model: In addition to ad revenues, Slide would take a cut of anything someone bought if it was delivered through a Slide slide show. Call it a Web 1.0 business plan with a Web 2.0 twist.

In many ways, the idea was the second coming of a once hot company called PointCast. Started in the mid-1990s, PointCast represented something similar, dubbed push technology because it would push what you wanted from the Web right to your desktop. In the early days of the Web, PointCast was thought to be worth hundreds of millions of dollars and was considered a real threat to big portals such as Yahoo! or AOL, but management missteps and slow dial-up Internet connections conspired to tank the site before it ever really got going. It went down in dotcom history as one of the biggest flameouts of the era.

Still, the idea continues to captivate people. This vision of bringing the Web to the desktop had hooked Allen and Vinod when Max was raising money. Allen had actually been the attorney for PointCast before his venture capital days, and he still had something called the tombstone in his office. Tombstones in the financial world are the announcements of good news—a funding round, an acquisition, or an IPO. Some run in publications like *The Wall Street Journal*. Others are just framed, bedecking venture capitalists' conference room walls as a way to show off their deal-making prowess. As they were signing the contract between Mayfield and Slide, Allen offered the PointCast tombstone to Max, who backed away, throwing up his hands as if it were cursed.

"I don't want to be near that thing!" he said.

Allen laughed. "Okay, it'll be your reward when you guys go public."

Think of push technology as a step beyond a search engine like Google. With Google, you can find almost anything. But you still have to go to the site, manually type in a query, and plow through the results. You are pulling the data. With push technology, you tell the engine broadly what you are interested in and it does the rest of the work for you, delivering a stream of results to your desktop.

But if PointCast was too early, Slide might have been too late. Today people live online, not on the computer desktop. For instance, a Gmail account now has just as much memory and functionality as Microsoft Outlook. Millions of users manage their photo collections through Web software like Picasa and Flickr. Google's online word processor and spreadsheet programs are even making inroads into the granddaddies of all desktop programs, Microsoft Word and Excel. The effect is even more pronounced in the business software world, where companies like Salesforce.com have helped companies slash their technology budgets by hosting all of their software for them and then leasing usage of the programs back to them over the Web.

Even within the Web browser, for example, Google alerts and RSS feeds have made finding what you want easier than it was in Web 1.0 days. Just enter topics you are into and missives from major national publications and niche blogs come directly to your email address or Web page. Although the original PointCast plan never really came to fruition, the Web and the way people use it hasn't necessarily waited around for it. It's unclear what exactly a modern-day PointCast would look like and what its business model might be.

By mid-2007 that was becoming increasingly clear to Max. Push technology was still a viable concept, but increasingly people wanted their stuff pushed to their Web sites, blogs, or social networking pages, not their desktops. Max moved fast to respond to that. He kept a handful of people supporting the desktop ticker slide show, but shifted most of the company's focus to Web-based widgets—where the growth, excitement, and competition were.

In general, Web 2.0 businesses have pretty clear business models. After all, most of them are based on advertising—a $20 billion market in the United States alone. But widgets were something else entirely. A cardinal rule of start-ups is not to rely on any other business for their success, and widgets were 100 percent reliant on the sites like MySpace and Facebook that they ran on. These host sites could ban widgets or dictate how advertising could be worked into their products. And ultimately MySpace and Facebook would own all that user data, not the widget maker. Most Web sites strive to get as many unique visitors and page views as they can; widget companies have similar goals, but count page views across the many different sites they run on. It's a bizarre model, and no one is yet sure how advertisers will take to it. Ultimately it's a mass market game. Both Slide and RockYou are striving to have so many page views and users that they eclipse Yahoo!, the biggest site on the Web in terms of users. (In December 2006, MySpace just eclipsed Yahoo! in page views.) Then they can offer advertisers not only a mass base but also one that cuts across MySpace, Facebook, and other popular sites. In other words, an advertiser would have the choice to target only MySpace users, or via widgets, target users on any of the mass social networks.

Slide's offices are intense. Start-ups are truly outgrowths of their founders, and walking into Slide was like entering a room full of Max Levchins hard at work. Scores of serious-looking coders are sitting in front of their screens for eighteen hours a day. Which is funny, because they are designing new and improved slide shows with glitter, swirls, and floating hearts. They're racking their brains to come up with anything to keep fickle teenage girls from defecting to Slide's archenemy RockYou. Most of the day the rooms are dead quiet. They have to be, because when Max addresses his engineers, it's barely above a whisper. Every once in a while he might joke, "Good job, everyone, take the rest of the minute off." By late afternoon, the engineers—all hopped up on Red Bull, coffee, and Diet Coke—start to go stir crazy, along with all the dogs they bring to work every day. After all, the engineers work far too many hours to leave them at home.

Max's crew has come far from the early days of the rolling stock ticker. Now your pictures can bounce onto the screen, pushing out the previous one, or rotate in a circle before a large image shoots to the forefront. Although RockYou has many of these same themes and effects—the hearts, the glitter, and so forth—it's easy to compare RockYou's widgets to Slide's and see why Slide is bigger. The animation, the fluid movement, the sophistication—it's just an objectively better product. Even Lance Tokuda, RockYou's chief executive, cedes the point. Everything has to be visibly better for Max to be happy. Everything has to be boiled down to what he can see, or preferably what he can graph. Max obsesses over metrics. One day he proudly proclaims: "I can build a slide show in three minutes. I've timed it!"

This has all been building to a nasty war between Slide and RockYou, with each maintaining it is larger, each ripping off the other's products. Having an enemy has helped focus Slide, and for now, it beats RockYou on every count. Max has raised more money, Max has a better track record, Max has a larger staff, and it'd be impossible to work more hours. In June 2007, Internet stat research firm comScore did the first study of widgets and named Slide the largest—with a reach as wide as 13.8 percent of the world's Internet audience. RockYou was second.

Lance isn't exactly Max's biggest fan. It's not that Max has done anything underhanded. He's honest and direct with the RockYou folks when they talk. He just beats them at their own game, and for RockYou, that gets old. There are two kinds of start-ups in the Valley: those who create and evangelize a totally new type of technology, and those who see what someone else is doing and just do it better. Netscape was an example of the former, changing the way people used the Internet forever, but ultimately taking a drubbing in the browser wars at the hands of Microsoft. Google was an example of the latter, tackling search once everyone thought AOL and Yahoo! owned it and executing search so much better that it won the market.

RockYou was the first to do slide shows in the browser. It was the first to come up with a portfolio of widgets beyond slide shows. But every time Max saw their early success, he reacted, countered, and beat them. RockYou made the costly mistake of growing slowly. Max, confident he would wind up with a big hit on his hands, hired smart engineers as soon as he could find them. As a result, Slide can simply do more than RockYou, faster and better—and sometimes that includes ripping off their ideas and perfecting them. "I'm not going to lie," says Lance's cofounder Jia Shen. "It pisses you off after a while."

It's a fiercely competitive world online, because anyone's site can have the same reach. Quality matters. "It's a Darwinian environment Slide is in, and that's a good environment for Max," Dave Weiden says.

But bragging rights and ego aside, Max still has no idea what the real business spoils of this great widget war would be. He just knows he needs to win. And as Slide continued to grow, it soon became obvious that a new battlefield was emerging: Facebook.

Mark Zuckerberg may be the only person that can make Max look suave. At Facebook's May 2007 big platform launch sweaty-palmed

Zuck introduced Max onstage as a spokesperson for companies hungry to build applications on top of Facebook. Max strolled out on the San Francisco Design Center's cavernous stage wearing his usual Web 2.0-compliant uniform: tight-fitting T-shirt plus designer jeans plus Pumas. He waved to the crowd, displaying his best all-American smile. He spent a few minutes talking up the importance of the Facebook platform and tried to pump up all the coders in the audience for the all-night hackathon ahead. Channeling some hip-hop flair, he managed to work *props* and *peeps* into the same opening sentence. He ended his spiel with a fist in the air and the words "Let's hack!" Facebook's PR department also pimped Max out to the press to help pump Facebook's platform plan.

The rapport between the two companies couldn't be more different than the sly "please don't notice how big we're getting" relationship Slide has with MySpace. Part of that is because Facebook has taken a different tack from MySpace: It wants other companies to take over its pages, knowing that in the history of high tech, the most open platforms have always won. Of course, there's also an obvious connection between Slide and Facebook: Peter Thiel. After all, if Peter had never had that 1999 meeting with Max, it's possible he wouldn't have made all that cash to invest in companies like Facebook.

But that's where Max's natural Facebook advantages end. Once the open platform was launched, Slide was launched into a free-for-all landgrab with every other Web company in the Valley. Facebook couldn't handle the load, and applications were crashing all over the place. Max watched in horror the first morning it was live as RockYou's slide shows worked and Slide's did not.

RockYou had another advantage too—horoscopes. Max had always made fun of RockYou's horoscope widget, which could be added to people's Web pages or profiles to deliver daily horoscopes. It took no technical skill to build and was frivolous. He'd considered buying a tiny company with a competing horoscope widget just to screw with RockYou, but pooh-poohed the idea. But on Facebook horoscopes were one of the fastest-growing applications. That got RockYou on people's pages, where it could push its slide shows over Slide's.

Max can admit when he's wrong and switch courses fast. Within hours, he sprang into action. His engineers worked nonstop to make sure the slide shows were working. At the same time, now he pushed them to build new, simple—even silly—applications that people might enjoy so that Slide could grab some real estate on Facebook profile pages before it was too late. The Facebook market was still smaller than the MySpace one, but Facebook openly published how many people had adopted each application. It was a place RockYou could build some bragging rights, and Max wasn't going to let that happen.

Slide came up with a Fortune Cookie and Magic Eight Ball application that could compete with Horoscopes. It also launched an idea stolen from MySpace, the Top Friends application. On MySpace your top friends are displayed on your page, but not on Facebook's clean profile pages. Anyone who'd used and liked MySpace found Slide's Top Friends application a no-brainer to adopt. To help it spread, Max and his engineers built in a somewhat annoying tool that would email your friends to let them know you'd added them as a top friend. The email would say something like, "Max has added you as a top friend. Does he make your top friends?" Obliged through social pressure to comply, your friends too would add the application, and it would spread on its own through the complex web of Facebook friendships.

Every single person who adopted it mattered, because they in turn would spread the word to their friends. Max even rotated all of his hundreds of friends through his own list of top friends so they'd get these passive-aggressive emails, prompting them to add the application. It didn't matter that most of them wouldn't stay in his top friends, few people would actually click onto his profile page to check. When a competing company launched Favorite Friends, Slide even bought them out for $60,000. Max was not playing around here.

It might seem a little clumsy, even desperate, but it worked. Within a month, between Top Friends and the Fortune Cookie, Slide had two of the top three applications, with a whopping 11 million of Facebook users installing one or the other on their pages. It took months for Slide to get that far on MySpace. RockYou wasn't going away, though; horoscopes were the fourth most popular application and RockYou was rolling out new applications as well. Even worse: It still led in slide shows.

The arms race was all Max could think about. Max's friends were even getting caught in the RockYou Slide cross fire. James Hong's company HotorNot released a "moods" application, where you could pick an emoticon to tell friends if you were feeling happy, sad, stressed, or one of a few dozen other moods, and within hours RockYou immediately launched a similar application called emote. James confronted RockYou's Jia, who explained that his engineers didn't copy James and said they'd assumed it was a Slide app anyway. The HotorNot engineers were so livid, they immediately started to bundle it with Top Friends. Even still, James notes that RockYou's intensity—its desire to see Slide fail—is nothing compared to Max's. He predicts that RockYou will end up getting bought by someone who really wants Slide but can't afford Max's price tag. "Slide is probably the best thing that ever happened to RockYou," he says.

This was a wild user-grabbing melee with more than a thousand applications grappling for real estate in people's online worlds. The only problem was, as with the widget economy as a whole, there was mass uncertainty about how valuable one of these

Facebook users were. Most of the applications were free, and Facebook controlled the ad sales on the pages. Plus people could delete the applications as easy as they could add them. It had taken more than ten years to divine the value of a page view. Widgets, whether on Facebook, MySpace, or some other site, could well turn out to be as useless as 1990s eyeballs in building actual businesses.

As the initial madness was dying down, a new strategy emerged. Slide would cede Facebook slide shows to RockYou for now. They didn't work as well on Facebook as on MySpace anyway. Slide shows get their bling factor from something called Flash animation that's usually automatic on any site, so when you load the page, the slide show just starts running, drawing the viewer in with its glitter and graphics and rolling captions. But in a bid to be less garish than MySpace, Facebook disabled automatic Flash animation. So on Facebook viewers had to click on the slide show to start it. And that made a big difference.

Top Friends was a different case. People loved it, and soon millions had installed it. Slide added little boxes underneath top friends' profile pictures, allowing people to message or "poke" them right from the Top Friends box, skipping the normal Facebook navigation. It also came up with something called the Fun Wall. On Facebook, your wall is like the marker board on the door of your dorm room that people can leave messages on; only on Facebook you can give virtual gifts and attach photos and other files to the wall. The Fun Wall was meant to top this, giving people fun tools to do things like put mustaches on pictures of your friends. On Facebook you could get someone's attention by "poking" him or her. Slide launched Super Poke, where you could poke, hug, punch, or virtually throw sheep at people. One by one Slide was rejiggering all of Facebook's central, most important applications. Max was trying to hijack the whole site, one widget at a time. (RockYou competed with SuperWall and X Me, but again, through sheer force of will Slide's applications were more popular.)

Maybe it was inevitable that Facebook would be the YouTube of 2007. But if that was so, Slide was going to become the most important part of Facebook. Peter's two protégés were going to become closer allies or rivals.

10

SELL OUT

On Presidents' Day weekend 2007, Kevin Rose hadn't been at the Digg headquarters for a whole week. He hadn't been at Fly Bar, his local watering hole. He hadn't even been at Mission Cliffs, the rock-climbing place that had become an obsession of late. He was actually on a vacation. In another week he'd be speaking at a conference in London, but for now he was in Amsterdam. He was turning thirty and celebrating it big-time. He put a good part of the festivities on his corporate Digg card—a privilege Jay had granted him only recently precisely because he was afraid things like this would happen. Kevin makes his patented hand-in-the-cookie-jar face when he divulges this. There's no telling how many times he has used it in his life to get out of scrapes.

But turning thirty wasn't just a milestone. Kevin Rose is actually growing up. He's drinking less and has lost a good twenty pounds since *BusinessWeek* referred to him as "Tom Cruise's doughier younger brother." He's shopping at Bloomingdale's, not at little shops along Haight Street. "I don't know... I want to buy something nice," he says sheepishly. Suddenly sitting around playing video games with his pals isn't all he wants out of life. Even

Brenda, Jay's wife, has noticed a difference. One day when Jay made one of his usual condescending jokes about Kevin, she admonished him: "Jay, Kevin is an adult. And you're not his dad."

Digg is also growing up, and the hype is running high. No longer do articles explain what Digg is. No longer do they talk about whether AOL's Digg clone will overtake it. They talk about real world problems facing any Web property that matters: how to manage its growth; how to make sure its voting results aren't getting manipulated and the company isn't getting sued for the stories people post there. This isn't an experiment anymore. The company is actually worth something. People's livelihoods depend on it.

All this newfound respectability also coincides with another major change for Kevin: He's a real money-in-the-bank millionaire. He has even hired a financial adviser to manage his riches and make sure his bills are paid on time. Guys like Reid Hoffman who were once Kevin's benefactors are calling to see if he wants to be a fellow angel investor in new companies. Kevin is clearly enjoying the money—or the idea of it, anyway. He is shopping for $1 million plus homes in San Francisco, although he hasn't bought one yet. And he swears he is upgrading his ratty Volkswagen Golf to a sleek new black Audi.

But Kevin gets nervous when he touches on the subject of his net worth. He may come off as flaky, but he's well aware his greatest asset is his low-key, geek-turned-hipster shtick that hundreds of thousands of geeky Kevin Rose wannabes can relate to. It's what has enabled him to build one of the most loyal communities on the Web. Kevin Rose as Silicon Valley mogul would be another matter. He's terrified that his fans will think he's profiting from all their labor Digging stories around the clock or has sold out. If he gave Digg to some lame has-been company like Yahoo! or Microsoft? That'd be it. To many of his fans, he wouldn't be the same Kevin Rose.

But the truth is, he has sold out, even if just a bit. When Digg raised its second round of venture capital in November 2006, Kevin did what's called a partial liquidation of his Digg stock. That is, he sold new investors about 10 percent of his then 39 percent ownership. The Digg faithful should actually be happy about this. A partial liquidation makes it far less likely Kevin will sell the whole company—at least for a while.

Partial liquidations have always been controversial in Silicon Valley. Most old-school venture capitalists want every dollar of capital going toward building a business, not lining some entrepreneur's pocket. The message goes like this: "Let's work hard and build a great company. Then we'll all make money together." Never mind that venture capitalists almost always make more on the upside because they own more of the company and they are less hurt on the downside because they get millions in management fees and have stakes in dozens of other start-ups. Smart investors quickly understood why the rules are different with Web 2.0, why partial liquidations make a company far more likely to post higher returns. It all has to do with the secret curse of success in the new Web world: the agony of the sell.

It's always a gut-wrenching decision when a founder who has spent years (or months, in some cases) of sleepless nights building out something he or she cares about then has to sell it to someone else. In Web 2.0, the anxiety is taken to a new level. As does everything else in this scene, the anxiety harks back to the dotcom bust. Back then, as companies continued to grow in users, employees, and valuation—and in some cases, revenues—everyone felt invincible. Selling was a convenience. Odds seemed high most Web companies could go public if they wanted. The question was, did they want to wait it out or cash out now and start something new?

But after the bust, going public was no more than a pipedream for Internet companies. When potential buyers waved even a few million in front of the founders, they feared if they didn't take the money right then, there might not be other offers. Many of the early acquisition prices for Web 2.0 companies were in the range of $30 million or less. A venture capitalist doesn't even get out of bed for a return like that. And during the first bubble, neither would an entrepreneur. They'd had to raise so much money that investors ending up owning far more of the company than the founders did. In the case of PayPal, it took a $1.5 billion sale for Max to make $35 million. This time around, though, founders had managed to hold on to such whopping stakes in their companies that selling to someone like Yahoo! for $30 million meant they would make $15 million, $20 million, or even $30 million.

That's hard to turn down, especially for someone like Kevin, who certainly didn't come from money and is constantly reminded by Jay how fast $55 million can disappear. Having some so-called fuck-you money is a powerful thing. Almost everyone would take a guaranteed million over the slim chance of making $100 million. And—making it even harder for these founders—in many cases the decision was solely up to them. Again, thanks to low start-up costs and quick-and-easy revenue streams, entrepreneurs had been able to keep board control of their companies in ways rarely seen in the Valley.

So it's no wonder a lot of the earliest and most promising start-ups were sold when Web businesses were starting up again. These were the companies who pioneered most of the features you think of when you think about Web 2.0. Flickr came up with a new collaborative way to share photos, del.icio.us came up with tagging and bookmarking, and Blogger and LiveJournal were pioneers of blogging. Each of them sold for $40 million or less. Flickr and del.icio.us went to Yahoo!, Blogger to Google, and LiveJournal to Six Apart. Had these companies held out, they could easily have been worth far more.

For Silicon Valley's sake—maybe even for the sake of the Web itself—it's a shame these companies were sold when they were. Inside larger, slower-moving organizations, start-ups can hardly be as nimble or innovative as they were pre-purchase. We'll never know how big they could have gotten, what new features the founders could have thought up in all-night Red Bull–fueled coding sessions. What ingenious twists they could have taken in the bob-and-weave of start-up survival. Or how many people they could have employed and how valuable their market capitalizations could have grown.

Perhaps they had all peaked at $40 million or so and were smart to sell. But this is unlikely when you consider the sites that have built off their success and are already worth far more. Photobucket and Slide were both developed after Flickr proved people wanted a better way to share their photos; Digg took the tagging idea from del.icio.us and applied it to news; and Six Apart only started once Mena had gotten swept up in the nascent blogging scene by using Blogger's software.

Here's where partial liquidations come in. Take $1 million or so. Now you've got your fuck-you money, so let's see what this company can really be worth. Zuck did a partial liquidation with Facebook, Ben and Mena did one with Six Apart, and now, in Digg's December 2006 funding round, Kevin had done one too. But this wasn't the first or last time he would agonize over whether to sell or keep trying to change the world.

Kevin had hit that same point in his entrepreneurial stride as Russ and Jeremy, Ben and Mena, and Zuck. They've done something well enough to get attention and beat the early wave of me-too competitors. They've made the first million and become successful enough to get magazine covers and be asked to speak at conferences. Even if their current ventures flame out, they've banked enough cash to be okay and have enough Valley credibility to get funded again easily.

Still, for people who never really set out to build the next great Web company, this period is less fun than the early days. It's definitely more stressful. And the whole to-sell-or-not-to-sell game is the single biggest thing they wrestle with. Life is like a high-stakes version of one of those TV game shows where you can take the money or gamble your winnings in hopes of making more on the next question. Half the audience is yelling, "Take the money!" and the other half is yelling, "Don't take the money!" As these entrepreneurs work their way through the real-life growing pains of building a big business, they vacillate between the two emotions.

Of course, there's one big flaw in that analogy. In a game show, at least a check is dangled in front of the contestants so they know what they're giving up. Companies have a prolonged acquisition mating dance. The big company calls to "talk about a partnership." The entrepreneur meets with representatives of the big company. Then some time passes. The big company sends out feelers again, wanting to learn more about the start-up. This back-and-forth continues until finally the subject of an acquisition is formally broached. Then there's a long negotiating process, all of this while a start-up is building out its business before another scrappy competitor outdoes them.

Kevin has faced the dilemma of whether or not to sell as much as anyone in the scene. Some founders—for example, Brad Fitzpatrick—know they want to sell, and others like Mark Zuckerberg know they don't. Then there is Kevin Rose, stuck somewhere in the middle. Each time he has flirted with selling—maybe even been tempted—but each time some element was not quite right. He dug deep within himself and ultimately said no. Still, that hesitation has always been there. It's one reason he's the quintessential Web 2.0 everyman—ballsy enough to start a Web company, but still not quite sure it won't all disappear in a moment's notice.

The first time Kevin got an offer was way back in 2005. It was the early days of Digg, and Jay was just an adviser. The company consisted of Kevin and his freelance Canadian coder, Owen. A very shrewd Los Angeles–based entrepreneur named Jason Calacanis emailed him an offer. Calacanis is a polarizing figure in the Valley. He's a master at self-promotion, and a lot of people feel he's more talk than walk. During the bubble, he presided over an ultimately defunct New York publication, the *Silicon Alley Reporter*, and a blog network called Weblogs, which he sold to AOL-Time Warner for about $20 million in 2005. Respectable, no doubt. Still, he shocked the Valley when he parlayed that into a job as an entrepreneur in residence at Sequoia Capital in 2006. He's in the middle of building a new company called Mahalo, which is working toward taking on Google in search by using people to write search results instead of algorithm-crunching computers. Think of it as a cross between Wikipedia and Google. Mahalo is clearly the most ambitious thing he has attempted yet.

But even his doubters give Jason credit for one thing: he excels at catching onto things just before they hit big. After all, he was one of the first people to build a sizable blog publishing business. Back in 2005, he became enamored with Digg. He offered Kevin $4 million, a stunning number to Kevin, who'd had only $10,000 in his savings when he started Digg less than a year earlier, most of which he sunk into the company. What made the offer more attractive than the cash was the fact that Kevin would still run the company and Jason would add "Digg This" buttons to the bottom of all the Weblogs pages. Weblogs' gadget site, Engadget, by itself had five times the traffic of Digg in those days, and much the same target audience. That kind of an audience would catapult Digg ahead of any of the other companies trying to do the same thing practically overnight.

Kevin read the offer. He read it again. "Holy shit," he thought. "I just spent six months on this and I can sell it for four million? Um, yes!"

Kevin ran the deal by Jay, who was far less impressed. There was some serious fine print here. The deal wouldn't pay $4 million upfront; it would be structured like an investment. Calacanis would take a controlling stake in Digg for less than that, with an option to buy it outright over time, the total coming to $4 million. The terms were worse than a venture capital deal, for what was ultimately not much money. And as Jay explained, once Weblogs owned a controlling stake in Digg, there would be little incentive to buy the rest of it, leaving Kevin to work away building something that wasn't even really his anymore. "This is a shitty deal," Jay said. "You're worth more."

Kevin listened. After all, Jay's bias is usually to cash out while you can. Kevin told Jason no. Looking back, he can't believe he considered the offer. "Calacanis is a very shrewd businessman," Kevin says. "When he spots a trend he will go after it and he will acquire it for pennies on the dollar. Props to him if he can pull it off, but in my case I had Jay telling me not to do it." He does admit that if it'd been $4 million upfront, he probably would have done it. The whole experience made two things clear: Digg was becoming valuable and Kevin needed someone who understood stuff like this. As the company grew, more and more dicey decisions like this would come up, and Kevin simply couldn't handle them and continue to build the site. He needed Jay.

When Jay agreed to be CEO, he told Kevin two things. One, Jay was staying in New York and would have to do the job remotely. Two, Kevin would always be in control of the company's fate. Even after they raised money, there were just three board seats, occupied by Kevin, Jay, and David Sze. And when it came to matters such as selling the company, Jay decided he would always vote the way Kevin did. "Jay always told me from day one, 'I am CEO. I will run the shit, but when it comes down to ultimate veto power over anything that happens to your property, it's up to you.' " Kevin remembers. "That's why I love Jay. Here's a guy who created what is now a multibillion-dollar company on the NASDAQ and someone he entrusted his power to betrayed him. He will never let that happen to me. I turned over the entire company to him because I believe he'll stay true to that."

Digg continued to grow with Jay in charge. It raised venture capital. It started to become a force in the online media world. And none of this was lost on the Web 1.0 giant Yahoo! It was the second player to look at Digg and realize its social media voting system could be applied across a wide variety of Web properties. Although the Valley perception is that Yahoo! is less Web 2.0–savvy than Google, in 2005 and 2006 it was making some smart bets. The company had already picked up del.icio.us and Flickr on the cheap; Digg could have been a third prescient move. But big companies like Yahoo! are far less direct than someone like Jason Calacanis. There was no offer with harsh terms emailed over to Kevin; instead it was more the Silicon Valley acquisition mating ritual: casual conversations, hints, talks, what-would-you-think-about-this winks and nods over cocktails.

Again, Kevin figured the promises were all too good to be true. Kevin knew a thing or two about how Yahoo! worked. He was close friends with Josh Schachter, who'd build del.icio.us and sold it to Yahoo! earlier in 2005. In fact, del.icio.us had been one of the influences for Digg. It was a way for people to "tag" things they were interested in online, but Kevin thought it wasn't designed well and didn't have anything to do with current events. In early 2006, Schachter started probing Kevin to see if he too would be interested in a sale to Yahoo!, likely in the range of $25 million or so. But Kevin knew that del.icio.us had sold too soon and that Josh now had far less freedom to pursue his vision for the company. "I wouldn't want to say they were putting the lockdown on the development process [at del.icio.us], but I knew they were putting more hoops in the way to get certain features out," Kevin says. Putting in more process can really weaken a company that's used to making quick decisions. It worried Kevin.

It worried him particularly at the time the two were talking. Digg was in the middle of building its all-important Version 3, which would expand the site beyond tech news for the first time. Selling to Yahoo! now could endanger Version 3's success. So after a couple of discussions, Digg opted out, telling Yahoo! they were going to focus on building their business. Kevin, who owned about 40 percent of the company at this point, waved good-bye to about $10 million or so.

That, too, proved to be a smart move. A few months later, Version 3 and the continuing hype of all things Web raised Digg's profile and street value even more. Forget blogs like Engadget; sites like *The Washington Post* and *The New York Times* had "Digg This" buttons now. By the fall of 2006, if anyone was going to buy Digg, the cost would easily be in the range of $100 million to $200 million. On paper, Kevin was worth at least $40 million. Of course, there's a downside to the hype. Suddenly Digg had big competitors. Now an executive at America Online, Calacanis was turning the old Netscape brand into a Digg clone and offering top Diggers $1,000 a month to switch teams. MySpace was also threatening to release a social news page as part of its mass social network. Hard as he was working, Kevin knew that Digg's lead—and his own paper wealth—could evaporate at any time.

Around that time, the fall of 2006, he got an email from Ross Levinsohn. "I'm in the Bay Area," it read. "Let's have breakfast." Levinsohn was the senior vice president for Fox's interactive media business and the tactician who bought MySpace for the bargain-basement price of $580 million—a sum everyone called outrageous at the time. Now he was into Digg. Kevin drove down to the Marriott by the San Francisco airport and met Ross. Kevin liked him immediately. He didn't come across as pushy, smarmy, opportunistic, or sleazy. Just a nice guy who, Kevin thought, seemed to be pretty good at seeing the future of the Web—especially as an old media type.

Both Kevin and Ross had ambitious ideas for social networking and media, and how it could transform the Web and culture. Ross told Kevin about the other Web properties he was eyeing. They were mostly sites Kevin was excited about too. As Ross unspooled his grand MySpace vision, Kevin got very excited. Ross wanted to take the great MySpace platform of millions of self-empowered users and meld it with sites like Digg to make things like people-powered news a mass phenomenon, something no media outlet could ignore. It was Kevin's original vision for Digg, only on MySpace-powered steroids.

Ross's idea was to take all of Digg's behind-the-scenes algorithms about people and what they like and feed these back into MySpace. In other words, if you're a regular Digger, the site knows the kinds of stories you like and hate. It's able to learn more about your interests than just what you may choose to list in a MySpace profile. It's again the idea of digitization of identity, just via a different route than that taken by Plaxo or Facebook.

Ross echoed what Kevin already believed: that the future of MySpace and any of these social networks isn't searching based on how people look or where they live, but on *who they are*. MySpace may be able to help you find a list of girls who are five feet five, have brown hair, and live in San Francisco, but Digg could find people with your same interests, based on what you inadvertently share about yourself through digging or burying stories. "The kind of algorithm that can match me with someone who is into the Democratic Party and into sailing and likes oolong tea is much more valuable than just a raw-stat-based my-hair-is-brown kind of search," Kevin says.

The more Kevin thought about it, the more excited he got about the possible combination. This wasn't just about cashing out, although he was sure to make a bundle off any deal. (The potential offer would have been a minimum of $150 million, a life-changing $60 million payday for Rose.) This was about making Digg a bigger, better, more powerful site. It was about pairing Digg with the single most powerful Web 2.0 company at the time, MySpace. The more he talked to his staff, the more excited they got just from the idea of playing with all that MySpace data. "If there's one thing we're good at at Digg, it's the analysis of data," Kevin says. "We spend our entire lives analyzing why stories should make it to the front page. The idea of being turned on to twenty-five million user accounts, to tear into that and create a farm of a thousand servers that do nothing but crunch and compare users to each other was very exciting. And we would have a huge social network of people democratically voting on news and what is hot."

Kevin thought about it every day. Of any deal he had been offered so far, this was the best, but he didn't want to jinx it. Finally, one day, Kevin was playing golf with Owen when he got a call from Ross. Ross suggested he come down to Los Angeles to meet with Rupert—as in media mogul Rupert Murdoch, CEO of News Corporation, which owns Fox. The same Rupert Murdoch who would buy *The Wall Street Journal* for $6 billion almost a year later. Murdoch was one of the undisputed giants of the old media guard. Kevin smiled broadly. This wasn't just Calacanis or Yahoo! trying to buy him on the cheap because Digg was getting some momentum. This was a major deal with a major player that could make Digg bigger than he'd ever dreamed. *This,* he was excited about.

As he, Jay, and a few other executives flew down to Los Angeles, Kevin had what he calls one of his "Why the hell am I here?" moments. All the hype and attention aside, running Digg wasn't really glamorous. It was hard, 24-7 work. And even the most optimistic valuations of Digg were no more than a rounding error on the valuation of Facebook or YouTube. Still, just two years ago Kevin was nobody. He had a good job, but he was miserable and his employer, the geeky G4 network, was going nowhere. He was fighting with his girlfriend about whether he should invest his paltry savings in his idea, and she thought he was insane. Even Jay thought Revision3 was a better idea. Now *Rupert* fucking *Murdoch* was courting him. As geeks like Kevin would say, woot.

Down in L.A., Kevin sat in News Corp.'s conference room, ready to demo the site and unspool the grand Digg vision, as he'd now done countless times. Murdoch came in, shook his hand, said "Nice to meet you," and sat down across from him. There were four people from Digg flanking Kevin and ten people from Fox flanking Murdoch. Every time Murdoch spoke, the Fox people shut up immediately and listened. Kevin was impressed, of course. But the more he looked across the table at Murdoch, the less nervous he became. "I know this is really fucked up, but the entire time I'm looking at Rupert and I'm thinking, 'He looks like my grandpa and I want to give him a piece of candy,'" Kevin says. "He was so disarming when I thought of him as Grandpa, it made the demo really easy."

After the meeting, "Grandpa" Murdoch said he would be in touch and the Digg crew left. They headed over to the Hyatt to have a few drinks and Ross said he'd meet them later on. By the time Ross arrived, Rupert was already sitting with them. "Everyone was really clicking," Ross said. "Mr. Murdoch was telling stories and we all left feeling great about the future." Jay was told to expect an offer.

But the offer never came. Murdoch had turned on the deal and Ross didn't immediately know why. Kevin and Jay were equally confused. Others close to the situation say the deal was scuttled by the MySpace guys, who didn't want to share the Fox Interactive Media spotlight. But Ross wasn't giving up. He thought Digg was a transformative company and wanted this deal badly. He and Kevin had drinks at the Clift Hotel around the time of the November Web 2.0 Summit and Ross told Kevin he thought he was getting talks back on track. He told Kevin he would quit if it didn't happen. Ross ended up leaving the company two weeks later, frustrated at the politics and infighting, and with him went the deal's sponsor.

Kevin figured if Ross was gone, it was for the best that the deal got scuttled anyway. "I think the problem with Fox is they acquired this company MySpace and they think to themselves 'Wow.' But one thing they are missing is that they have to continue to invest in this company. You can't just milk them for their ad revenue for the next fifty years," Kevin says. "MySpace hasn't launched a new feature in a year. It's going to hurt them because Facebook is kicking some major ass."

So Digg moved on. Jay told Fox to call if they had an offer on paper; otherwise they were going to go back to building their business. TechCrunch and other blogs later reported that Digg had been offered $150 million and had turned it down, balking because it wasn't more. But given how gaga Kevin was about tying Digg to MySpace, it's hard to imagine Kevin would have had that reaction. Says Jay, "If we got offered $150 million, no one told me." Once again, talks came and went. And once again, something had screwed up the deal. Digg was still on its own.

By now it was almost Thanksgiving, and as he prepped to go home to Vegas for the holiday, Kevin reflected on what a roller-coaster year 2006 had been. But 2006 wasn't over yet, and there was one more offer to buy Digg that year that the blogs never reported. And this time Kevin was seated across the conference room table from someone more impressive than Murdoch. This time Kevin was nervous.

It was Al Gore. The former vice president of the United States was at the height of his popularity. Not only was he fresh off the release of *An Inconvenient Truth*, but he held a board seat on one of the sexiest companies in all of techdom, Apple Computer. Gore was also chairman of a company called CurrentTV, based in San Francisco. Current is user-generated content on TV, not the Internet. People upload clips of themselves doing stuff—say, confessionals as they try to quit smoking, or drumming on upside-down tubs on an urban street corner. The network allows people to vote on these clips and broadcasts them all day long. In many ways, it's like Digg for TV, only with video.

Current called on the heels of the News Corp. heartbreak saying they just wanted to talk about some ways to partner with Digg. Current was frustrated they couldn't get more people voting on their shows and were interested in seeing if some sort of arrangement with Digg could up the number of votes. They wanted users to really mold and shape their schedule. The same way Digg had made editors irrelevant, Current wanted to do the same with programming executives.

Kevin drove up Third Street to Current's headquarters in San Francisco and sat down in the conference room. In walked Gore. "Kevin, it's nice to meet you," he said. Kevin was utterly dazzled. All he could think was, "Al Gore is sitting across the table from me interested in talking to me about my company that I started out of my apartment. What the hell is going on?"

"I like what you've done with Digg," Gore said. Kevin smiled and maybe nodded. He doesn't really remember. *Al Gore actually knew what Digg was!* "He's got the whole accent, you know?" Kevin says, retelling the story, grinning, and doing the worst Gore impression you've ever heard. He was thinking to himself, "I don't care what comes out of your mouth next, I'm going to say yes to it, so let's just do it."

At the meeting Gore ran the room. He charmed everyone on

the Digg team. He remembered everyone's name, and if someone got cut off, he was careful to come back to him and ask him to finish what he was saying. It was quite a contrast to the meeting with Murdoch. "It made me feel so good to know this guy is legit," Kevin says, remembering and still glowing. "You could just tell."

By the end of the meeting it was "made known" that Current wanted to acquire Digg. Kevin had been so focused on the obvious suitors like Yahoo! or Fox he hadn't even considered a deal with Current. He had to think. The Digg crew left and Current invited them to come back to talk about a formal offer.

They came back a few weeks later. Gore was there again, with a glossy PowerPoint presentation that showed the CurrentTV and Digg logos coming together. Gore was standing in front of the screen, eyes on Kevin, with the Digg logo projected across his forehead. Kevin was trying his hardest to pay attention to what Gore was saying, but he was focusing at this large Digg logo on Al Gore's forehead, thinking, "Oh. My. God." That night twenty-nine-year-old Kevin called his parents. "You're never going to believe what I saw on Al Gore's forehead today," he said.

Ultimately, Current did make an offer. Kevin is bound by nondisclosure agreements not to repeat the terms, but he says it was "a very fair offer," which likely means at least in the range of $100 million. But again Digg and Kevin walked away. Another offer, another caveat. This time it came down to control. Under terms of the deal, Digg would be part of Current, not an independent entity, and Kevin and Jay weren't ready to give up that kind of control, especially since Current's main focus was TV and Digg's was the Internet. It came down to a fundamental disagreement. Current saw Digg as something that would fuel their TV network, and Kevin saw Digg and the Internet as the next step after TV. "I'm not sure they saw eye to eye on the importance of that," Kevin says. "There's so much more value in us winning that war than the old media television war."

So for the fourth gut-wrenching time, no sale.

It's about ten-thirty P.M. on June 19, 2007, and Kevin and Jay look exhausted. They're dressed up. Well, dressed up for Web 2.0 guys. They've each got on a mostly ironed collared shirt and a jacket. Jay is nursing a beer and Kevin is mostly looking at a glass of pinot noir. They're trying hard to be lively and not just slump down into the cushy chairs in the lobby bar of San Francisco's W Hotel and doze off. They're in a small gang of Digg executives and one Microsoft exec; the Microsoft exec has just treated them to dinner at the swanky San Francisco restaurant The Fifth Floor.

The two are discussing an ad deal, much like the one Microsoft has already negotiated with Facebook. It would basically outsource Digg's banner ads for Microsoft to sell, in exchange for a guaranteed revenue stream. This arrangement gives Microsoft space on another hot site to sell to its base of advertisers. But it's also good for Digg. It brings them a step closer to profitability and a viable business model. And with each ad outsourcing deal, Digg puts off having to build its own ad sales force. That keeps the head count at the company a low twenty-five people and lets them focus 100 percent on the site itself. "Kevin can just go nuts with ideas," Jay says. And Jay can get a little breathing room. Life as a long-distance CEO of Digg and Revision3 hasn't been easy.

Still, you wonder if Kevin and Jay are secretly wishing this meeting was about selling the company instead. Digg is weighing on both of them. Kevin still has millions of ideas for the site, but is frustrated at how long the ideas take to become real features Diggers can actually use. He makes a point of signing off on every single feature that goes on the site—especially the home page. But frequently he gives them only a cursory glance. There are so many features in the Digg queue that he spends a frustrating amount of time mapping out something called page flows, or how people will navigate through the increasingly complex site page by page. For instance: If people click on, say, "add a friend," they're directed to this page; if not, they go to another page instead. Kevin used to be a huge tea devotee, but the endless screenshots and procedures of Digg have gotten so mind-numbing that recently he has switched to espresso.

Meantime, Kevin is increasingly drawn to his newest venture, something called Pownce. It's new, fun, and nimble, and unlike Digg, is a blank slate right now. In fact, it's a lot like Digg was in the early days when it was just Kevin and Owen. "On a scale of one to dope?" he says just before it has launched. "It's dope." More specifically, Pownce is an easy way to swap big files and small messages with your friends all at once, in groups, or one at a time. Updates on your days and your whereabouts, similar to a blog or Facebook status update, are melded with a far prettier and so far legal version of something like KaZaA or Napster. If Digg is like Kevin's wife and kids, Pownce is like a young, fun mistress.

He is building Pownce with Daniel Burka, the Robin to Kevin's Batman. (Daniel hates to be called this, saying Robin was the lamest superhero ever.) Daniel, like Robin, doesn't get the same attention that Kevin, or Batman, gets for Digg's success. But as the site's graphic designer, Daniel has been a big factor in making all of Kevin's brainstorms work on the screen. Kevin will scribble something onto a yellow Post-It; Daniel will practically read his mind, translating it into an idea that can actually be coded. The early days of Digg were the most fun for them: coming up with new ideas on the fly, bouncing the ideas back and forth. As they'd refine an idea they'd yell things like "Yeah, dude, that's sweet!" or Kevin's trademark, "That's aaaaaawwweeeesome"—a word that seems to have about seven syllables when he says it. Now any idea has to go through endless process and troubleshooting before it's ready to be used by Digg's millions of users. With Pownce, they can just play. They can even test out ideas for Digg on Pownce.

Pownce's launch could hardly even be called a launch. There was no press release, nothing formal. And no venture capital: The company was totally funded by Kevin. Despite Digg's success, he still knew what got him there: building something cool and just seeing how it did. Not drafting a big business plan and raising millions. The site was initially by invitation only. This is a common way to roll out a new site, especially if it's high profile—as anything Kevin Rose does is these days. They watch how people use the site, and where it breaks down under real usage, making tweaks along the way. Too much traffic and the whole thing may just break down. The guys didn't even grant interviews to press anxious to see what Kevin was doing next. This was smart: No matter how low-key they tried to be, there was going to be a lot of pressure on Pownce to live up to Kevin's hype, and many people wanted to see him fail.

Even Pownce's pseudo-launch party was no-frills, nothing like the increasingly flashy parties Digg and Revision3 have in clubs and bars around San Francisco. Kevin and Daniel rented a house in San Francisco's Castro District for a couple hundred bucks, got a keg, and put out some chips and salsa. The house is owned by one of the state's biggest proponents of legalizing medical marijuana, and the garden was filled with pot plants. Tapestries and baubles hung from the ceiling. It was like an off-campus frat party. Kevin and Daniel even called it a kegger in the invites. Aside from a few bloggers, there was no press there, no business types, no opportunists. Just people who were into the Web. A nineteen-year-old kid from Vacaville who's starting his own company was there and took a photo of himself with Kevin, posting it on Facebook the next morning with the caption "The All-American Icon, Mr. Kevin Rose." His friends were impressed.

Of course, in part Pownce didn't need PR or a lavish launch because it had Kevin. James Currier, a local Web entrepreneur, remarked in a summer 2007 blog post that Kevin Rose may be the first Tom Cruise of the Web. Just as fans will go see a movie simply because Tom Cruise is in it, so too will the throng of techy early adopters rush to check out anything Kevin Rose starts. "Certainly there are a few serial winners in Silicon Valley, but each time they've succeeded they've done it from scratch... [battling] their way to the top," Currier wrote. "But... if [Kevin Rose] is involved with something, it gets high adoption, which creates value, as long as it's a network effect business."

In just a few weeks, thousands of people signed up for so-called premium Pownce accounts that allow them to send larger files over their network for $20 a year. The four-person company had raked in some $40,000 in revenues with no more marketing than a sign on the site telling people premium memberships exist. Before he even launched Pownce, there was a Facebook group called Fans of Kevin Rose's New Start-up with hundreds of members. Once Pownce launched, invitations to join were actually being sold on eBay. "Okay, now this is ridiculous," Kevin wrote, sharing the link with friends over Pownce.

Ridiculous? Yes. But that's not to say Kevin didn't love it. Everything about Pownce is marked with wide-eyed enthusiasm. Some days it's hard for Kevin to go back to the rigors and reality of Digg. And that's the very reason Jay wasn't too keen on Kevin starting a new company. The two bickered about it in the months surrounding Pownce's launch. Jay insisted Kevin needed to focus on Digg. Kevin countered that Jay has Digg and Revision3, asking why he can't have a side project. "Be very careful what you say here," Jay warned testily. "Revision3 was first. I stepped away from it to run Digg because you asked me to." Jay says he doesn't get Pownce, either, perhaps an indication of the five-year age gap between the two, Jay's irritability from the stress of running two companies at the same time, or some jealousy that Kevin is starting a new venture without him.

Not that he dwells on it. Jay has far more pressing issues. He has been trying to do the impossible for nearly two years now: run Digg, run Revision3, and live in New York. From the outside, all is well. Digg is growing in users, revenues, and overall value, and Revision3 has just closed a second funding round at a $23 million valuation. Not amazing, but also not bad for a company that in essence has one hit so far in Diggnation. In fact, Jay is holding it all together so well, *Business 2.0* magazine named him one of "The 50 Who Matter Now" in the summer of 2007. "Kevin Rose may be the camera-ready face of news aggregator Digg and online video network Revision3, but Adelson is the quiet guy in the background who builds them into successful businesses," it read. "Without Adelson, the people-powered content revolution wouldn't be quite so powerful." (Of course Kevin placed in the online reader poll. As always, the fan favorite.)

Potential acquirers have continued to pay attention to Jay too. On a balmy July 2007 day, Jay and Reid Hoffman were having coffee, only it wasn't at a regular spot like Farley's in San Francisco or University Coffee Café in Palo Alto. They were in Sun Valley, Idaho. And as Jay looked over Reid's shoulder he saw a large telephoto lens emerging from a thick bank of hedges that protected several hundred emerging and established captains of media and technology from the outside world. Jay was at the illustrious Allen & Company Sun Valley Media Conference and was starting to feel as if he had arrived. He spent most of the week starstruck. Fortunately Andreessen—an old hand at these things by now—was there to help shepherd Jay around.

While Brenda and his kids went fishing and horseback riding, Jay spent most of the conference having a series of surreal moments. The time Jay and Marc were chatting when Sumner Redstone sauntered up. Jay's heart leapt. "Viacom wants to buy Digg!"

he thought. Redstone merely asked him the time. The morning Jay walked into a crowded breakfast area and saw Wendi Murdoch, Rupert's wife, waving at him, motioning him to come sit with the News Corp. crowd. He looked around to make sure she was talking to him. She was. That afternoon he chatted up Anderson Cooper about his upcoming trip to Iraq. And then there was the moment of ultimate wonder: when Jay met Bill Gates. And Bill Gates said he *loved* Digg. In fact, nearly everyone he met knew Digg. Most talk about purchasing Digg was vague, save one executive of a major East Coast media empire who remarked he was interested in Digg but concerned about the price, because the company had just done another big online deal.

"I'm not sure we can afford you," the exec said.

"Only one way to find out," Jay told him, smiling.

But accolades aside, Jay knows the truth. This bicoastal arrangement is hurting Digg, Revision3, and his marriage. Digg is at a pivotal point. It's no longer an experiment; it's worth something now. There is something to lose. And the company needs to move quickly to prove it can be more than just a news aggregation and voting site, novel as that concept was. There are only so many people who want to get that involved with news online. Digg badly needs to branch out into a forum to vote on other things. Images? Products? Vacation destinations? Something else big that will hit. Something that could make it more of a platform company, like LinkedIn or Facebook. Otherwise Digg is a one-trick pony that will start to slide into irrelevancy. This is the sad truth of start-ups. Those nosebleed valuations aren't based so much on what you are doing now, but a start-up's potential to keep doing more. If it stagnates, the company can unravel quickly.

In the case of Digg, the vision is there. It has been there for more than a year. But Kevin, Jay, and the crew have had to rearchitect a lot of the code to make it possible, and with a skeleton twenty-five-person crew, innovation is grinding to a halt. Digg also isn't the typical work-twenty-four-hours-a-day start-up. The culture of any start-up emanates from its founder. You walk into Yelp and it's loose, jokey, hip, and fun, much like hanging out with Russ and Jeremy. You walk into Slide and it's quiet and intense, much like hanging out with Max. Facebook is a coding-all-night-eating-junk-food dorm room. You go in to Digg after five P.M. or so and it's empty—much like Jay's desk in San Francisco most of the year. "There is absolutely no question in my mind—no question—that Digg has been hurt and its future has been mitigated because of a lack of leadership here," Jay says. "What I'm saying is, I've hurt the company significantly. It's weird to know what you're doing is bad for business."

That said, for Jay to step aside wouldn't necessarily be a better option. Kevin isn't the chief executive type. He doesn't even manage anyone at Digg. He's too unfocused, and besides, his real strength is coming up with ideas and tweaking the product. Jay's value is shielding Kevin from all the rigors of the business so he can focus on creating. As much as Jay typically defers to Kevin on the product stuff, Kevin usually defers to Jay on everything else. There is a lot of trust and mutual respect between the two. Disrupting that relationship at this critical point would be worse than having an absentee CEO.

That leaves only one other option, which to Jay isn't an option: his moving back to San Francisco. "You think I can just pick up my family?" he asks over coffee one morning. His eyes are bloodshot and he keeps getting interrupted with calls about a Revision3 press release that's about to go out. He has another long day ahead of him, cramming in everything he can before he takes off for New York again. "That is not within the realm of possibility. The exit from San Francisco to New York was an epic, dramatic, emotional turning point in all our lives that saved my relationship with my wife and saved my relationship with my kids. Family is first. Fuck Web 2.0. Fuck Digg. Fuck everybody. My family is number one." No matter the toll on Digg; no matter the toll on him. And it is taking a toll on him. He flies to San Francisco twice a month and has twenty-hour days when he gets here. He is more exhausted than he's ever felt. He knows he can't keep up this pace.

There is a constant tug-of-war in Jay's soul between work and family. He's an entrepreneur; it's in his blood. As much as running Digg has cost him, it also saved him. He was stagnating in New York. He was miserable and so sick from stress-related arthritis that he was basically immobile for a year. Digg and Kevin reinvigorated him. But entrepreneurs tend to live their work. If you want to succeed, there's no choice. And after Equinix, he can't quite go there again.

Add up all these factors, and it seems Digg is headed toward sale. As is typical of Kevin and Jay's relationship, they are sending mixed messages. Jay seems to be the one who wants to sell, although for the right price to the right company. But Kevin says Jay doesn't really want to sell. Kevin—although he is clearly exhausted and annoyed with a lot of details of company building—insists he doesn't want to sell. He wants to see if he can pull off his greater vision. But Jay says Kevin craves the security of a big cash-out and free time to work on other projects. All accounts are likely true, in their own way. Clearly Digg isn't desperate, but it's hard to believe they wouldn't sell if the right price (a couple hundred million) and the right terms (a cool company who would let Digg be run as a separate, autonomous group) came along. Mostly it depends on what day you catch them on. And lately there just seem to be a lot of wrong days.

Kevin finds himself reminding people of something a lot in these days: He started Digg because he was bored and thought it'd be cool. His wildest dream was that one day it could pay his rent.

He never thought he'd have twenty-five people working for him, never thought he'd be on the cover of national magazines, never thought it would make him a millionaire. Of course now that he is, he has to remind himself of those early days too. The money, the glitz, all that attention may not have been his goal, but they don't suck either. When a Parisian conference invited Kevin to speak, he refused unless the sponsors paid for a business-class flight. Other overseas conferences have been known to give his whole entourage business-class flights. Kevin may think he truly pines for the simple life, but all these luxuries and attention would be hard to give up.

Somewhere along the line, part of that passion—the fire he felt just talking about Digg—receded along with those early modest ambitions to just do something cool and pay rent. In the early days of Digg, Kevin used to slap his Treo down in front of him everywhere he went, checking it every few minutes to make sure that no one was trying to reach him, that too much traffic hadn't overwhelmed Digg's servers, or that people weren't trying to game the site with illegal voting schemes. He'd pick his Treo up midsentence, grinning, saying something like "Oh, I see what you're trying to do!" to some wayward Digger or texting Jay immediately if something was going wrong. He couldn't mentally step away. He didn't *want* to. He never does that anymore, or if he has to, it's with far less enthusiasm. In August 2007 he's taking a month off Diggnation, saddling fellow Diggnation host Alex Albrecht with guest cohosts. "I just need a break," he says in late July, rubbing his eyes.

About a week later, Jay is getting a ride home from some friends after a swanky party at the de Young Museum announcing popular blogger Om Malik's new Revision3 show. An exhausted Jay is nodding off in the backseat. "I hope I can get one of those electric sports cars," he says dreamily. He's talking about a Tesla, an electric car that can go from 0 to 60 in less than four seconds and has a top speed of 130 miles per hour. The first production is about to roll out in the Valley and every entrepreneur, executive, and venture capitalist wants one. Jay sneaked off to test-drive a Tesla more than a few times on his visits here. "You think I deserve an exit, right?" he says wistfully.

Back in the summer of 2006, when *BusinessWeek*'s cover on the Web 2.0 scene was being decided on, the editors wanted to pick one main character, a literal cover boy for the new Web movement. There were two obvious candidates: Kevin Rose and Mark Zuckerberg.

As entrepreneurs, the two share a lot in common. Neither had made a fortune in the Web 1.0 days, nor had they outright failed. Kevin worked in entry-level jobs, and Zuck was in middle school. Both came up with their companies out of their own lives and own desires for sites that didn't yet exist. Both have an uncanny mind-meld with their core Web audiences, and both have a dead-on instinct when it comes to features, user experience, and the evolution of their sites. Neither was a strong coder or manager, but rather a visionary who just built his site from his gut. And both had a cult-like following among users. Everyone in the college scene knew Zuck by name. And, well, Kevin's hold on techy people was like a mini Steve Jobs–Apple fanboy worship fest.

Of course, both Zuck and Kevin have their detractors. Zuckerberg has been called arrogant with delusions of grandeur. People resented that a nineteen-year-old could waltz into the Valley, make venture capitalists his bitches, and later turn down billions of dollars. In the early days, few people thought Facebook could elude Friendster's fate, and later, few thought it could compete with the great social networking juggernaut MySpace.

When it comes to Kevin, people hate that he isn't actually a coder, just a guy with ideas. Kevin's aw-shucks manner makes him seem like he just got lucky his entire career. He came to the Valley with no pedigree or connections and managed to get a job working on TechTV behind the scenes. One day he discovered a security flaw in Microsoft's operating system—who in tech hadn't?—and nervously went on the air to warn viewers about it. That turned into more segments, and the next thing you knew, he was hosting the channel's most popular show.

And when Digg first debuted, people thought it was even more gimmicky than Facebook. Journalists and bloggers hated that it made millions of dollars by linking to their original work, contributing nothing original of its own. "It's a parasite!" one journalist screamed in the wake of the *BusinessWeek* cover. Not surprisingly when Pownce launched, many blogs almost immediately turned negative, simply because they wanted the cocky do-no-wrong Kevin Rose to get his comeuppance, never mind that the site was just a few hours old and still in test mode. Even David Sze got his share of ridicule when he invested a tiny $2 million in Digg and a larger sum in Facebook at the gaudy valuation of $500 million. Few doubt now that Sze will make a handsome return on both.

Another thing Kevin and Zuck shared, like so many members of the Web 2.0 generation, were influential friend-tors who were key in shaping their companies during the early days and perhaps later as well. Kevin's was Jay. Zuck's was Peter Thiel. The two couldn't be more different. And those differences resonate in Kevin and Zuck and in Digg and Facebook.

Peter is somewhat of an enigma in Silicon Valley, even to his friends. For all the jokes that Max is some sort of robot, in many ways Thiel is more machinelike. Every day he wakes up early in his almost-unlived-in four-thousand-square-foot San Francisco mansion before heading off to his futuristic-looking San Francisco offices. Tapping a code into a keypad sends his office door whooshing open. At home and at work, he surrounds himself with immaculate chessboards and shelves of books. And rarely—even to his closest friends—does Peter talk about his personal life. The description makes him sound like some cold, Mr. Burns–like figure, which isn't really true. Once you get to know him, Peter loosens up. He is warm, genuine, and even charming one-on-one. Or at least charming by Silicon Valley's generally low social standards. "No one in their right mind would describe Peter or Max as charismatic," says longtime friend Allen Morgan, laughing.

Peter has distinct, almost quirky mannerisms, shaking his head side to side as he unspools some cunning counterintuitive market theory, then listening intensely as you talk, nodding, glancing off to process the thought, then emitting a rapid "Yes! Yes! Yes! Yes! Yes!" if he agrees with you. It's not just that Peter is smart, even by Valley standards. His brain works differently from most people's, which is why he's known as Silicon Valley's consummate contrarian. He can take the same set of data as anyone else and process it in a completely different way, which usually leads him to a completely different investment thesis, whether it's in a private company or a publicly traded one.

One day he explained why older tech companies are eventually worthless investments. Tech companies' greatest assets are their engineers. A hot start-up attracts the smartest people, which ultimately makes it even hotter. But after the company goes public, all those smart people become rich. Either they wind up working less hard, or worse, they cash out their shares and leave. The company will never be able to replace them with anyone nearly as smart, because those people will either start their own companies or flock to the next hot start-up. After all, the one big money-making opportunity of the IPO is gone. Peter argues any tech company will eventually decline in value as a result. "You could argue," he concludes, "that a company like Intel is actually worth nothing." It's not just theory. Ever the chess master, Peter acts on his contrarian instincts too, forecasting where his opponent will go and then going another way to win.

Taking PayPal public at a time no other company would dare to was an obvious example, but just as striking was the time Peter essentially saved PayPal from bankruptcy. It was March 2000, just a few days before the NASDAQ crashed, and PayPal was seeking another round of funding. Back then, Peter was PayPal's vice president of finance. The company had merged with Sequoia-backed X.com, and Moritz had insisted on a grown-up CEO to run the combined company. The offer that came back from investors was a $200 million round at a $500 million pre-money valuation. Sounds rich, right? The PayPalers were insulted. It was the height of the bubble; they all thought PayPal was the next great Valley company and should be worth far more than that. Everyone in the room voted to hold out for a better valuation—that is, everyone except Peter. "The market is inflated and we have to take this right now," Peter told them, eventually convincing everyone. Within a few days, the entire NASDAQ collapsed and many companies who'd been holding out for better deals were bankrupt within a year. "It's really psychologically powerful when you are in a bubble like that," David Sacks, PayPal's chief operating officer, remembers. "Peter was the only one who saw it. He saved the company."

Such general market pessimism makes Peter's outright bullishness on Facebook stand out. In December 2006, while much of the Web world was still reeling from the news that Facebook had turned down Yahoo!'s $1 billion offer, Peter was of the belief that the company was worth closer to $8 billion. And this was a good six months before the opening of Facebook's platform caused the Valley to erupt into full Facebook mania. It's not that Zuckerberg needs help believing in the outsize value of his company. But having a mentor like Peter to back him up, not to argue that he should take the easy money, has shaped Facebook in ways Zuck probably doesn't even realize. And Peter has always gotten that Facebook's biggest asset is Zuckerberg's gut. In a Valley where most venture investors would be insisting on adult supervision,

Peter has always been convinced Zuck should stay Facebook's CEO no matter what.

Jay believes in Kevin's gut just as steadfastly, but in almost every other respect he and Peter couldn't be more different. His rural home just outside New York City is littered with the toys, clothes, and clutter that comes with three kids. The aluminum siding needs to be replaced and the deck is cracking. And unlike the highly rational Peter, Jay is ruled by emotions. He couldn't sell his Equinix shares even as the market was tanking because he wanted to show everyone he still believed in the company. And he didn't quit Equinix long after he had been pushed to the sidelines because he always had an irrational hope he'd take it back. He largely agreed to be Digg's chief executive because of loyalty to Kevin, not on the sheer logic of the move. And now he's constantly torn between his family and his Silicon Valley dreams of redemption. He always ends up on the side of family. Still, there is a constant pull west he can't fully ignore.

Of course, as Digg's chief executive, Jay is far more intimately involved in the company's dealings than Peter is with Facebook. But that means his hang-ups are even more welded into the company. Both Jay and Kevin insist that Jay's Equinix scares are nothing but a plus as the company grapples its way through hype and acquisition offers. But you could argue that Jay's mind-set held the company back too. The insistence that Digg run on a shoestring budget has kept the team intensely focused on the core product—no doubt a plus in the early days. But it has also kept Digg from moving much beyond it.

Culturally, Digg has always set its sights on a modest success. If it became a major home run, great, but they don't *expect* it the way Peter and Zuck do with Facebook. You can tell the difference in everything the two companies do. Digg has a skeleton person staff while Facebook employs hundreds. Digg has one floor of a

Potrero Hill building; Facebook has taken over four buildings in Palo Alto. Digg has raised just $11 million in venture capital; Facebook has raised nearly $300 million. And Digg is still largely a news site; Facebook has become an all-encompassing platform. For Digg, a purchase price of a couple hundred million is thinking big. For Facebook, there doesn't seem to be any limit.

Still, *BusinessWeek* chose Kevin for that cover because he is the everyman of this wave of Web companies. He's well aware that all this could evaporate and is more motivated by creativity and having enough money to fuel his future business ambitions. He rarely, if ever, dreams of the company going public. He somewhat accidentally hit on something that has gone nuts. Yes, he enjoys the money, the fame, and the attention, as anyone would. But ultimately he feels somewhat lost. Not only "How did I get here?" but many times, "How do I get out?" In his dreamier moments he says, "What people don't understand is I just want to go to Oregon and chop wood, and have a dog that I can throw a ball to. I want to have a designer and a coder who work for me. And we can just create cool stuff."

At times Zuckerberg yearns for the early days too. But he's more like the long line of Silicon Valley boy wonders such as Steve Jobs, Bill Gates, and Marc Andreessen. The kid who came to the Valley during its deadest times and started something that seemed modest, that people even dismissed as a fad, but ultimately helped connect the world. Tucked away in an office building in Palo Alto, Zuck is practically invisible to the Web 2.0 scene. He can't be bothered by it. He is building his dream. His dream that he believes will help "make sense of the world."

The day after Facebook's big F8 platform launch, Kevin sent Zuck a message over Facebook. "Way to go yesterday, dude. Next time you're in San Francisco, drinks are on me." This one line illuminated much of the differences between them. Zuckerberg never attends any of the scene parties, whereas Kevin is among the biggest celebrities. Facebook itself never has parties, with the lone exception of the all-night hackathon at F8—notably an event for geeks, not PR folks, media, and hangers-on. And notably, the hackathon wasn't at a club. Water and Red Bull were the libations, not free cocktails and beer. As much as the two have in common, as much as they like each other, the smart money would bet Zuck never takes Kevin up on his offer.

Smart money would also bet Digg sells and Facebook doesn't.

11

THE NONTREPRENEUR

Zachary A. Nelson is the quintessential Silicon Valley entrepreneur. He grew up in the Midwest, the seventh of ten kids. He still comes across as that gangly corn-fed Nebraskan boy. Only now he is driving a Bentley and wearing designer suits. Growing up, he always knew he was different and would get out of his hometown, no matter what. He didn't lose his virginity until college out of the fear that he would accidentally get a girl pregnant and get stuck. His sisters joked that holding out so long wasn't difficult; in high school he sported large glasses so ugly they called them the "birth control glasses."

When Zach landed in the Valley he climbed the Silicon Valley software ladder with aplomb. When he made it to Oracle Corporation in 1992, he'd hit the big time. He remembers the first time he interviewed with Larry Ellison, Oracle's iconic chief executive who at one time eclipsed Bill Gates as the world's wealthiest man. It was terrifying and exhilarating all at once. Nelson did well at Oracle, holding the vice president of marketing slot longer than any predecessor—no small feat under the mercurial Ellison. Then he went to Internet security company McAfee in 1996, bringing some much-needed flair to the company. He brokered the stadium naming deal with the Oakland Athletics, forming a fast friendship with Oakland general manager Billy Beane.

Nelson may have seemed happy-go-lucky, but he was hardly content. He had moved to the Valley for one reason and stayed there through the bruising tech downturn for that same reason: to become the CEO of his own up-and-coming software powerhouse. His dream would all culminate in one day standing on the floor of the New York Stock Exchange, or in a pinch the NASDAQ market site, and ringing that opening bell the day *his* company went public.

His shot came in 2002, when Larry called to offer him the job of chief executive at a small company named NetSuite. Larry had invested in NetSuite in 1999, and it had managed to grow through tech's nuclear winter. It was the brainchild of one of Larry's closest engineering lieutenants, Evan Goldberg. Larry had also invested in Salesforce.com, one of the first so-called on-demand software companies. Typically businesses buy multimillion-dollar software packages, then spend millions more having them installed, customized, and maintained. But both Salesforce and NetSuite had a new idea: they would buy, run, and maintain all the software for their customers, allowing them to access it over the Web. It was almost like renting software instead of owning it. And of course this was all made possible by the Internet.

Salesforce was the higher profile company of the two, and focused on software to manage sales teams' leads and contacts. NetSuite was aiming to do something much grander: "rent" to a business all the software it would need, everything from accounting to online stores. Zach was standing in his kitchen one day, talking to Larry on the phone and wondering if this was finally his shot. "I know this company will be bigger than [German software giant and Oracle rival] SAP one day," Larry said. "The only question in my mind is whether it'll be bigger than Microsoft." Zach was sold.

By late 2006, all of Zach's hard work was finally getting rewarded. The company filed its intention to go public and although a year of SEC scrutiny and banker meetings awaited him, Zach was pumped. "Are you kidding me? This is what everyone in Silicon Valley dreams of!" he said, envisioning the moment he'd ring the opening bell.

Or it used to be. True Valley entrepreneurs like Nelson are a dying breed, especially when it comes to Internet companies. For a long time the path of a start-up was simply a given: entrepreneurs take venture money, they build the business, and one day if everything goes well they get to go public. More than just the financial windfall, going public was the ultimate validation that your company had made it. But just as the crash was a cautionary tale of the unseemly side of venture capital and start-up life, so too was it a cautionary tale that going public isn't always the fairy-tale ending it seems to be.

For one thing, all that control and ownership this generation of companies have worked so hard to maintain? That's all gone once you're publicly owned. The founders' ownership gets diluted in exchange for all the cash they raise by selling shares to the public. And no public company chief executive has a board-level voting majority. He's just one voice in the boardroom.

Public companies also have to openly state their revenues, losses, and profits, which a lot of fast-growing tech companies consider a competitive disadvantage. Still, that's the least of the hassles. There's also the all-important quarterly earnings dance, in which a company has to make sure it beats its expectations by a penny, does a conference call where the managers talk in vague terms about their world-class management team's execution, and listen to an hour of questions from analysts trying to figure out how well the company is *really* doing. Then the company sets its expectations for the next quarter—always high enough so the stock doesn't tank, but low enough so the company can still beat them. Preferably by a penny.

Then there's the Wall Street addiction to growth. Sure, companies need to have profits, but even wildly profitable businesses don't do well in the public markets unless they have gaudy revenue growth figures attached to them. If growth stalls, watch out, because here come activist hedge funds to pound the management team, demanding they buy a company or do something dramatic to juice up the stock. Building a business for the long haul rarely happens on Wall Street now that we all live in a world of 24-7 news and short attention spans. It's all about *this quarter*. And happiness in a public company, especially a tech one, is all about the stock price. Nothing can kill morale more than a stock price that just doesn't move, while a new hotshot stock zooms past.

The government has only made the harsh reality of life as a public company worse in the years since the bust, thanks to something called Sarbanes-Oxley regulations. SOX, as the act has been annoyingly nicknamed, was intended to make companies more honest and open in the wake of corporate scandals, but it has only caused more problems. Companies now have to jump through hundreds of new auditing and regulatory hoops, boosting the cost of being a public company by millions of dollars a year. SOX was a boon to accounting and legal firms, but to no one else. Most investors were still befuddled by confusing quarterly reports, having little idea what was really going on behind the scenes at the companies they owned part of. Instead of punishing bad people, the government just made an already imperfect system worse.

Other regulations piled on top of SOX, making public life even less attractive. Silicon Valley big shots spent much of the years after the bust locked in an all-out battle with the government over the accounting of stock options—the lifeblood of working for a high-growth start-up or tech company. And to make sure supposedly independent Wall Street analysts weren't pumping up companies just because the other side of the firm was getting massive banking fees from them, new rules on Wall Street encouraged analysts to cover only the most widely held stocks. That meant analysts wrote hundreds of research reports on companies like Cisco and Genentech, but finding such a report on a small tech or biotech company that had just gone public was nearly impossible. Companies with market values of less than $1 billion were simply lost in the shuffle, hopelessly ignored by most investors. And it wasn't just tech. Companies in all sectors started eyeing the London Stock Exchange instead of the NASDAQ, as London became the nouveau financial center of the world.

"No thank you," said much of the Web generation, looking at the mess. Guys like Kevin Rose, Mark Zuckerberg, and even Ben and Mena Trott didn't spend their days dreaming of that NASDAQ moment. The thought made them queasy. They didn't want to spend a quarter of their time dealing with investors, analysts, and accountants. They wanted to make cool stuff. That's how they wound up starting Web businesses at a time no sane businessperson would anyway. They hated the management and process and red tape that come along with running several-hundred-person private companies. If Zach Nelson is the quintessential Silicon Valley entrepreneur, these are the Silicon Valley nontrepreneurs.

Of course the sentiment isn't really as much "no thank you" as it is "not until I absolutely have to." Because when an entrepreneur takes venture capital, the truth is that sooner or later he has to do one of three things: go public, sell the company, or bring in a new CEO who will. But entrepreneurs who came of age during the bubble have seen just how often each of those options can ruin a company.

A few Web 2.0 entrepreneurs have managed to bring in new management, but the results are hard to measure. Barak Berkowitz was brought in to run Six Apart as soon as it started to become much more than Ben, Mena, and Andrew. Barak was working with the Japanese company that first funded Six Apart when he met the Trotts. Over a getting-to-know-you dinner, he infuriated Mena almost immediately. She was describing Six Apart's somewhat modest goals of hiring only one or two people and trying to build a nice, profitable little business. "You're not ready for venture capital," he said condescendingly. It kept her up all night: "Who is this fat fuck, and why does he think he knows our business?"

But eventually she and Ben realized Barak was right and that they needed someone like him if they were going to move forward. Their first offices had two rooms: one where Ben could code in silence and one where Barak, Andrew, and Mena all sat together in very close quarters. The first day Barak came in with a tool belt and was fixing loose wires that were hanging from the ceiling. They laughed and made jokes about his CEO job description. Still, "that's what we needed then," Ben says. "A guy who could fix shit." While Ben, Mena, and Andrew are all creative types, Barak is organized and obsessed with numbers. Early in his career he was a floor manager at Macy's, and Mena says he still runs the company that way, interrogating each of them about whether they have sold their quota of suits for the month.

But Barak wasn't the guy to lead the company to an IPO. In August 2007, there was concern that Six Apart wasn't growing fast enough. It had focused so heavily on giving authors and blog publishers what they needed that it had neglected the readers of blogs. There were few tools to help readers find new blogs, which ultimately hurt people trying to make a living writing them. Externally there wasn't a good spokesperson for the company either. Barak didn't enjoy dealing with the press, Ben was too shy, and Mena was too emotional.

Ultimately, the company felt it needed new leadership and tapped Chris Alden, a more traditional media guy, to be chief executive. Chris had been the original founder of *Red Herring* magazine. The magazine was mostly known for its go-go dotcom days, but it had been started back in the early 1990s, when the tech industry was in a deep freeze. Later in the bubble, when billion-dollar media conglomerates like IDG and Time Inc. launched competing magazines, Alden raised venture capital and hired a grown-up CEO. It turned out to be a bad move. When the downturn hit, the bulked-up magazine went under. If he hadn't fallen for the Valley game, he believes *Red Herring* would be in business today and worth half a billion dollars, and TechCrunch would not exist. He's probably right.

Chris may be the perfect person to run Six Apart at this point. He was promoted because he helped revive the company's Movable Type product, which had been neglected. The board wanted him to do the same thing company-wide. He's mild-mannered enough to get along with the company's strong personalities, but intense at the same time. He likes being a CEO but is also entrepreneurial, which Six Apart still needs. In fact this is the first job he's ever held at a company that he didn't start.

Reid Hoffman has also hired a real chief executive at LinkedIn, Dan Nye. It was a risky move because Dan is a software guy, knowing nothing of the consumer Web—a scenario that didn't play out well in the late 1990s when a rash of managers replaced visionary founders. Dan even looks the part: a balding white guy of medium height and medium build. But after interviewing some seventy people, Reid decided he didn't need a Web expert. He was still going to be the chairman, and he knew the Web. He needed a good manager. He needed someone who would actually *want* to be a public company CEO. Reid didn't even like being a private company CEO, struggling with blurring the lines between friend and boss and missing the technical visionary part of the job.

Dan, on the other hand, is one of those Zach Nelson types who dreams of the IPO moment. He had a cushy job at an accounting software company called Advent Software, with assurances of career advancement if he stayed. As he got to the later rounds of interviewing, Dan told Reid and each of his investors, "If you are looking to sell this company, please leave me where I am. I want to come here only if we're building a big public company." Reid assured him he was in no mood to flip a company he'd labored since the earliest days of social networking to build, and thanks to being one of the first PayPal board members and executives, Reid was already financially secure. LinkedIn was about something more.

David Sze was certainly not pushing for a sale now that LinkedIn was one of the largest social networks on the Web and one of the only solidly profitable ones. His job was about getting Greylock some big Web bragging rights, and LinkedIn was one of the most promising companies in the portfolio. That left LinkedIn's main investor, Sequoia. First, Mark Kvamme, the Sequoia partner in question, gave Dan the marketing spiel that Sequoia-backed startups make up 12 percent of the value of the NASDAQ, that Sequoia is a firm that builds companies. Then he put it in more practical venture capital terms: "LinkedIn and YouTube were both funded out of Fund XI," Kvamme said. "And YouTube has already repaid it." In other words, Sequoia was under no pressure to post a quick return and had every incentive to see LinkedIn through to something bigger as well. Dan was relieved. Upon joining the team, he sent the word out to bankers and the usual suspects that might make an acquisition offer: "Don't even call unless it's bigger than YouTube. Way bigger."

But so far Six Apart and LinkedIn were the exceptions. More common were the founders who just mulled the three-way no-win situation of not wanting to sell (bigger companies always screw up the product and kill innovation), not wanting to hand it over to a real manager (they don't get the Web and will kill the authenticity with the community), and not wanting to go public (all busywork; no cool, creative work). A few were trying to create a new option. By the summer of 2007 every nontrepreneur's hero was a shy, unassuming guy named Evan Williams.

Like Zach, Evan is a corn-fed Nebraska transplant from a large family. But he's about ten years younger than Zach and the two hardly share the same Silicon Valley dream. In the summer of 2007, while Zach was shuttling around in suits and limos, courting Wall Street bankers and gearing up for his big moment, Evan was sitting in an obscure café in San Francisco's South Beach neighborhood, wearing the usual Web 2.0 ensemble of T-shirt and jeans. The contrast between the two was more pronounced when Evan looked up from his grilled fish and definitively said, "I would never create a public company. Ever."

Like so many others, Evan came to the Valley in the late 1990s and started an Internet company, called Pyra Labs. But it was almost an anti-dotcom. Pyra never took venture capital funding, and the twenty-six-year-old Evan and his crew made a point of calling themselves Web people, not dotcomers. He credits those decisions with making it out of the dotcom bubble alive. Pyra never got used to having money, so when it went away, the company was able to scrape by.

Pyra would give birth to Blogger, one of the very first tools for writing your own Web log, as blogs were called back then. It was even earlier than LiveJournal or Six Apart. When the economy crashed in 2000, Evan fired the whole staff except himself. The $10,000 he had in the bank when he started Pyra was long gone, but he always managed to sell just enough Blogger ads, T-shirts, and partnership deals to bring in the $800 a month he needed for his Noe Valley rent. He had no money to go out to bars or dinners, so he just stayed home, slaving away on the product and trying to make Blogger into something.

It may seem strange to be so committed to a nascent Web phenomenon such as blogging so far ahead of the user-generated content revolution and at a time when it seemed like the Net would never come back. But this was Evan's baby. He wasn't plotting to take down old media or anything grandiose. He just knew people liked blogging and liked his product, and he was convinced it could eventually make money. Maybe it wouldn't be a lot of money, but enough to get by. Besides, this was the epic Silicon Valley bust, and it wasn't like other jobs were plentiful. Better to work on building his own thing than wait tables.

By the end of 2002 things started to change, and Blogger started to make more money. Evan even hired a few people and began running it like a real business, not as an obsessive side project. He started to talk to some real venture capitalists about funding. That's when a mutual friend set up a meeting between Blogger and Google. Google was still private at this point. The company was doing well, but few people knew exactly how well. Google was so focused on its core business that it had never done a real acquisition. So when they asked Evan down for a meeting he assumed it was just some sort of partnership. It's hard to believe, given the large shadow Google would soon cast over all of Silicon Valley and tech, but Evan didn't really have any preconceived notions about the search giant. He headed down Highway 101 to meet with Google founders Larry Page and Sergey Brin. "We were so naive," Evan says. "We thought maybe they just wanted to search the blogs."

As it turned out, Google wanted to buy Blogger. And Evan faced a really hard decision. Like anyone else in the Valley, he'd seen most acquisitions turn out badly, and by now he'd invested so much of his time, his money, and himself in Blogger that it felt intensely personal. As if *he* were on the auction block. He'd stuck by the company, nursing it along when no one else would, when anyone else would have thought he was crazy.

But at the same time, another thought nagged at him. A thought that convinced him he should sell. As much as he loved Blogger and wanted it to live forever, he didn't necessarily want to be the one running it. It had been a long, exhausting slog, and while Blogger was doing better, pushing it to the next level was going to take more years of hard work. Evan simply didn't know if he was up for it. He was part of this new breed of creative Web nontrepreneur. He wasn't the world's best coder. He didn't like being the CEO. He just liked coming up with the idea, the look and feel of the site, all the details of how it worked, the name, and then releasing it. If it was successful, he was happy, but he was anxious to move on to the next project—much like a filmmaker or an author might pour his heart into a project for years, finish it, take a break, and then attack a new one. But Web companies don't work that way. "You are never done with them, unlike lots of other creative endeavors," Evan says. "It's such a commitment, and that makes getting acquired very attractive. It's a way this will survive and I can move on eventually." And of course as part of Google, Blogger would have far more resources to reach its full potential. So Evan sold.

The deal was modest, less than $10 million. Evan and his investors got paid in stock they couldn't sell until after the company went public. They would get jobs at Google to pay the bills in the meantime, making sure Blogger kept innovating and working to integrate the product with Google's quietly dominant search business. Thanks to Google's rocket IPO two years later, the deal would turn out far better than expected, with Evan himself netting a reported $50 million. (Evan has never commented on what he made.) He would even meet a new girlfriend at Google, a stunning dark-haired girl in human resources named Sara (now Evan's wife).

Still, this wasn't a storybook ending. Evan was frustrated by life post-acquisition. He still had to wait two more years for his payout, and instead of having all these vast Google resources he'd imagined, he couldn't seem to get anything done. He wasn't even allowed to hire people without running it past bureaucrats. And all those synergies that had been promised just weren't happening. Blogger was just another division in the vast, growing company. After Google went public, it was even worse. Evan wasn't good at navigating the political animal Google was becoming, and many nights he wondered why he'd sold. He needed to get out. And once he had fulfilled his contractual obligations to Google and Blogger, he did.

Looking back, he's glad Blogger survived and is still used by millions of people. And of course he's glad the deal turned out to be so lucrative. Still, he suspects, no true entrepreneur ever feels great about selling his or her company. "Google tried their darnedest to create an environment where entrepreneurs thrive, and I just don't know if that's possible because true entrepreneurs want it to be their thing," he says. "The day you sign the papers, it's not your thing anymore." But nontrepreneurs have the worst of it, because they don't want to run it forever either. Something Evan would realize with his second start-up, Odeo.

When Evan left Google he was exhausted and emotionally drained. His plan was to take some time off. But he started to get very excited about something called podcasting. Spurred by America's burgeoning love affair with Apple's iPod, podcasting was the audio equivalent of blogging. People recorded audio shows and mainstream radio shows and simply digitized their archives. The idea was, people would grab them via iTunes or other Web sites, throw them on their iPods, and listen at their leisure. Evan became addicted to them on his forty-five-minute drive to Google's Mountain View headquarters and back. As in the early days of Blogger, he started to get very excited. This, he decided, was the next big thing.

There were several legitimate reasons to think that. Podcasting borrowed from so many exciting consumer trends. It had the personal self-expression of blogging, the niche-audience appeal of satellite radio with its endless networks of music and talk, and the play-to-it-whenever-you-like appeal of TiVo. And of course anything connected with the iPod was hip. People were carrying these things with them everywhere. This was a new way of carrying around content that a television, Walkman, even satellite radio couldn't really match.

Evan bought the hype and helped his neighbor, Noah Glass, start Odeo. It was Noah's idea, and initially Evan was just going to be an adviser. Then he became an early investor. And before he knew it, he'd signed on to be CEO, they'd raised venture capital, and they'd hired a dozen people. And he still had no real idea what the company would be doing or what this awesome new podcasting product would be. It went against his gut and everything he'd learned from Blogger. It was like Evan had chronologically flopped his two experiences. In the dotcom times he was disciplined, but with Odeo he got caught up in all the excitement. "I totally got sucked in," he says, and then amends the statement quietly to himself. "I sucked myself in."

Evan may be known as one of the Valley's true nice guys, but he wasn't immune to Silicon Valley's ego trappings. He got caught up in his own myth and in the great Silicon Valley start-up game. He began to feel desperate to show he could do it again. That Blogger wasn't a fluke. "I didn't want to be one of those guys that got lucky and then went and sat on an island, but I don't know why I couldn't have done that for a while," he says. "I was looking for a win and I was getting so much external encouragement that this was *the thing*." When he talks about Odeo now, it's like he's discussing some horrible past relationship and is working as hard as possible to be polite about it.

By most standards, Odeo failed. It turned out podcasting was different from blogging in some key ways. Other than long commutes, most people don't have the time to listen to one long, continuous show. Audio programs don't provide the instant gratification of shuffling through three-minute songs or reading terse blog posts, nor do they have the easy navigation of TiVo. Odeo was never able to find that killer product or service that would take off the way Blogger had. In trying, Evan started to betray all of his own rules he'd published on his blog about building a successful start-up: "Be narrow"; "be tiny"; "be wary." He'd go into board meetings with a new strategy and a great pitch of why it was *the* plan. The board would be sold. Only the strategy wouldn't pan out, and he'd have to come up with something different. Evan was miserable. He hated being the CEO, and he knew he wasn't doing a good job at it.

In February 2006 there was a tiny ray of hope. Jack Dorsey, an engineer at Odeo, had been obsessed with this idea of a universal status message, something inspired from instant messaging. Status messages would tell your friends if you were available, away, or idle; you could also write your own to tell people you were, say, on deadline or out shopping. Jack wanted to create a status message that could work across the Web, email, instant message, and cell phones to tell everyone what you were up to. It would be like a tiny blog, just a sentence or two long. By now text messaging had become ubiquitous enough that the idea was technically feasible. Jack developed a quick prototype, and the Odeo crew started playing with it. They soon got addicted to the instant gratification of swapping witty updates with one another, a cross between a public blog and a personal text message.

Evan considered putting all of Odeo's resources behind it, but there were two problems. First, the new thing had nothing to do with podcasting. Second, Evan was worried the weight of this fourteen-person, venture-backed start-up would crush a fragile and beautifully simple idea. So he just told Jack and a few others to keep working on it, and he got back to trying to save this moribund podcasting company he was growing to hate more and more by the day.

Finally in May of 2006, Evan decided to quit trying. Most other entrepreneurs in his position would have kept pushing until they got there or ran out of money, motivated by an unwillingness to admit failure or the eternal hope that that killer product was just around the corner, or simply because that's how the Valley's game is played. Instead Evan did something practically unheard of in Silicon Valley. He told his board that it just wasn't working. That he'd gotten away from his beliefs and values. That he wasn't happy. That they'd tried to find a buyer and couldn't, so he personally was giving them their money back. Evan was essentially digging into his own pockets to buy the company back himself. He sold Odeo's assets to a new company he started called Obvious.

The investors were thrilled. Many Web 2.0 workers saluted Evan as a hero who cut through all the pretense, admitted Odeo was a dud, and created his own life without meddling investors. Others thought he was a chump. After all, venture capitalists are paid to take risks, and they were making millions in management fees while the bet on Odeo and others rode. They probably wouldn't have done the same for Evan. Even Evan admits he could have bought the company for far less. Valleywag wrote at the time about him: "Nice guys finish last."

Evan bought out his investors partly because he thought it was the right thing to do. He wasn't sure he'd really lived up to his commitment to build a podcasting company. And with more than a dozen angels and venture capitalist firms invested in the company, he didn't want to burn those relationships. But Evan wasn't just being nice. When he bought Odeo, he knew he was also buying that idea he loved so much: the universal status message. It hearkened back to those old instant-relay chat rooms where most of these geeks got their first online pals.

With this version, you didn't even have to download anything if you didn't want to; you could just post notes and read them online. To the right would be little squares showing the faces of people you were "following," who might or might not be "following" you. If you chose, you could get these messages pushed to your computer desktop or delivered to your phone. But how much you used it or didn't was largely up to you. It even had a prompt to make it easy for people: "What are you doing?" That simple prototype would become a site called Twitter, and within the geeky Silicon Valley confines it would become an instant phenomenon when it was launched at the South by Southwest conference in 2007. The digerati would flash-mob bars and parties in Austin as people "twittered" where they were and those "tweets" popped up on everyone's cell phones.

Evan always had a sense Twitter could be big if it was done right and broken out of a larger, struggling company. For all its simplicity Twitter could surprise you when you used it regularly. By blasting out the details of your day, you get a truer sense of what your friends are up to than with more formal blog postings, emails, or even sporadic meetings over drinks. Evan felt a rush getting messages from people he didn't have time to talk to every day but liked and cared about nonetheless. "I just thought people might like to hear from people," he says. "It was like blogging, but with dramatically lowered barriers to getting that endorphin rush. I couldn't really describe it, but it just seemed potentially huge."

Hours before Evan and Sara's July 2007 wedding, the two sat in different areas getting ready, visiting with friends and family, and twittering personal notes about the day and their feelings. Far-flung friends reading these notes felt like they were there, living the moment with them. "When I talk to someone every six months,

I get a news report of their life. I get the headlines and that's not where intimacy is created," Evan says. "People say Twitter is so superficial, but I think it's almost the opposite." Knowing all this, Evan did not want Odeo's investors to think there'd been some bait and switch, as if he'd purposely sold Odeo to Obvious for a loss only to spin out the potentially successful Twitter. If he repaid their investments, they couldn't very well complain.

By mid-2007 Twitter was successful enough that Obvious did spin it out, and the company took venture funding from Odeo's former venture firm Charles River Ventures and prominent angels like Marc Andreessen. Evan got angry letters from fans saying things like, "We thought you hated venture capitalists!" But they misunderstood his Odeo experience. It wasn't venture capital itself he had a problem with, it was that he took it before he had a clue what his killer product was, and then wasted that money flailing around trying to find it. In contrast, Twitter had already taken off in geek and early adopter circles—even getting picked up by MTV for real-time twittering from the Video Music Awards—well before it considered outside funding. All the while, Evan, who was months before deemed a chump too nice for his own good, owned nearly 100 percent of it.

There's another key difference between Twitter and Odeo—and even between Twitter and Blogger. Evan isn't running it, Jack is. In fact, Evan isn't even an employee of Twitter. He went through being the CEO of Blogger and then having to sell it. He was miserable. He went through being the CEO of Odeo and trying to build something big through the traditional start-up route. He was miserable then too. He learned something about himself. He didn't want to be a CEO. "It's not what interests me," he says. "I don't want to build a big company. I want to be involved and I want to create things. I know I can do that best if I'm not the guy. Being the guy just sucks."

After Twitter spun out, Evan stayed at Obvious. It's hardly obvious what his job actually entails, and that's part of the idea. It may prove his greatest innovation yet, the creative founder's dream of living just the fun part. Evan owns 100 percent of Obvious and has just a handful of designers and coders working for him so he can work on any idea that strikes him. In the wake of Twitter's spinout in the summer of 2007, that means getting married to Sara and going on a nice long honeymoon through Asia and Africa. Friends were regaled with Twitter updates like "Watching a lion. Shhhhh." After that, he'll see. He'll still be very involved with Twitter, but his real day job will be poking around and coming up with the next great Web app. No pressure of investors. No board to report to. No focus on making money. Just building cool stuff and seeing where it goes. It's much like what he did at Pyra Labs, which led to Blogger. It's what he wanted to do after he left Google, before he got seduced by the Valley game. Not this time, even with a nascent hit like Twitter to tempt him. He's not getting sucked back in.

At least for now Evan Williams had found a way to build cool new Web sites without having to build them into companies—and if Twitter is only a modest success, he'll still make money doing it. Everyone was watching him closely. This was the secret Web 2.0 dream of having your cake and eating it too, and so far Evan is one of the only Web guys actually managing to do it.

Hardly anyone outside the Web microcosm gets the whole nontrepreneur pull. Wall Street, the press, East Coast hangers-on who were now turning their attention to the Valley again—none of them wanted to hear it. News and the markets were slow in the summer of 2007, and all they wanted was an IPO. A big fat Web 2.0 IPO.

It seemed to be all that was missing. By this point, there was serious hype and froth surrounding everything Web in Silicon Valley. The tug-of-war between giddiness and wariness that characterized 2005 and 2006 had mostly gone to the side of giddiness. Parties were everywhere again, although still nothing like the lavish affairs of the late 1990s. One night in April as the spring Web 2.0 Expo conference was starting, there were more than six parties on one night within a few blocks of San Francisco's SOMA area. The NetVibes party—celebrating the belated official U.S. launch of a hot French Web 2.0 name—was the most reminiscent of the bad old days. Thousands of people were trying to get in, and the line was wrapped around the block. Free drinks for everyone. Clubs like 111 Minna and Mezzanine seemed to be doing an entire business in start-up parties.

Even the kingmakers were growing weary. In a controversial post, TechCrunch's Michael Arrington yearned for 2005, when a few people could sit in his living room with burgers and beers and bat around ideas. Now he was practically stalked by wannabe companies dying for his Web 2.0 blessing. One start-up group bearing latte and pastries even borderline-broke into his house in the wee hours of the morning. His summer 2007 TechCrunch party was swarmed with more than nine hundred people—and that few only because he strictly capped it. You had to show a photo ID to get in. *Newsweek* called it harder to get into than Studio 54 in its heyday. Some onlookers were alarmed at the number of blue-shirt MBA posers there.

No doubt some dumb companies were getting started. A company called Reality Bedding allowed people to go online and pick a picture of a celebrity, or two women making out; for a fee they'd print it on a comforter and mail it to you. Ostensibly, so a lonely guy could say he was sleeping with Angelina Jolie. Not surprisingly, they went out of business by summer of 2007, the founder remarking that the idea was "too visionary and ahead of its time." Or maybe just too lame. While this was an extreme example, some people were clearly getting carried away. Some of the discipline that arose from the pain of the bust was disappearing. As with any

Silicon Valley cycle, many of these companies were going to be out of business soon—maybe within a year. One important element was still missing from this so-called bubble: IPOs. Indeed, even acquisitions of Web companies were still slow. Aside from MySpace's $300 million purchase of Photobucket and eBay's $75 million purchase of a Digg-inspired site named StumbleUpon, not many sizable deals were happening. No one had come near YouTube's $1.65 billion payday—a high-water mark that was looking more and more like an anomaly.

Wishful thinkers in the media, on Wall Street, and on blogs had started the year saying 2007 would be a banner year for tech IPOs, and by midyear, there was indeed a pickup in activity. But the companies going out were more like one-off companies that had been held out of the public markets for the previous few years. There was no unifying theme signaling the next new thing; and the companies had nothing to do with Web 2.0. The only Web companies serious about going out were selling Web software to businesses, such as NetSuite or potentially OpenTable.com, a 2000-era company that had managed to stay alive but made most of its money selling reservation software to restaurants. Six Apart and LinkedIn were rumored to be strong IPO candidates, but anyone who knew anything about them knew this was at least a year off.

The one IPO that people were foaming at the mouth just thinking about was Facebook. With MySpace and YouTube purchased, it was the giant of Web 2.0, and after the F8 platform launch, that became obvious to everyone. It had also become obvious that Zuckerberg wasn't going to sell. Thanks to the rich advertising deal the company had cut with Microsoft, it even had revenues to back up all those eyeballs. Some bloggers began asserting the company would definitely file before the end of 2007. Just like with YouTube's purchase nearly a year ago, wishful thinkers were hoping this could be Web 2.0's "Netscape moment."

By summer 2007, CNBC shows were doing regular segments about the upcoming Facebook IPO, never mind there was no real evidence this was in the works. Bloggers and business publications kept talking about it too. Any little thing was an indication. They hired a CFO who understood the ins and outs of granting stock options: must be about to file. A cheeky music video Zuck's sister produced had a reference to Facebook turning down Yahoo! to go public: must be about to file. She pulled the video from YouTube: must be about to file. Everyone assumed that the iconic Valley dream was still there, and that surely someone like Zuckerberg just couldn't wait for his IPO moment.

But they were wrong. Yes, unlike some others, Zuck would rather go public than pick a new CEO or sell the company. He knows his investors need a return and his employees want to cash out their stock options. Instead, in late 2007 he brokered the $240 million investment deal with Microsoft to buy him some time. He'll take Facebook public one day, but he thinks it's not too much to ask that they wait a few years. He's thinking 2009 at the earliest. People close to the company wonder if crossing the five-hundred-employee mark might push up the date. When a company has more than five hundred shareholders, it has to report as if it is public, and in the Valley almost all employees get stock. This was ultimately what forced Google to file when it did.

But Zuckerberg isn't even sure he would then. "Publicly reporting numbers is the least of my concerns about being a public company," he says. When Peter and Max were building PayPal, Peter used to tell people success wasn't profitability, nor was it beating rival online payment systems. It was going public. This is a sentiment Zuck doesn't share with his mentor. And it's one of the clearest indicators of the Web generation gap.

In all the pundits' talk about who will be the next Google they were missing a crucial point: Google became such a behemoth because it *waited* to go public. The company could have gone public for years; the growth, revenue, profits, and management team were all there. But it waited, amassing a huge lead in the lucrative search-advertising market, and debuted only when it was so huge no one could take it down, bully it, or launch any kind of Google takeover.

Google was big enough it could thumb its nose at many of the hassles of being a public company. It eschewed the usual banker-led IPO, in which friends of Wall Street firms get the most of the proceeds, for an open auction where everyday people could bid on and purchase shares. That cut fees for banks as well and wasn't popular. What's more, the company made clear it wasn't going to give quarterly guidance and that founders Larry Page and Sergey Brin would retain sizable control over most things Google.

Wall Street balked at all of this, insisting the IPO would be a flop. Several big institutions boycotted it. Then Google soared from a modest opening price of $85 a share to more than $600 a share. Google and its cubicles of new millionaires won, and the smarter investors and entrepreneurs in the Valley learned a valuable lesson about waiting to go public until their businesses were so huge they could do it on their terms. This approach wasn't too different from the new way of looking at venture capital. If a founder really had something great, hold on to that ownership (that is, shares) as long as possible. Just as with venture capital, the longer he or she could wait, the more valuable those shares would become.

And Facebook, despite its success, had plenty of kinks to work out before it could be anything like Google. The company was struggling to recruit managers that Zuck could work with and trust, creating high turnover in some positions. It was scrambling to keep the site up and running as hundreds of new applications launched on it and millions of users were snapping up those applications in days. And of course there were the marketing challenges of continuing to expand outside the college market and figuring out more sustainable revenue streams than Microsoft's selling its banner ads. Those are hard problems to solve without Wall Street. Facebook didn't have a shortage of cash, and it wasn't looking for a stock currency to go buy other companies with. It simply made no sense not to wait. And unlike the situation in late 1990s, the psychological allure—the sense that this would *make* their company—just wasn't there.

Again, the PayPal crew seemed to be the exception, that psychological happy medium between naive giddiness and crippling wariness. The group that had managed to learn from the lessons of the bust and still believe the Valley system wasn't broken. PayPal's IPO day had still been the happiest of Max's life. Now locked in competition with himself, he was hellbent on doing it again. In January 2008, Slide closed its fourth funding round: $50 million from Wall Street heavyweights T. Rowe Price and Fidelity. The company was now valued at a steep $550 million. He was one-third of the way to PayPal. Only a massive acquisition or total bankruptcy was going to stop him.

In the midst of all of this excitement and subsequent hand wringing over the excitement, not every party in San Francisco was screaming *"BUBBLE!"* On July 4, 2007, a few hundred select individuals gathered at Peter Thiel's huge San Francisco home to eat, drink, and watch the Crissy Field fireworks from his rooftop. Parking is nightmarish in this area even when fireworks aren't on display, so Peter arranged for valet parking at his hedge fund's nearby offices and shuttles to transport his guests to his home.

This was no barbecue. Guests milled around dining on sushi from four-star Ozumo Sushi and were waited on by a full staff. But it was hardly opulent or showy. If anything, it was understated. Just a gathering of Peter and his friends that could be happening in 2001, 2007, or any time in between. Not surprisingly, the PayPal crew was in attendance. Jeremy Stoppelman was there with his brother and usual sidekick, Michael. Keith Rabois, who'd just left LinkedIn to join Max at Slide, was there too. Max and Nellie were of course there, with Max looking all-American in an Illinois baseball cap. Yu Pan was there too. The unassuming multimillionaire was decked in a *Transformers* T-shirt and was gushing about the movie, which he'd just seen. He brought a friend who lives in Los Angeles and was considering a move to the Valley. Yu Pan's argument: "You're focused on business now and there are no girls up here to distract you." Some of Peter's newer acolytes were there, including Sean Parker and a few other Founders Fund portfolio companies. (The party-shy Zuck was surprisingly a no-show.)

Valleywag trolled for dirt on the party, but there was simply none to dish. No one was bragging about paper wealth or stock options or even talking much about business. Okay, Max could be heard talking about the Facebook application wars. But mostly these were people just happy to be in the Valley. To be surrounded by people like them. To be able to wake up every day and work hard at creating something that just might change the world. That most of these people had known each other since the late 1990s, through poverty, wealth, and for a few, poverty again, said something about the deep bonds that existed between them.

When someone made a reference to the Valley scene, Yu Pan's Los Angeles–based friend waved his hand at the roof of unassuming, somewhat geeky men (and a few ladies) waiting to see the fireworks and said, "What scene?" Indeed, people weren't lavishly dressed or looking around to see who was there worth talking to. But gatherings like the one on this roof are the core of the real Silicon Valley. Launch parties come and go. Parties like these, where people who'd be misfits anywhere else feel at home, where they can get away from press, bankers, and copycats—that's the real glue of the Valley that never goes away. It's why these people didn't leave in 2001, and why many of them never will. It's why the Valley will always be the Valley.

12

THE FAIL WHALE

"WE'RE THROWING WHALES, PEOPLE!"

In the summer of 2008, no words were more hated at Twitter's headquarters, or possibly anywhere in the Web 2.0 world. Twitter was the hottest site of the moment, but it found itself in the grips of what Web entrepreneurs refer to as "a great problem to have": usage was soaring. Millions of people were sending millions of Tweets per day, and the system two Odeo employees had cobbled together to test an idea simply couldn't handle it. But every time a Twitter engineer yelled those four words, it certainly didn't feel like a great problem to have.

Twitter's unreliability had stretched nearly a year by that summer, getting worse by the month. The site could be down for hours a day, for days at a time. Twitter users were getting impatient. People had started to rely on the system as a sort of personal news feed, a way of connecting with friends, and a tool for tracking events. When it went down, people flew into a rage. It only made them angrier that Twitter's staff wasn't saying much of anything about why the outages were occurring or when they would end. The Twitter team wasn't trying to be obtuse; they just didn't know what to say. They were just as stumped.

All of that anger got aimed at a whale. Not a real whale, but a blithely grinning cartoon whale being lifted inches above an orange-and-white ocean by a net pulled by a flock of very hard-working cartoon birds. Before 2008, this was just a cute piece of clip art developed by an Australian illustrator. Biz Stone, one of Twitter's founders, grabbed it from a clip art site on the fly because Twitter needed a screen to show when the system was down. This cartoon soon became known as the Fail Whale.

The Fail Whale was cute at first. In fact, undeniably so. But when you saw him every time you tried to message a friend or Tweet a new blog post, his oblivious grinning expression became maddening.

As furious as users were, they stopped short of tearing Twitter down or abandoning the site altogether. There was something about Twitter that Silicon Valley rooted for; a remarkable sense of goodwill for a company that was continually letting its users down for months. Friendster certainly hadn't been cut that kind of slack.

Even the whale itself developed fans. The problem went on long enough that a weird Stockholm Syndrome developed. A Fail Whale fan club emerged. One guy got a Fail Whale tattoo. The woman who'd designed the art started to produce T-shirts and mugs. She sent a box of Fail Whale T-shirts to Twitter's offices late in the summer, but the joke was wearing thin on a staff battling the problem day and night.

Sure, some staffers found it funny. After a point you just have to laugh, right? But ask CEO Jack Dorsey about wearing a Fail Whale shirt and you'll get this answer: "I won't wear any shirt with a whale on it, ever. It has put me off the whole species." Twitter's cofounder Evan Williams agrees: "I hate that fucking whale." In the summer of 2008, that was one of the few areas where Jack and Evan were in sync.

The very first thing Jack Dorsey says to people is this: "I didn't come from the Web. I came from the dispatch industry." This tells you why Twitter was one of the only companies to launch after the Web 2.0 mania had begun that actually did something new. It wasn't a me-too, overengineered version of MySpace, Facebook, or YouTube. It was its own thing, beautiful and simple. The type of thing that should have sprung up as sites like del.icio.us, LiveJournal, and Flickr were beginning to unknowingly define Web 2.0.

That's because Twitter didn't really start in 2006. It started in Jack's head back when he was fifteen years old. He was just a geeky kid living in St. Louis in the 1990s who had an unnatural obsession with the dispatch industry. Particularly the armies of couriers who physically took something, put it in their messenger bags, and dropped the packages off somewhere else. He thought about it the way other fifteen-year-olds think about half-naked girls or *Star Wars*—with sheer awe that never seemed to end.

And when he thought of dispatchers, he would picture a huge map of New York City with blinking lights of couriers all acting like a flock of birds navigating the city individually, but also as one. A symphony of bikers fanning out in different corners of the city, crossing paths seamlessly, each on their own route, then coming back to the same place at the close of business. All controlled by one conductor; one master plan. "I wanted to write software to do it," Jack says. "*I just had to.*"

So throughout high school and college while the Marc Andreessens and Max Levchins of the world were starting their first Web companies and moving to the Valley, Jack was obsessively writing dispatch software in St. Louis. It was absurd; the city had no need for any of it, so as a sophomore in college, Jack quickly discovered the world's largest dispatch firm—headquartered in the dispatch city of his dreams: New York. He dropped out of school, moved there, got a job, and got to be close friends with the CEO. Like almost anything else in 1997, the company had just gone public on NASDAQ and was growing rapidly, its stock soaring. "It was everything I'd ever wanted to do," Jack says.

When Jack got to New York he saw that dispatch was more than couriers—it was taxis, limos, town cars, emergency vehicles, and public transportation all operating on the same system. More blinking red lights on a map moving individually and yet in concert with each other like some beautiful colony of ants. Jack was giddy. It was an invisible map that was virtually running New York City! When he watched a dispatch map, he felt like he was seeing Manhattan breathing and moving.

It was almost an anthropological study of how people work in swarms, particularly the low expectation of swarms. If someone cries out for a cab, and that cab is on the way to another destination, it's not a personal slight. You just reach out for the next cab. "The expectation is so low, that the friction is very low as well," he says. To Jack it was all magic.

He was so obsessed; he saw dispatch everywhere—even in instant message status updates. Status updates used to be as simple as "online," "offline," or "idle," but soon IM service providers let you customize them and people got creative. Jack loved being able to passively know what each of his friends was doing, the way a dispatcher could look at a map and see that Cab No. 2345 was picking up a passenger at 26th and Lex. The problem was you and your friends had to be at your computers to get those status updates.

Jack wanted them wherever he was; whenever he wanted it. So when the first rudimentary BlackBerrys came out—then just called a Rim 850—Jack got one. The device was short and stumpy and only did email. Jack wrote a program to take his email from his phone and broadcast it out to a number of friends' inboxes. It was basically Twitter, but it didn't work because no one else had these devices. Friends were generally befuddled by seemingly unimportant details of Jack's life landing in their email box long after the information was relevant.

Nonetheless, the idea continued to play out in Jack's mind. He continued to write dispatch software, even moving to San Francisco and cofounding an Internet dispatch software company in 1999. He and a cofounder raised $2 million from angel investors and hired a "grown-up" CEO from General Magic. They blindly turned over control of the company to him. Jack didn't want to be management; he just wanted to work on the product itself. They hired five engineers in Montreal, and Jack temporarily moved up there to work with them.

Then, like so many other start-ups in the dotcom bubble, things went horribly wrong. The CEO got caught up in the Internet excitement and lost sight of the idea that the product was being built for dispatchers. He started hiring salespeople like mad and those salespeople were making wild promises to customers that the company's tiny engineering staff couldn't fulfill. Finally, about nine months into the whole thing, the CEO called Jack and his cofounder and said, "I want to take the company in another direction and you two are out. I'm laying you off."

Jack choked in disbelief and was escorted out of the building with a box of his belongings. He couldn't quite process the larger picture of what had just happened; all he knew right then was that he was twenty-two years old, in Montreal, and on a work visa that had effectively just expired. He had no friends there and no family and no idea what he was going to do. So he did what any normal twenty-two-year-old would do: He got drunk. (It was actually the first drink Jack had ever consumed, not terrifically surprising for a kid who'd been obsessed with dispatch software since he was fifteen.) A week later, the investors found out about the move, pulled the plug, and gave the company back to Jack and his cofounder. But it was 2000, and the market was crashing. There was no hope of raising more money. They'd missed their window. Brutally schooled in how the start-up game really works, Jack started to pick up contract work wherever he could. "I knew then whatever I did next, I would run," he says.

Jack went back to New York, but not for long. Having spent his whole career focused on the behind-the-scenes magic of dispatch, he decided it was time to grow up. The Internet bubble was over and if he wanted to make something of himself he needed a real job in tech. He moved back to San Francisco and got a job at an uninspiring company named RiverBed, which makes software that makes broadband networks move faster.

But he was immediately bored at RiverBed. It was 2005 by now and Evan Williams had started Odeo, and a good number of the Web cool kids in San Francisco had flocked to there to work with him. Jack was an outsider with no experience building Web apps. He didn't know any of them, but he knew of them. He'd eat lunch in San Francisco's South Park neighborhood every day and see them. He fantasized about working with someone like Evan, or "Ev," as he's known amid the Web hipsters.

Odeo had put out a request for a contract engineer, and one day, Jack was eating lunch in South Park mulling over whether he should make the jump. He didn't love podcasting—truth be told he was still obsessed with dispatch and there was no Venn diagram that featured podcasting and dispatch, try as he did to find one. But something about working with Evan called to him. He saw it as a way to work with top front-end designers and get a belated introduction to the Web. Just then, he saw Evan breezily heading into Café Centro for lunch. Jack took it as a sign, and applied. He was given a contract and a few days later got hired full-time.

Little did Jack realize at the time no one at Odeo was into podcasting and that was precisely the problem. There was no passion around building tools for podcasting, but the team—including Evan—was desperate to find something about which they could be passionate. At the same time SMS was becoming popular. You could finally send a text from a Verizon phone to, say, a Sprint phone. And the ability to text was found in even the most low-rent phones. Jack had been disappointed by early SMS progenitors and assumed this version would be just as lame. But an Odeo colleague who was addicted to texting encouraged him to play around with it. The clouds parted and birds started to sing: *This was it!* Jack was in love with SMS. "It's this rough form of technology. It barely works. It's sketchy, but when it does work it's amazing!" he gushes still. "It's so simple. Just one message. No subject line. No malice or forethought. You just made it and hit send and it was received and your friends loved it. It was the best form of communication I could think of."

It was also—finally!—the way to make the system, the thing, the universal status message that Jack had dreamt about for nearly eight years, work. All you had to do was take the one-to-one texting model and somehow add in a buddy list or dispatch service and you'd have what would soon become Twitter. Jack could hardly contain his excitement. Within days he found himself agonizing over whether to contain it or not. Odeo had about seventeen people and they were all grappling for something about which to care. Two ideas were percolating: how to get podcasting (ugh, podcasting!) on mobile and a way to do something around like-minded groups. One day, the team went out to the leafy playground in the park, just outside Odeo's offices. The same park where Jack used to eye the Odeo team. Evan divided them into groups and asked them to brainstorm.

One of the things developers love about working with Evan is he can throw any assumption for the sake of wild brainstorming. This was why Biz Stone had followed Evan from Google to Odeo—again, despite a total lack of interest in podcasting. If Biz had an idea that defied gravity, Evan's approach was, "Let's just write on the whiteboard 'no gravity'; now, what's your idea?" This was one of those anti-gravity days.

Jack was sitting in his small group trying to decide whether to share his idea he'd carried around with him for the better part of a decade. The universal status message had nothing to do with podcasting, after all. But more worrying: He knew the second he uttered it, it was no longer his. He was terrified about trusting the wrong people again. He had a decision to make: Should he clam up and leave and try it on his own? He wasn't being challenged at Odeo and was thinking about quitting anyway. But looking around he saw a creative team that had a lot of skills he lacked. It was a team he liked and trusted, and a team that was growing to hate podcasting more by the day, desperate for a new idea to rally around.

Jack took a deep breath and told everyone his idea. They got it. When the groups all came together to pitch their best ideas, he pitched it again. People got it again, but many thought it was too simple. Also, it was a pretty big conceptual leap from an audio-based company. Jack's impression was people found it interesting. But not *that* interesting.

Days later Evan, Biz, Jack, and a few others had a meeting about how to expand Odeo's friendship model and Jack talked up the idea again. Evan told Jack and Biz to take another programmer and work on it for two weeks. The three of them built the entire system—with SMS going in and out of the Web interface. But what to call it? Jack had been calling it Stat.us in his head, but it was a dreadful name. Jack and Biz wanted something fun and something that captured the motion and emotion of a phone buzzing with a message. The feeling of something buzzing in your pocket, interrupting you, but immediately delighting you as well. That was the rush for developers working on the project: Creating something that could make your friend's phone buzz. "Twitch" was the first idea, inspired by the dance the phone actually does when it vibrates. But Twitch doesn't have the best connotations. So they looked up *twitch* in the dictionary, hoping to find words that sounded like it. They saw *twitter*: short, inconsequential bursts of information or chirps from birds. Since the earliest days of watching dispatch maps in New York City Jack had thought of the blinking lights moving individually, yet in concert, as some sort of animal flock. The name was perfect and they reserved the dorky domain, "Twttr." (The more palatable Twitter was bought months later.)

Jack sent out the first Tweet to coworkers, inviting them to try Twitter out. As soon as they sent their first messages they were in love. They started to invite friends and family. Soon users soared to five thousand. Biz vividly remembers one day he was ripping up disgusting carpet in his new house. While he was gagging at the maggots and mold and whatever else he was finding, his phone buzzed and it was a Twitter from Evan. It read something like: "Ahhhh, sitting outside, enjoying some wine in Napa. . . ." "You bastard!" Biz shouted at his phone. Then he started laughing. It was so diametrically opposed to what he was doing, and somehow the real time juxtaposition was hilarious. That was when he knew they had something.

As Odeo's employees and friends and families started having their own Twitter *aha* moments, Odeo was increasingly falling apart. That's when Evan finally called uncle on the whole Odeo thing, personally bought out his investors, and launched Obvious. Twitter was Obvious's most, well, obviously good idea. In April 2007, Evan spun Twitter out and kept Jack as CEO. It wasn't a, well, obvious choice. Jack not only had no experience as a CEO, he'd never managed anyone. He'd only been a programmer. But Evan had decided he never wanted to be "the guy" again. The Valley's ultimate nontrepreneur, he wanted to have creative ideas and sit on islands, not be bothered by boards and VCs. But Jack wanted this. It was his idea. And there were plenty of less experienced kids running companies. (Mark Zuckerberg, anyone?) So Evan said yes.

Having vowed years earlier that he wanted to be the boss of the next thing he did, Jack was thrilled. But he was tested immediately. For one thing, everyone from Odeo was invited to come to Twitter and Jack immediately went from peer to boss. He had a difficult time gaining people's respect, and had to fire several of them. And no sooner did Twitter break out at the South-by-Southwest conference in 2007 then did the scalability problems start. The system just wasn't designed for that much rapid growth. That set a dangerous survival tactic of continual patching rather than solving underlying problems. And as Twitter became even more popular, it only made things worse.

People frequently blamed Twitter's lightweight "Ruby on Rails" programming language for the failure problems, but Biz, Jack, and Evan say the problem was more cultural than technical. Twitter had been written so ad hoc that no one person knew the whole code. So when something went wrong, no one immediately knew what it was. And because the system was being continually patched on the fly, if one thing failed, the whole thing failed. "We just weren't approaching it the right way because we just didn't think it would grow that quickly," Jack says. It was especially frustrating for him, given his long history in real-time networks that couldn't fail. But he'd never built one as a Web service.

The other problem was that Twitter released its so-called APIs on day one. APIs give outside programmers the underlying data to write applications on top of another site. In essence, Twitter had opened up its platform to outside developers from its launch, something Facebook waited years to do. That helped Twitter take off immediately and drove a lot of early alpha-geek adoption and evangelism. But anytime you let others on your system, you introduce uncertainty. "Before [Facebook's platform release] I never once saw an error page on Facebook," Jack says. "After that, I saw them all the time. You saw the same thing when Apple released its iPhone [software developer kit]. The battery would go down and you'd have all these weird bugs. We had all these people hitting our servers every second in a non-optimized way, and we weren't ready for that."

The only answer they could come up with was having two people comb through and tweak the entire code, then assign individual engineers with sections to continually monitor. It would eventually work, but it was a painstaking process and a brutal summer. Jack went through every imaginable emotion. "You get to this point where you have so much stress, where you feel like you are physically underwater, and then suddenly you find a way to get your head a little bit above," he remembers. "I actually had that physical feeling one day. I was sitting in South Park and I thought, 'Oh my God. I can't take this thing. There's too much going on and this is just not going to work out.' Then you get this little burst of strength and think, 'Oh, this is what we need to do,' and you go back to the office."

Jack spent a lot of time in South Park during that time. Every week, he'd go on a walk around the park with every employee, talking through the tough times and the solutions the company was working on. "It was so freeing for me and them because we could just commiserate and talk about what we needed to do to get out of this place," he says. "But in the office, it was pretty terrible most days. It was long and dark and looked like a tomb, and the world was falling down around us. We loved Twitter. We loved using it. We had all our family members and our best friends on it and it pained us to put those people through that experience. And we were reminded of it daily."

As luck would have it, during this time, Twitter also had to go raise more venture money. It was the company's third round of funding; the first was from Evan, and the second from a New York–based investor named Fred Wilson. Amazingly, the team had refused money from the Sand Hill set, despite their proximity and obvious hunger to invest in Twitter. And this time too, the team was leaning toward an East Coast firm, Spark Capital of Boston. The Sand Hill set was just a little too breathless to invest in Twitter. There was no questioning of the strategy, or the business model, just a smiling, "Great, you should hear from us by the end of the day." Jack and Evan considered fund-raising like hiring an employee you can never fire. So they looked for critical board members who would help Twitter become better.

As the deal was wrapping up at a heady valuation—which Evan considers nothing short of amazing given how many whales the team was "throwing"—Jack got some bad news from St. Louis. His youngest brother, Dewey, was in a Vespa accident and had been rushed to the hospital. Jack's family told him that everything looked okay, and that they were just holding Dewey in the ER. Jack was concerned, obviously, but assumed everything was going to be fine. The next morning he got a call from his mother. Between sobs she told Jack that Dewey was going into surgery to have part of his skull removed because there was too much pressure on his brain. "Things are not looking too good right now," she said. "You have to come home. You have to come home."

Jack had a meeting with potential investors that day. He was utterly shaken up and afterward told Evan he had to fly to St. Louis. Before boarding the plane, he sent a note to Twitter's staff telling them what was happening but to keep it confidential. He offered a meager pep talk to the effect of, "We're in the middle of a lot of things and I need you all to keep working. I'll be in touch." By the time Jack landed, Dewey had made it out of surgery, but he was in a coma. Jack was told the three days after brain surgery are crucial. If something goes wrong, it's over. But if everything goes right, he'll be okay. Three days never lasted longer. On the third day, Dewey was still in a coma. As one of a battery of tests, the doctors asked Dewey for a thumbs-up and were getting nothing. Jack was in despair watching it. The funding didn't matter, Fail Whale was nothing, he just wanted his brother to give him a thumbs-up.

Finally, the third time the doctors asked, Dewey weakly extended his thumb. At that moment Jack Twittered, "My brother just gave me a thumbs-up." To anyone who knew his situation, it spoke volumes. Twitter's headquarters exploded into tears and relief. Jack was immediately flooded with congratulatory emails. At the same time he got a few notes from hopeful suitor VCs that said things like, "Well, your brother better give you a thumbs-up, Twitter is great!" It was a perfect example of how a seemingly frivolous 140-character-or-less note could also be the most profound thing to people who knew the context. "Everything I needed to say was in that one message, and everyone I cared about instantly knew," he says. He was stunned by how powerful his own idea had become.

Just as Dewey came through the surgery, Twitter raised its funding, and finally conquered the Fail Whale. In August, September, and October, Twitter had almost 100 percent uptime even as events like the election drove traffic higher and higher. Jack had every reason to feel on top of the world. Everywhere he looked there were signs that Twitter was getting mainstream. Companies like Comcast and Dell were relying on it for real-time customer service. The Red Cross was using it as an emergency messaging system. CNN's Rick Santos was soliciting on-air comments from viewers via Twitter. Twitter was even mentioned in a Sally Forth comic. "I mean, who even reads that anymore?" Jack says. In typical cyber-fear-mongering, the government was even scared Twitter was so powerful it could become an indispensable tool for terrorists.

The crowning moment was an October trip to New York—the city whose blinking lights of cabs and couriers had first given Jack the universal status message idea. He Twittered he was going to be at a bar and people could come join—a phenomenon known as the

"Tweet-up." It had become a popular activity among users, but ironically Jack had never been to one. Within three days he had a bar in the East Village donating space, a sponsor for an open vodka bar, and three hundred people attending. He knew Twitter was big in San Francisco, but this stunned him. These were media people, ad executives, bankers, and models—not a geek among them. Jack had been so heads down in San Francisco fixing Twitter for so long that it was the first time he really saw how far it'd spread and how fast.

Looking back on the previous eighteen months or so, Jack remembered all the stress, but he realized he'd never felt like being CEO of Twitter was the wrong choice for him. It had taken him a while to recognize where he was good and where he needed work, he granted. But even during his moments of doubt, he had never felt the depression of, "I don't want to do this anymore." If it were up to him, he would stay CEO of Twitter forever.

"This is something I've always wanted to do and something I love doing," he says, sitting in Twitter's redesigned, light-filled, new headquarters under an artistic rendering of a flock of birds.

The day after he uttered these words, Jack was fired.

Just a little more than a year ago Evan Williams sat in a café in South Park and definitively said, "I don't want to build a big company. I want to be involved and I want to create things. I know I can do that best if I'm not the guy. Being the guy just sucks."

Now, he was sitting in a café in China Basin, a few blocks over, and he was all but confessing that he not only wanted to be "the guy" now; Evan "nice guy" Williams was about to become "*that guy*"—the guy who ousts the founding CEO. Evan and the Twitter board were firing Jack today. Clearly, a lot had happened in a year.

The change started in March 2008. Evan had spent the better part of a year doing everything he'd always thought he'd wanted. He was living the nontrepreneur dream. He had a bona fide hit on his hands in Twitter, and he was by far the largest investor. But he didn't have to run it. He could just play. He could speak at conferences, sit on beaches, travel to Japan. To his great shock, he wasn't happy. All this time trying not to get sucked back into the Silicon Valley game, and he found he missed it. He missed building something, and he'd given up the chance to build the single hottest, new Web 2.0 company, Twitter.

The longer he watched from the outside, the bigger Twitter got, the worse the Fail Whale issues got too. Because Evan was Twitter's largest shareholder, a founder, and so closely associated with the company, but didn't have a day-to-day role, watching the whales pop up made him feel helpless and angry. Like users, he'd send messages with subject lines like, "WHAT IS GOING ON OVER THERE?" By March 2008, Evan knew he wanted back in the Valley game and back in Twitter.

As the company's largest shareholder and chairman of the board, he didn't exactly have to ask permission. But it wasn't clear what role he should take. He still didn't think he wanted to be CEO, grimacing as he remembered all the things he hated about Odeo. He thought back to the time he was happiest—working on Blogger. And decided at his core, he was a product guy, and he should be in charge of the product.

That meant Jack—the contract programmer Evan had hired a few years back—was technically his boss. And several others who'd joined Odeo just to work for Evan, like Biz Stone, were now his peers. Jack had finally asserted himself as the CEO, and here was Evan coming back to the company, as an employee, but also chairman of the board, the largest investor and, like it or not, a CEO-like figure. Although Evan would say Jack was "technically" his boss, ask if he *considered* Jack his boss and he blushes guiltily and awkwardly confesses, "No."

It's not surprising then, that Jack and Evan never really got along under the same Twitter roof, although they hid it well. It wasn't that they were fighting or having any big disagreements on where the company was going. They just didn't talk. Evan grants it was an awkward situation and adds that he probably didn't make it easy. "I'm not necessarily that easy to work with. Maybe I was too critical or something," he says. "It could have been that I am just not happy not being the top guy." Evan and Jack tried to make a greater effort, having regular meetings to force communication. But things were only getting more strained.

Meanwhile, Evan was discovering he couldn't just be the product guy. It had been the ideal role back in the Blogger days. He regarded business details and dealing with people a necessary evil to get his product out. That was one of the reasons he sold to Google. But it had been ten years and his interests and skills had expanded. He hadn't realized that everything he'd gone through—selling Blogger, navigating Google, starting and surviving Odeo, recognizing Twitter and helping create it—had actually made him pretty good at "business stuff." And once he started working at Twitter, he couldn't not think about the company as a whole, the culture, the money, the system. He actually liked digging into spreadsheets. Evan realized it was impossible for him to sit at Twitter having the experience of the last ten years' ups-and-downs and not want to take over the whole company and do things his way.

The question of replacing Jack first came up for the board during the summer of 2008, while Twitter was raising another round of money. Taking the money meant that the company likely wasn't selling, and the board asked whether Jack had the chops to take the company to the next level. Nothing was decided then, but it kept coming back up for two reasons: Things weren't getting better between Evan and Jack and, increasingly, Evan was discovering that he did actually want to be the CEO of Twitter. Both Jack and Evan complained to the board, and the board decreed that one way or another, it couldn't go on. So Fred Wilson asked Evan, "Do you want this? Do you want to be CEO?"

Evan had to do some soul-searching. He didn't want to get sucked in again the way he had with Odeo. But, he started to think, Twitter wasn't Odeo. Twitter was something he got and loved from day one. It had done everything right. It had started small, with a simple product, then taken funding. It followed all of his rules. No matter what, he was already heavily personally and financially invested in Twitter. Why not jump in all the way? Every time he thought about his options, there didn't seem to be anything else he wanted to do. Even the administrative stuff he'd hated at Odeo could easily be delegated to a VP of some type. Why not? They were a well-funded start-up. "This could be awesome," he finally decided.

Of course, there was one problem: Jack. Even though he and Evan hadn't been getting along, they didn't hate each other. Evan had always been the entrepreneur's entrepreneur. He wasn't comfortable with being the new ousting-CEO, the villain of the Web world.

That kept the whole thing in a holding pattern for a month or so—just the time that Twitter was coming out of its Fail Whale woes. Everyone on the board knew it had to be done, and Jack had been warned. It was only going to get worse between them, and as a start-up, they couldn't afford further distractions. But Evan was stalling. Finally, he had lunch with a close friend and advisor who was also an experienced CEO. His friend asked what he was waiting for. Evan said, "I don't want to be the guy who kicks Jack out. Everyone is going to say he was such a nice guy."

"Do you think it's the right thing for the company?" his friend asked.

"I know it is," Evan said.

"Then you have to be that guy."

His friend was right and Evan knew it. This is what being a CEO was all about. He called his investors and started the paperwork. It took about two weeks to draw up—during which time Evan could hardly look Jack in the eye. After his warning, Jack had started hustling, working even harder to prove they shouldn't kick him out. Evan found it admirable, and it made his job harder. Nearly ten years earlier, Jack had learned how easily you could lose control of your idea. But Evan was learning an even harder lesson of Silicon Valley survival. Sometimes, for the good of the company and your investment, you had to be the bad guy.

Twitter's investor Fred Wilson and Spark's Bijan Sabet were in town for a board meeting and the three of them decided the investors should deliver the news, not Evan. It would be easier for Jack that way. And really, the news wasn't all bad. Jack would be awarded the second largest individual stake of Twitter stock and would be named chairman of the board. It was generous by any standards. Later that night, Jack went out with a few now-former coworkers. "Come on! This is a celebration," one of them said. Jack smiled, but he couldn't feel very celebratory on the inside. The next day it was announced with the ubiquitous face-saving line, "Jack Dorsey has decided to step down."

Evan was an emotional wreck for the next week, but soon enough he started to get excited about his new job. He was more excited than he'd been about any job for a while. And while he'd felt badly for Jack, he didn't feel *that badly*. After all, Evan points out that he too was a founder. If it wasn't for Evan, Twitter may have never become a reality. It might have stayed an idea in Jack's head for another ten years.

Talking about it, Evan all but screams: *It was just an idea!!* "I don't want to take anything away from him, but I just don't put that much value in ideas," Evan says. "Ideas are everywhere and there are a million little decisions and lots of hard work you have to do to make ideas worth something. Everyone on the team helped do that. No one worked harder over the last couple years than Jack, and he's walking away with a large stake in the company, and we're going to work on this for many more years to make that worth tons financially. He's going to be connected with the company forever. He's always going to be able to say Twitter was his idea and always be able to say he was the cofounder of Twitter and the first CEO of Twitter."

Evan adds that he thinks Jack will have more ideas, now that this one has finally been realized. "I don't know if he regrets handing over the idea, but I certainly think it was a good thing for him, not only for us," he says. "I think given who he was and what he knew at the time this was a hell of a platform for him to unleash this idea on the world. Most companies don't get here based on the solidity of the idea. It's lots of other stuff. So it seems fair to me."

Of course, at the end of the day, Evan was right. Anyone can be the visionary with a good idea. Being an entrepreneur who can create a billion-dollar company is about so much more. After all, Facebook wasn't the first social network, and as an idea Slide is practically unrecognizable from Max's original conception. Perhaps the harshest reality of being more than just lucky is you can't stay the nice guy forever.

As 2008 draws to a close, Evan finds himself once again presiding over a promising company that's entering a brutal downturn. Of course, there are differences between Blogger and Twitter. Evan has made a name for himself and a fortune, and Twitter is way farther along than Blogger was in 2000. Even as the credit crunch ripples down the financial food chain to worried venture capitalists, Twitter could still raise money. It's the other Web 2.0 companies that keep hearing, "You can only get a B-round if you have revenues or Twitter-style growth and no one has Twitter-style growth."

Usage of Twitter is exploding. No one knows exact numbers—not even Twitter because so much of its traffic is through third-party Web applications and SMS networks. Third-party traffic sites estimate that only 45 percent of Tweets come through Twitter.com. Twitter is grabbing cult status, as one of the single most important sites during the 2008 Presidential election, giving people a real-time chat room for the debates and real-time updates on polling conditions. Twitter even partnered with Al Gore's CurrentTV for a "Hack the Debate" program that allowed users to jump in via Tweet.

As Twitter has developed, it has turned into a Web 2.0 hybrid of the best parts of del.icio.us, Facebook, Digg, and others. Via the acquisition of Summize, a top-notch Twitter search engine, you can track what people are saying at any point in time. It's not too different from the bottoms-up search engine that Marc Andreessen thought del.icio.us could have become had Josh not sold to Yahoo! And Twitter has frequently been described as a real-time news feed of your friends' lives—a way to keep in touch with the world around. That's an almost verbatim version of Zuck's mantra that Facebook "makes sense of the world around you like a daily paper." And, given the millions of links and stories passed around on Twitter, it's almost a lightweight Digg 2.0. Companies troll Twitter to find out what customers are saying about them and intervene, à la Yelp. Perhaps most striking: Many Twitter users have a desktop application that brings their friends' messages, videos, photos, news topics, and retail deals to their desktop. Sound familiar? It's reminiscent of the early push-media vision of Slide. Could Twitter be the ultimate Web 2.0 Frankenstein?

Interestingly, as the population of Twitter users has doubled several times in the last nine months, the proportion of active users—those posting at least once over the last month—has stayed constant. That's not something Facebook, YouTube, or other rapidly growing social software sites can boast, according to a report by O'Reilly Media. Tim O'Reilly—the head of the group—was Evan's first employer in the Bay Area, and even he initially found Twitter frivolous. But in 2008, he compared the power of conversational marketing on Twitter to the cell phone and blogs. "The future often comes to us in disguise, with toys that grow up to spark a business revolution. Twitter is like that. Ignore it at your peril."

That said, Evan isn't done. He says Twitter is going to change a lot, but not at the expense of that simplicity. "I think if we didn't evolve the user experience and functionality, it would be lame," he says. "All the things we want to change about the product are to serve things people are already doing." Forget user-generated content; as the O'Reilly report points out, Twitter is one of the first sites to have user-generated features. Early on people started directing messages at people with an "@" sign and the person's Twitter name. Twitter dubbed them "replies" and worked it into the site. There's a half dozen similar examples where users are telling Twitter how they want to use the site. Within reason, Evan sees his job as making that easier.

Indeed, that's how Evan is thinking about Twitter's business model too. The plan is to let corporate Twitter users use the service the way they want to—and charge them for it. There's been a lot of debate over whether Twitter would have some sort of partial subscription business model or an ad-based one. Evan says neither. He's planning something more creative that's every bit an extension of the product as any free feature. "There are lame ways we could make money now. We have enough of a user base and enough traffic," he says. "But it needs to be part of the system."

Evan uses the word "system" a lot. He thinks of Twitter as a living, breathing organism—not unlike a flock of birds—that he needs to keep moving together, now that he's taken over the lead position in the formation. Revenue is as much a part of that "system" as company culture, features, the user interface, and the behavior that happens on the site. "The revenue piece is pure product design," he says, getting excited. "What are people trying to do and how much are we going to help them do it? Is this something only companies want? Then how much can we charge? And where's the credit card field?"

He won't say much more, but is planning on rolling it out in the first half of 2009. It's earlier than he expected, but in the current economic climate he wants to know if his plans will work, so he can budget the rest of Twitter's venture money accordingly. His goal is to not have to raise money in 2009—a fund-raising year that's expected to be brutal.

Whether with free features or those to drive revenues, much of the future of Twitter will revolve around search. Since Twitter acquired the Twitter search site Summize in the summer of 2008, it has changed the entire team's thinking about Twitter's future. Summize allows people to see what anyone is saying about them, or any topic, moment-by-moment, whether you commit to following them or not. People use it to track mass events—like the fallout from a natural disaster or where the hot after-party is. Says Evan, "A lot of people have called Twitter a personal news feed, and that's the direction that makes a lot of sense."

Eventually, he wants people to log onto Twitter and get the latest stuff, from anyone, which will interest them the most. It could be friends, companies, or other people who you don't know, saying something you care about. It could be a news story, a note from your mom, or a sale on shoes. And unlike other Web 2.0 properties, Twitter doesn't rely on the social graph. It's almost an evolved social Web. You don't have to "friend" someone—you can follow them, and they don't have to follow you back. Or via Summize, you can read about anything the Twitter universe is saying without following anyone.

To Evan, that has been the single most important thing Twitter got right in the early days. It better re-creates the social world around us. After all, we talk, message, and email with people all day long who we wouldn't declare "friends." "We wanted to create social software without social awkwardness," Evan says. Imagine that, coming out of a place like Silicon Valley.

EPILOGUE

In May 2007, *The Financial Times* ran an article about the seventeenth-century tulip bubble, widely considered the king of all economic bubbles, referred to over and over again whenever anything gets frothy. You heard it mentioned constantly in Silicon Valley after March 2000. But to Marc Andreesen's great delight, word is spreading that maybe it wasn't really a bubble after all, thanks to a new book, *Tulipmania*, by Anne Goldgar. According to legend, tulips got bid up out of control, and when the futures contracts on them crashed, so too did the Dutch economy. People were so ruined they committed suicide.

But in truth Goldgar couldn't even find a single person who was bankrupted by the so-called bubble. Tulips, seen as a status symbol for a short time, did appreciate outrageously in value, but only a very small group paid these exorbitant prices. When those prices fell by some 90 percent, the economic effects were actually very modest. Wealthy Dutchmen had agreed only on futures contracts, to buy the plants when they bloomed. When the market tanked, the most overbid bulbs were still in the ground. So the wealthy elite simply didn't pay up. The crash didn't even devastate tulip traders, because most of them were selling the contracts only as a side job. But just as with the dotcom bust, the crash had a crushing social impact: When people reneged on these payments, it hurt the social contracts that were the basis of Dutch capitalism. In other words, the damage was cultural and emotional, not economic or financial.

About the same time Goldgar was busting the myth of the tulip bubble, researchers from the University of Virginia and the University of Maryland came out with some research on the dotcom bubble. Ask people what percentage of dotcoms went out of business and they'll guess something in the neighborhood of 90 percent. In reality, nearly half of the companies funded in 1999—the peak—were still in business five years later. Those odds are better than those for opening a restaurant. Most of the tech companies getting bought or going public in the so-called comeback year of 2007 were those self-same companies, finally working their way through the venture capital system seven years later.

The researchers included David Kirsch of the University of Maryland, who has cobbled together a database of emails, prospectuses, and legal documents from the insane period from 1995 to 2000. His conclusion was staggering: If the failure rate for high-risk businesses was that low, perhaps *not enough* companies were started. The problem, he argues, wasn't the number of businesses that were tried, nor was it the unproven business models. It was simply the huge amount of money that went into each one, money that was mostly wasted.

Both reports point out the discrepancy between the emotional memory of a great crash and the actual facts. What actually happened versus what it felt like.

It was an interesting time for both reports to come out, as the Web scene leading into 2008 was getting more frenzied by the day. Venture capital levels and valuations were rising, companies were being minted daily, and there was at least one Web party a night in San Francisco. To many, 2007 *felt* like another Web bubble. But, as the world would soon see, in the fall of 2008 far greater economic woes would fell the U.S. economy. The plain fact was if every single dotcom went under, it would have been a blip on the macroeconomic radar. But as history shows, emotional devastation would be another matter.

Not that Web companies weren't impacted by the popping of the very real bubble created by the housing and credit markets. There was a sense of resentment in the Valley that this time the Web guys got it right. This time they were disciplined with low costs of capital and quick-and-dirty revenues from day one. This time, Wall Street tanked the economy. And just like the Valley's excess in the late 1990s dragged down Wall Street, Wall Street was now dragging down the Valley. Growth in online advertising was flattening, and without one-time catalysts like the Olympics and the Presidential election, no one expected 2009 to be pretty. Start-ups immediately shifted from growth-at-all-costs to cut the deadweight in staff and expenses and maximize any revenue opportunities immediately. The glory days of passion and big dreams are giving way to the stark realities of scarce additional rounds of funding and falling valuations.

Still, there was plenty to be optimistic about. The better Web 2.0 companies saw this coming. They raised huge "recession rounds" back in late 2007 or early 2008 that gave them huge valuations and enough money in the bank to last several years without even making a dime. It was true that aside from LinkedIn, few had nailed their business model; that never-before-seen ways to sell ads online that would make the difference between a company worth hundreds of thousands and a company worth billions.

But, several things about this new wave of Web companies seem obvious. At least a few large billion-dollar-plus companies will emerge, Facebook and LinkedIn being the most obvious bets. Slightly more will sell for a price in the hundreds of millions. The rest will get bought for below $100 million, or will simply go under. A new class of Internet millionaires will be minted, probably more of them than people expect, thanks to the large stakes founders have retained in their companies. As with every single Silicon Valley cycle, the people who make the most money off of it all will be the people who believed in the power of the Net before it was fashionable again. Out of investors, David Sze, Jim Breyer, the partners at Sequoia Capital, and friend-tors such as Marc Andreesen, Peter Thiel, and Reid Hoffman will make out like bandits. Many other will lose money. People may call it a bubble, but it's actually just business as usual in the Valley.

But the emotional toll in store for this generation of Web entrepreneurs and the people who've helped them build their dreams is far less predictable. Both success and failure can be dangerous things. Too much success, and everyone gets cocky and careless. Too much failure, and it's hard to believe again. But if the rise of Web 2.0 from the ashes of the bust has taught us anything, it's that Silicon Valley will never get so scorched that things never rise again. It's that old cliché that a rose grows even in the desert. And it takes only a few successes. The people who flock here want to believe; they just need a little help sometimes.

When historians and economists look back on the Internet waves of the late 1990s and mid-2000s, they will likely see a clear difference. That the dotcoms of the late 1990s created more wealth, jobs, and public companies—even if many of them would eventually go away. The Web 2.0 companies of the mid-2000s may never have the same financial impact, but it's hard to imagine they won't have a far greater social impact.

Some people believe the more we socialize online, the bigger the rift in the real-world social fabric. That interacting with each other via machines makes us all more antisocial. Nothing could be further from the truth. The Web isn't a replacement for offline relationships; it's merely an efficient tool to keep in touch with people more easily, reconnect with friends and family once lost, or discover new friends that you may never meet in the real world. There are no online or offline friends; friends are friends.

Everyone who has experimented with social networking has his or her *aha!* moment. The moment you rediscover a long-lost friend.

The moment you meet someone you get along with so well, you can't believe you never met in the offline world. Or simply the seamless ability to stay in touch with everyone, to be reminded of your friends' birthdays, to have all of their up-to-date contact information at your fingertips for as long as you can get online. It's not a dramatic moment, but the thousand little moments that make life easier and social bonds richer. It's undeniably powerful. Anyone who thinks social networking is just a fad simply hasn't tried using it.

To be sure, there's a dark side to having super-efficient human relationships, and to the Web's general ubiquity. Terrorist cells can convene more easily. Identity theft is rampant. Parents fret that pedophiles roam MySpace looking for victims. And in the Web 2.0 world, people increasingly expose their nasty sides. In March 2007, *The Washington Post* reported on some Yale law students who were anonymously posting slanderous comments about gay, female, and black students at Yale on a chat board, even including lies about some of the students having sexually transmitted diseases. The posts were so damaging that some of the targets say they were denied jobs as a result. As the *Post* wrote, it wasn't simply a cautionary tale about the ugly side of social networking, it was a scary window into the soul and character of the Yale law students.

In many ways, it's worse than identity theft. It's certainly more emotionally devastating. Entrepreneurs have always been optimists about technology and business. But increasingly, as the Web plays a larger role in society, they need to be optimists about human nature as well. "The Internet is neither good nor evil, in and of itself, but people are mostly good, so that makes the Internet mostly good," Andreesen says. You have to believe that to build and champion those companies. Because more than anything, the social Internet allows our true selves to come out.

Entering 2008, Slide was doing well. It had 134 million unique visitors a month, or more than 30 percent of the U.S. Internet audience, according to the latest numbers from Internet researcher comScore. It had three of the top four applications on Facebook, with more than seven million active daily users. In terms of overall reach online, Slide ranked an amazing ninth, just after Amazon.com And they were starting to make some money, with major brands launching in-widget ad campaigns.

But to say it had been the YouTube of 2007 was a stretch. The company was only starting to experiment with advertising, and big questions still remained: Would advertising work on widgets? Would the growth continue? Was Slide really solving a big problem, as PayPal did, or just ordering people's photos online? Could it ever be worth anything close to $1.5 billion? According to Fidelity and a few other financial powerhouses, it was at least worth one-third of that. A January 2008 venture capital round valued Slide at a whopping $550 million and gave Max enough cash to wait out the recession.

Such a coup not withstanding, nothing Max Levchin ever does seems to be easy. In the fall of 2007, Max finally decided to propose to his long-time girlfriend Nellie. He spent weeks learning the intricacies of diamonds: the many variations of the cut, the color, and the clarity. What an inclusion was and which kinds to avoid. He graphed the beauty of the diamond against the cost and discovered at which point the beauty only increases linearly, while the costs shoot up exponentially—the point you should buy. Finally he settled on exactly what he wanted and found three diamonds in the world that fit the criteria. But he knew—scientifically—they were all the same. So he picked the one that weighed 3.14 carats. In the final justification that Nellie was the woman for him, when he told her the weight she said, "Pi?" Max was proud. Not only had she been with him since before PayPal, she knew pi.

As all of the hype around Web 2.0 began to wane, the only company that seemed to be poised to be the Google of this generation was Facebook. Zuck had matured as chief executive, even wearing real shoes from time to time. He didn't even really go by the fratty Harvard moniker "Zuck" anymore. His site was maturing too. As its audience grew beyond college kids, people even wondered if it might tank LinkedIn. But social networking isn't a zero-sum game—people don't go to one site, any more than people read one magazine or watch one television network. There are people on LinkedIn who may never join Facebook, just as there are people who may never switch from MySpace. Or the very Web savvy will use all three but tend to favor one over the other depending on age, demographics, and interests. Had MySpace not been sold, it's quite likely all three could be solid IPO candidates—once the markets recover of course. Each site has grown up differently, influenced by its founders, investors, and communities.

But as for becoming the next great technology powerhouse, MySpace was part of Fox, and while LinkedIn had a better business model, Facebook was the bigger phenomenon. And that business model was starting to emerge. In November 2007, Facebook unveiled the beginnings of its ambitious advertising plans. The idea was that in the real world, advertisers spend a lot of money getting people to discover they want something, whether its via TV ads, billboards, or glossy pages in a magazine, and spend far less money hooking up people who want to buy something with, say, a coupon or list of stores selling the product. It's roughly $250 billion for so-called demand creation and $30 billion for so-called demand fulfillment. But somehow on the Web, those statistics had gotten flipped. The vast majority of online advertising was in demand fulfillment, specifically giving someone searching for *Harry Potter* the Amazon link to find the books and movies. But what about all the people who might buy a Harry Potter book, but don't know it yet?

That's where Facebook was hoping to build a new advertising system. If Google was trying to find the online equivalent of direct mail, Facebook was trying to find the online equivalent of the Super Bowl ad, all based on information the company could glean through its social graph, like who you were and what your friends liked. Done well, it would mimic normal social patterns such as word of mouth. But it was an enormous undertaking and the company was only now taking the highly controversial first steps. Chamath Palihapitiya, Facebook's vice president of product marketing and operations, told his staff this would be a system the company would be perfecting for decades.

Still, that uncertainty aside, for Zuck, it was no longer a struggle to prove his gut was right, it was a struggle not to believe his own hype. There is a pattern in the Internet economy that Peter Thiel compares to a Greek tragedy. One company gets so huge it dominates everything else in the scene. Entrepreneurs, investors, Wall Street, and the press all rally around it, pushing the hype up higher and higher. That company eventually begins to believe it is infallible—the sin of hubris, just as in the Greek tragedies. And then inevitably it stumbles. And all that love and adulation goes sour. It usually takes about four years, once a company has gone public. It happened to Netscape. It happened to Yahoo! It happened to eBay. And as Google pushes past $600 per share, people in the Valley know it will one day happen to Google as well. Back when Facebook was in only thirty schools, Peter told Zuck, "Just don't fuck it up." Once the company was valued as high as $15 billion and had more than 100 million active users, his challenge to Zuck was "Not only do you need to become the next Google, you need to break the four-year curse." No pressure.

Meanwhile, as the downturn hit Six Apart and Digg were all facing the same threat: owners whose hearts just weren't in it for the long haul. In the case of Six Apart, the Trotts have at least done a better job than most of bringing in managers who do want to turn their 2002 experiment into a big business. And the two have a rare ability to care deeply about Six Apart, but be able to hand it over at the same time. They used to call Movable Type their baby, but in the fall of 2007, as a very pregnant Mena started thinking about the real baby she was about to have, she wasn't even sure that she'd go back to work full-time. Ben beamed in the days before Six Apart shipped the fourth version of Movable Type, under Chris Alden's leadership. He was quite proud of it, even though for once, he'd had little to do with its development.

People thought growth at Six Apart was topping out, but many didn't realize how vast their blogging interests were. That's because most of their customers blogged under their own brands, and a big percentage of the blogs they powered were private. For instance, Procter & Gamble has five hundred blogs in-house running on Six Apart's software but only people within the company read them. In total, Six Apart estimates it powers nearly twenty million bloggers and delivers them some hundred million readers per month. That rivals Facebook's audience, only spread across millions of blogs. That said, Vox, the company's blog site with a social networking bent, wasn't growing as fast as they'd like. In another sign of trouble, one of the company's most creative forces, Brad Fitzpatrick of LiveJournal, had grown bored with Six Apart and quit. Usually that happens after an IPO. At Six Apart's last funding round it has raised money at a steep valuation. It was now up to Chris Alden to prove investors weren't wrong.

Brad Fitzpatrick may have left Six Apart, but he didn't leave the Web 2.0 world. In the summer of 2007, he joined Google to help leads its "Open Social" initiative. Open Social was Google's way of answering Facebook's platform success. The search giant signed deals with every major social network and widget maker—everyone except Facebook. Google was pledging to build its own platform and scripting language that would work on all of these sites, giving developers just one "site" to design applications for. Some press prematurely hailed it as a Facebook killer, and it was one of the first big events to knock the increasingly cocky Facebook back on its heels.

But it also showed just how frightened Google was of the Valley upstart. Insiders say the haphazard alliance was thrown together rapidly to make a statement more than anything. Indeed, it was one of the first big Google announcements ever made where not a single line of code had been written. It was all so-called vaporware. Symbolically, it marked Google's own maturity as well: In the past it was the one taking on giants like Yahoo! and Microsoft. Now it was the giant reacting to a scrappy up-and-comer. That Halloween, at Google headquarters, Brad Fitzpatrick showed up for work in all white, with blue bars and letters taped up all over him, wearing a blue baseball cap. Ever the mischief maker around the office, he was dressed as the scariest thing some Googlers could imagine: Facebook.

Like Ben and Mena, Jay too has tried to give up some control. In the summer of 2007, he finally hired Jim Louderbeck, former editor of *PC Magazine*, as chief executive of Revision3 so that he could focus on Digg. Kevin too was focused on Digg, admitting that splitting his time and energy on Pownce was probably a mistake. While Six Apart bought Pownce for a small amount in late 2008, Revision3's fate is more up in the air. And unlike the financially cautious Digg, Revision3 raised a sizable $9 million funding round and was building studios and hiring expensive traditional media people to bolster its business. For all its attempts to become a major online content force, Diggnation still made up a sizable chunk of its viewers. Revision3 was increasingly looking more like an online version of the old TechTV more than anything else.

Still, it had the biggest hold on Jay's heart. Standing in Revision3's new offices, showing off the state-of-the-art editing rooms and pacing along the elevated floors of the four-thousand-square-foot studio under construction, Jay gets wistful. He wonders what would have happened if Digg hadn't grown faster. If he could have focused all his time on Revision3. If he could have ever had the strength or freedom to move back and do it full-time. "Digg feels like work," he says. "Every time I'm here it feels like . . . . just like *fun*."

Jay asked one day in August 2007 if I thought he had accomplished his goals as Kevin's mentor; if I thought he'd done right by him. It's an odd way of measuring how Digg was doing, but to Jay, it's almost as important as making sure he gets his own payday this time around. Protecting Kevin from the sweater-vests was just the first step. Now he wants Digg to make Kevin rich enough that he can do whatever he wants for the rest of his life. Sometimes, he says, he is more motivated by Kevin's success than his own. Somehow, if he can just steer Kevin right, Jay feels he will be absolved from all the ways his own journey went wrong. It's as if he's playing a video game and Kevin is his avatar on the screen. He laughs describing this, and adds, "Or maybe I just want to be Kevin."

Jay ticks off the qualities he envies in him: young, smart, good-looking, cool, effortlessly likable. The fanboys worship Kevin because he's successful but comes across as just a slightly better version of themselves. They watch *Diggnation* and imagine they too could just hang out with Kevin on his couch, drinking beer and talking about girls and the Apple iPhone. He's no aloof, mysterious genius like Zuckerberg; just a guy who had a good idea and went for it. In this sense, Jay is his biggest fanboy, seeing in Kevin his virtual do-over. And that's why, while it's riding high, before something goes horribly wrong, Jay wants to sell Digg. Unfortunately, the right deal still hasn't come along. So in October 2008, Digg raised a big round of funding; hired more people; moved to a bigger, more professional office space; and vowed it'd become more than just a home for the fanboys.

Of course, how much Digg is actually worth continues to be a subject of heated debate. Naysayers insist the company hasn't proven it can be much more than the next version of CNET, the same way Revision3 looks like the next version of TechTV. But there's no doubting Digg's impact. At least a dozen sites have directly copied its voting and burying features—even down to the exact look and feel of the buttons. And Kevin's cult status continues to rise. In October 2007, Marvel Comics released a comic book announcing who the next Captain America would be. It showed a mob of people—potential new Captain Americas—holding shields. Toward the front, there's a kid with shaggy hair and a Digg T-shirt on. It seems even Marvel Comics has its Kevin Rose fanboys.

Then there are the other PayPal mafia companies like Yelp and Geni. They're less likely to sell, simply because Max and Peter are the biggest investors and neither of them is pushing for a quick and easy sale to boost their numbers the way a more beleaguered venture capital firm might. Jeremy and Russ made their fuck-you money at PayPal; now they want to be build something. And so far so good: By the fall of 2007 early competitors InsiderPages and Judy's Book had already gone out of business, but Yelp was still growing. Russ and Jeremy were hopeful they were on their way to their own PayPal-like win. The same goes for Geni's chief executive David Sacks, who is already one of the few people to make it in both of the West Coast's most risky markets: Silicon Valley and Hollywood.

That leaves Ning and Slide. Both Marc and Max have something to prove and need something to do. They have substantial personal financial means to pump into their companies, and they both still fervently believe in them. Marc had got his win with Opsware and when Ning raised its most recent round of funding, it was at a $250 million valuation. On paper, he was a quarter of the way toward his third $1 billion plus company. Ning was quietly growing in popularity at a rate of about 10 percent more page views per week in the shadow of the almighty Facebook. By fall 2007, more than 100,000 niche social networks had been created. Gina and Marc expect it to take years to build Ning into a huge business, but so far all signs were pointing in the right direction.

The reclusive Marc was even starting to come out of hiding. In September 2007 he was on a panel at TechCrunch's inaugural conference. It was in the same ballroom of the Palace Hotel where he and Gina had demoed Ning a year earlier. Hundreds of people stuffed themselves into the room to catch a glimpse of four guys you rarely see at these things: Yahoo! founder Dave Filo; YouTube founder Chad Hurley; the most dominant venture capitalist of the Internet, Mike Moritz; and Marc Andreessen, the guy whose start-up began everything.

The interconnections between them was classic Silicon Valley. Early on, Netscape gave Yahoo! data center space; the Web was so young back then, there was nowhere else Yahoo! could get it. Netscape and YouTube had a subtle connection too: Chad is married to Jim Clark's daughter. And of course Mike Moritz's firm invested in more successful Internet companies than anyone else, among them Yahoo! and YouTube.

The three entrepreneurs typify each Web movement they belonged to. Chad is wearing jeans and has chin-length hair. He's the new Kevin Rose–style hip-geek combo, just bordering on heartthrob. Dave Filo was wearing pressed khakis with a white-and-blue checked shirt. In true dotcom style, he looked like the MBA guy, or any middle-management businessman, for that matter. Marc seems to defy any stereotype in khakis, a black T-shirt, and a purple zip-up jacket with yellow piping, fitting since at the time Netscape debuted no one quite knew what to make of it or the Internet.

The Marc onstage at the Palace Hotel this day was different from the Marc of a year ago. He was chatty and charming, openly talking about Netscape and Loudcloud, his failures and his successes. He seemed comfortable in his role as three-time entrepreneur and Web elder statesmen. That said, he again escaped backstage and through a side door once the panel was over.

But while Marc wants to prove something to the world, Max wants to prove it to himself. Entrepreneurs are notorious for self-identifying with their companies. But Max does it more than anyone. Slide is even more of a projection of himself than PayPal, since he's the CEO this time. He wakes up every morning—when he sleeps—knowing exactly what's on the line. He's never happy-go-lucky. At Slide's offices he is constantly at his desk, sitting on a stability ball and intensely staring a hole through his computer screen.

Reid knows a lot of guys in the Valley who've made money. But he says Max is one of the only ones who never changed. He's amazingly just as hungry as he was when he got here nearly ten years ago. It's hard to bet against intensity like Max's. Slide's business has been tweaked and changed over and over again. If the current iteration doesn't work, odds are Max changes it again and invests more cash until it does. Slide investor Allen Morgan can enumerate all kinds of business reasons why he believes Slide will beat RockYou, but the single biggest reason he's confident in his investment is this: "I wouldn't want to compete with Max Levchin."

Max may be both lucky and good, but more to the point, Max is simply determined. He isn't the visionary entrepreneur who comes up with the next huge thing and then watches it take off like a rocket. His initial business idea is almost always wrong. But that doesn't stop him. His companies seem to make it by sheer, steel-eyed force of will. It's hard to believe Max would want it any other way. His work ethic he can measure; he could graph it if he wanted to. But a runaway success might just be a fluke. "Very few people can work as hard as I do," he says. "And I mean the collective I. The guys that I've hired are not going to be okay with second place. If it's us versus another start-up, I would not put money on another start-up."

When Max was born, doctors told his mother he wouldn't live past three. He did, so they revised it to seven. When he lived past seven, they said, "Well, we can't really predict how long he's going to live. But watch out."

Max had chronic bronchitis and chronic asthma. He remembers coughing all the time. He was in the hospital at least two months out of the year, which soon became a self-fulfilling prophecy. If he went to the doctor for anything, they'd take one look at his chart, and back to the hospital he'd go. "This kid's clearly a death case waiting to happen," they'd say. Socialist medicine at its best. As Max once said, "It's hard to be a socialist when you grew up in a socialist country."

This was life until Max turned nine. He barely left the house. He read a lot. He never got in trouble. Most kids spent their summers at camp riding horses or making lanyards. Max went to these weird Russian sanitariums. "The word doesn't have the same meaning in Russian," he says. "If you were weak in the mind or body, you'd get sent to them, but there were no nuts in the one I used to go to."

He'd go on walks and take lots of salt baths with other sickly kids. He hated it. He was bored out of his mind, and worse, the older sickly kids beat up on him. He remembers throwing one of his few tantrums one year when they dropped him off. "This sucks and I'm not staying here!"

Warnings were the soundtrack to his youth. When he tried to run: "Don't run so hard!" When he'd play with friends: "Don't jump!" When he'd go outside: "You have to wear a hat!" When he was eight he remembers doctors pumping half a liter of phlegm from his lungs. "Nasty," he says, remembering it and making a face.

By the time he was nine he got sick of being so sick. He learned to *fake* clear breathing when doctors would listen to his lungs. He knew how to flex the right muscles in his chest to make sure it sounded like he wasn't wheezing. He got to go to school for an entire year. Quite an accomplishment.

His mother was stunned he hadn't been sick for *a whole year.* So she took him to get a physical with a new doctor. Max's mom brought her folder, containing all of his medical history, all of his hospitalizations, and the litany of what was wrong with her sickly boy.

"Breathe for me," the new doctor said to Max.

Max did his trick.

"Nah, you're faking it. Breathe for real," the doctor said.

Stunned, Max faked it better.

"You're still faking it."

Max was stuck. This guy was too good. He knew his tricks. He closed his eyes, and breathed for real, terrified he'd go back to a life of bed rest, baths, and sheer boredom.

Max took a deep breath. And then heard, "Okay, you're fine."

The doctor wasn't done. "Can you do a sit-up?"

Max's mom interceded, "No, he doesn't do sit-ups!"

He did one. It might have been one of the first of his life.

"Can you do ten?"

Max did ten sit-ups.

"Can you do one hundred?"

He knew that was too much. He'd been doing well just to be in school!

"No, I can't do one hundred," Max said.

"Eh, just try," the doctor said.

He did one hundred sit-ups.

Ten pushups?

"No, I don't think I can even do one," Max said.

He did ten.

The doctor looked at his mother and asked, "So what's the problem, ma'am?"

She stammered, "But he was sick."

"Yeah, well, that's what happens to kids," the doctor said. "They get sick and then they get better." He grabbed the folder from his mother and threw it in the trash. Then he turned to Max. "You're healthy and strong. Just go to school and forget about it."

It was a pivotal moment. And one that still messes with Max's head a bit. Was he ever really that sick? Or just told he was sick so often that he played the part?

This was the last time Max ever let anyone convince him what he was or wasn't capable of. Counting this, the near drowning in the Black Sea, and his narrow escape from Chernobyl's toxic mushroom cloud, he has cheated death at least three times. It puts the daunting task of building two companies worth at least $1 billion each into perspective.

Maybe Slide hasn't beat PayPal yet. But to Max, invincibility is simply a work in progress.

AUTHOR'S NOTE ON SOURCES AND REPORTING

This book is based on eighteen months and hundreds of hours of interviews with the main subjects of the book and even more interviews with executives, venture capitalists, and employees throughout Silicon Valley. There were a few conflicting accounts of stories; in these cases I've done my best to report the truth. CurrentTV, Yahoo!, and News Corporation did not comment on the acquisition talks with Digg. In chapter 1, Max Levchin's girlfriend's name is a pseudonym, because he requested she not be named.

ACKNOWLEDGMENTS

I want to thank Peter Thiel, Marc Andreessen, Kevin Rose, Jay Adelson, Mark Zuckerberg, Reid Hoffman, Ben and Mena Trott, Jeremy Stoppleman, Russel Simmons, and especially Max Levchin for inviting me into their personal and professional lives and sitting through countless hours of interviews. You trusted me with your stories, and I hope I did them justice. Thanks also to David Sze, Andrew Anker, Evan Williams, Zach Nelson, David Hornick, Gina Bianchini, Sean Parker, Ben Horowitz, Scott Banister, Allen Morgan, Brooke Hammerling, Matt Cohler, Tammy Nam, David Weiden, Jim Breyer, Nicole Williams, Randi Zuckerberg, and Brandee Barker for their invaluable help.

Thanks also go to Peter Burrows and Meredith Pierce, who read my manuscripts in various states of distress. Thanks to Michelle Conlin, Frank Comes, and the rest of the *BusinessWeek* crew who worked on, championed, and defended the cover story I co-wrote with the brilliant Jessi Hempel that lead to this book. A small amount of thanks goes to the bloggers who reacted so violently to said cover that it only gave me more press and legitimacy.

This book would have never happened without Hilary Terrell and my agents Daniel Greenberg and Jim Levine. Thanks also to Patrick Mulligan, who picked it up mid-project and kept me grounded with tepid praise and laughing with his emails. Thanks too to Bill Wellborn, who gave me my first job and changed my life when he wandered over to my desk in 1999 and asked me to look into something called venture capital. And thanks to my family and my in-laws for endless support.

Last, I want to thank my husband, Geoffrey Ellis. He has lived this book along with me, whether it was being awakened during sleepless nights or getting dragged to endless Web 2.0 parties. I promise we can stop talking about Web 2.0 now. (Maybe.)

INDEX

Page numbers in *italics* refer to illustrations